THE ARABIAN SHOW HORSE

THE ARABIAN SHOW HORSE

Lesley Skipper

Happy Birthday,
dear Christine,
and many, many thanks
for page 87!

Love Gudrun
1.12.07

J. A. ALLEN · LONDON

British Library Cataloguing-in-Publication Data.
A catalogue record for this book is available from the British Library.
ISBN 0.85131.681.6

Published in Great Britain in 1997 by
J. A. Allen & Company Limited,
1 Lower Grosvenor Place, Buckingham Palace Road,
London, SW1W 0EL

Designed by Paul Saunders
Typeset by Textype Typesetters, Cambridge
Printed by Dah Hua Printing Press Co.Ltd, Hong Kong

For all my horses
but especially for Zareeba
who taught me to listen

CONTENTS

ACKNOWLEDGEMENTS

I SHOULD like to thank the following people for all the help and support they have given me, together with much valuable information.

In the Arabian horse world: Rosemary Archer; Barbara Campbell; Nina Campbell; Anita and George Chadfield; Pat Coward; Lynn Debnam; Kath Deschenes; James Fleming; Melanie and Nick Gaddas-Brown; Margaret Greely; Jackie Howe; Karen Langridge; Carol Lawton; Heather Moffett; Sandra and Albert Nevin; Mr & Mrs Alun Prothero; Mr Anthony Rice; Lisa Smith; Kandice Trusler; Peter Upton; Jane van Lennep; George White; Diana Whittome; the staff of Windsor House, in particular Caroline Mitchell, for their endless patience and courtesy in responding to my many and varied requests for information, and many many others, too numerous to mention.

In the field of equitation: my patient instructor Caroline Jackson, for putting up with one who must often have seemed like a very slow and inept pupil; Sylvia Loch, for her depth of knowledge, limitless enthusiasm and her patience and never-failing encouragement; Michael J. Stevens; Kandice Trusler; and Mary Wanless for some valuable insights into the bio-mechanics of horse and rider.

For information about veterinary matters: the staff of Oaklands Veterinary Centre, Cleveland, in particular Graham Russ whose vast experience of horses was most invaluable; for insights into the problems of cosmetic shoeing and horse locomotion in general, my inestimable farrier, Neil Jackson; to our tooth-man, Tommy Nevin, for much advice over the years on calm and humane methods of handling horses in potentially stressful situations; for help in matters concerning horse welfare, Heather Parsons of the International League for the Protection of Horses; Malcolm Clay of the Association of Circus Proprietors of Great Britain for information about circuses in general and for details of the Kiley-Worthington report.

For help with illustrations: Rosemary Archer; Nina Campbell; Gill and Chris Cook of Pleasure Prints; Pat Coward; Lynn Debnam; Kath

Deschenes; Her Grace the Duchess of Rutland; Peter and Marilyn Sweet; Kandice Trusler; Jane Van Lennep; George White and Diana Whittome.

The staff of the London Library, Stockton Library, Cleveland County Libraries Inter-loans service, and the British Library for their patience, courtesy and efficiency in dealing with my numerous requests; Ian and Jean Healey of the Sportingman's Bookshop in Devon and the staff of Allen's Bookshop in London.

My thanks also to my non-horsy friends Sue Coulthard and Tony Harris for checking my writing for 'readability'; and most of all to my long-suffering husband Brian and our Girl Friday Joanne Husband, for putting up with my frequent abstraction while I worked on this book, for acting as sounding-boards for various ideas, and for their endless patience in listening to my various arguments and discussions.

My undying gratitude goes to Caroline Burt of J. A. Allen for her enthusiasm, faith, endless patience and encouragement; and to my editor Elizabeth O'Beirne-Ranelagh for her expertise, constructive criticism and, again, enthusiasm and encouragement.

Last, but far from least, my thanks to all the Arabian horses I have known, for whom this book has been written – and most of all to our own Arabians: Zareeba, Roxzella and Nivalis, for their beauty, elegance, affection and understanding.

My thanks for permission to use quotations from various publications go to:

J. A. Allen (Akrill, Caroline, *Not Quite A Horsewoman*; Albrecht, Brigadier-General, *Principles of Dressage*; Belasik, Paul, *Exploring Dressage Technique*; Greely, Margaret, *Arabian Exodus*; Guérinière, François Robichon de la, *The School of Horsemanship*; Kiley-Worthington, Marthe, *The Behaviour of Horses*; Lisjen, H. J. and Sylvia Stanier, *Classical Circus Equitation*; Loch, Sylvia, *The Royal Horse of Europe*; Marquis of Mashanaglass, *Training from The Ground*; Oliveira, Nuno, *Reflections on Equestrian Art*; Spooner, Glenda, *Handbook of Showing*); Alpine Publications Inc. (Byford, Sharon, *The Arabian: A Guide for Owners*); The Arabian Horse Trust of America (Edwards, Gladys Brown, *The Arabian: War Horse to Show Horse*); James Fleming (*The Crabbet Arabian Stud* and *Lady Anne Blunt: Journals and Correspondence*); the Earl of Lytton (Wentworth, Lady, *The Authentic Arabian Horse*); Colonel David Hancock (extracts from his article 'Are We Producing Pedigree Chumps?' *The Field*, January 1995); Michael Joseph (Poole, R. W. F., *The Cheviot Ranter*); Alan Rice (for extracts from his grandfather, Fred Rice's, book, *Chestnuts, Greys and Rodeo Days*); The Sportsman's Press (Loch, Sylvia, *Dressage: The Art of Classical Riding*; Peter

Upton (*The Classic Arab Horse*, Arab Horse Society); to the magazine *Horse and Rider*, and to Jane van Lennep for permission to use extracts from her article 'They Do It Their Way' (*Horse and Rider*, April 1989).

Every effort has been made to contact copyright holders but if any have been inadvertently overlooked, the publishers will be pleased to make the necessary arrangements at the first opportunity.

INTRODUCTION

'The demands of competitive success in the Show Ring and its weight as an assessment of the value of a horse is a break with tradition.'

MARGARET GREELY

IF YOU OWN Arabian horses and should happen to mention that fact to non-Arabian-minded members of the horse world, you will in all probability be asked, 'Do you show them?' Showing is such a dominant aspect of the Arabian horse world, whether in Britain or abroad, that to the general equestrian public it must often seem that it is the only activity to which Arabians are suited.

It was consideration of this opinion, and all it implies, that led me to write this book. It is not intended as a comprehensive description of Arabian horse showing practices throughout the world; this would almost require a book for each country, although much of the material is applicable to practices in other countries. Nor is it intended as a catalogue of show winners, though some of these are, of course, mentioned. No doubt I will have omitted many horses, and failed to explore a number of aspects, that some readers will feel I ought to have included; I beg their pardon in advance for any such omissions.

It is not a 'how to' book about showing. There are numerous excellent books which cover all aspects of showing (see Bibliography); I have certainly touched on practicalities where these relate specifically to the Arabian, but in the main this is a general study of the Arabian show horse and an intimate look at the world he inhabits.

The immense rise in popularity of showing over the last few decades has had a tremendous impact on the Arabian as a breed. The prestige attached to a champion show Arab has led a greater number of people to aspire to ownership of these beautiful horses and the result has been a population explosion within the breed. Unfortunately, as we shall see, many of these horses have been regarded as status symbols or exotic pets so that the increasing popularity which, in the early part of the twentieth century, saved the Arabian from oblivion and ensured its survival beyond any possibility of extinction, also worked to the detriment of the breed, by indiscriminate overproduction, and an overemphasis on certain qualities at the expense of others. In the eyes of many, this, together with various eccentric or abusive showing procedures, has led to the downgrading of the Arabian from a superbly practical – as well as supremely beautiful – riding horse, to the other extreme of an extravagantly refined animal whose role is purely ornamental.

That this cannot be good for any breed of animal should be clear from the fate of other species which have followed the same path. Chapter 10 considers the fate of certain breeds of dog, and how breeding for showing has had a deleterious effect, not only on breed type but on soundness of constitution. In the horse world, as we shall see, it is not only Arabians that are affected by the popularity of showing and some of its detrimental practices. In Chapter 10 the concerns of lovers of the native British pony breeds regarding the blurring of distinctions between the different breeds (caused by breeders' efforts to please show judges) are also aired.

It seems that humans are born 'tinkerers' and cannot resist attempting to 'improve' various breeds even when these have reached the peak of excellence in the form most suited to the purpose for which they were originally intended. Unfortunately, this 'improvement' is too often undertaken with a view to exhibiting the 'improved' stock and thereby winning prizes at shows. Some humans are notoriously easily snared by passing fads and fashions which are often the creation of one or two individuals out to make a name for themselves. The effects of such 'improvement' are therefore frequently detrimental. It is with this in mind that some breed societies frown on the idea of showing and, indeed, I am informed that one cattle breed society outlaws shows so as to avoid the problems associated with breeding specifically for showing as well as some of the abusive practices that inevitably creep in.

Let it be said now that I am not against the idea of showing as such. Indeed, I believe it can give much pleasure to both humans and horses. In its original form it was a means of selecting the best breeding stock; while in the field of equitation it was a way of showing off one's horses (and one's style) which, theoretically, like any healthy form of competition, should lead to raised standards. In practice, however, these ideals have gone badly askew so that, like so many other forms of competition, showing has gone from being a means towards an end to becoming an end in itself. As to many people 'the end justifies the means', this inevitably means that abuses and short-cuts creep in.

In a kind of sentimental haze, so many people like to imagine that now that horses are no longer generally required to work the land, pull carriages or sacrifice their lives in battle, their lot is invariably much better than in the past. After much thought, I would question that statement. Certainly in ages past many horses suffered the most appalling bad treatment at the hands of ignorant people; they were often required to work far beyond their capacity, or to risk their lives and suffer horrible injuries in battle. Yet it is unlikely that too many of them were *deliberately* starved, overworked or beaten to death. For a start, they were generally too valuable to waste in such a manner. Except in cases of extreme ignorance, a man of small means who owned only one horse was scarcely likely to ill-treat it to the point where it could not work as he would not easily be able to afford a replacement. Cavalry horses were generally looked after well as their riders' lives depended on them in battle, although certainly throughout the nineteenth and early twentieth centuries there was a huge wastage of horses from causes other than death or injury in battle, mainly because of ignorance of the principles of horse care. The Turks were extremely gentle in their breaking and schooling of horses; while the Arabs maintained for their horses a curious mixture of extreme devotion (as in the case of mares which practically shared the family's domestic life) and extreme indifference (for example regarding horses left to die rather than be humanely destroyed, or colts tethered interminably in the burning sun). The point is that all these horses were *necessary*, and more or less valued accordingly.

Today's horses are no longer necessary in a purely practical sense, yet there are more horses in Britain today than there were before the First World War. The growth of equestrian competitive disciplines since the beginning of the twentieth century has meant that there is a greater demand than ever for competition horses; that is, horses destined, and in some cases specifically bred, for competition.

This is all very well. Competition can be healthy in stimulating effort, in giving competitors a goal to aim for or in measuring progress in training. The problems start when competition – whether it is dressage, showjumping, eventing, showing or whatever – becomes an end in itself. The danger then is that the horse becomes merely a living 'tool', the means by which a rider or a trainer satisfies their ambition. It is then too easy to put that ambition before the horse's welfare; the higher one climbs in one's chosen sphere, the greater the pressures to win and to take short cuts in order to achieve that aim. So we see in showjumping – arguably the most pressured of the equestrian sports outside racing – accusations at the highest international level of cruel practices designed to make the horses jump higher. We see splendid horses ridden in a punishing manner to get them over Grand Prix courses which sometimes seem to have been designed deliberately to catch the horses out. It must make any thinking rider cringe to see the jabbing spurs and punishing, yanking hands of some riders, yet it is accepted because there is so much money at stake.

It is not only at higher levels that we see such abusive riding. Attend any unaffiliated showjumping class (and some affiliated ones) and you will see some truly sickening examples of harsh riding – savage, tugging hands, thumping legs and heavy seats landing with a thud on the horse's or pony's tender back, coupled with abuse of the whip which, in some cases, should result in the rider being banned from competition for life. All this takes place while spectators stand complacently by and do not utter a word of complaint; indeed there is evidence that complaint in some cases is not only ignored but actually abusively received. For a nation of horse-lovers, we are remarkably slow to act when witnessing abuse.

Nor can showjumping alone be singled out, although it is arguably the biggest offender in this respect. In competitive dressage – the purpose of which was originally to test the progress of a horse's training, hence the term dressage 'test' – we see far too much crude, uneducated riding. Too many horses are brought on far too quickly, overtaxing both their mental and physical powers. This is not often recognised because few people who are not actively involved in dressage realise the immense power and concentration needed by the highly trained dressage horse, but overtraining is all too common as is the practice of never turning some of these horses out so that they can kick up their heels and have a good gallop around like 'normal' horses. I believe it is no coincidence that such a high proportion of dressage horses seem to suffer from colic and related illnesses. Some of them never seem to be given the chance to relax properly, always expected to be 'on parade', as it were.

The racing industry is notorious for its phenomenal wastage of two year olds, whose immature frames are subjected to immense strain in order to satisfy the greed of their owners who want an early return for their often ludicrously inflated investments. It is to the credit of the Arab Horse Society that its minimum age for Arabian racehorses is four, although, at the time of writing, it seems likely that changes proposed by the Society will reduce this age limit to three. We can only hope that Arab racing does not succumb to the pursuit of gain above all else, which afflicts Thoroughbred flat racing.

Nor is showing the least guilty of the equestrian activities. Quite apart from the abuses discussed in greater detail in Chapter 9, we hear of so many show horses distressed by unnatural regimes and by the pressures of overshowing, sometimes seeming to spend the whole season dashing from one show to another.

In the light of all this, can we really claim to be any better than the past generations of horse owners who treated their working horses like drudges? At least their horses were necessary and they may perhaps be forgiven for thinking of them merely as living machines. They were, after all, a part of everyday life and, as we know, familiarity too often results, if not in contempt, at least in indifference. But we, who keep horses purely for pleasure – what excuse do we have?

Of course, I am not suggesting that all competitors are so unthinking and cynical about their horses. This is certainly not the case; at all levels of competition, in all fields of equestrian sport, there are countless people who give prime consideration to the horse's welfare and who would not dream of overstressing their horses. Many top competition horses are still competing well into late middle and early old age, precisely because they have *not* been overworked or abused in any way. However, the fact remains that it is so easy – whether through ignorance or through ambition – to fall into the trap of overriding the horse's needs and wellbeing. It is too easy to say of a bad practice: 'Oh well, everyone does it, so it must be all right.' Well, 'everyone' does *not* do it. It is precisely this kind of woolly thinking that leads to so much abuse and which provides those who would curtail or even abolish equestrian sport with so much ammunition.

The purpose of this book is to look at the world of the Arabian show horse and to see how and to what extent the popularity of showing has affected the breed. It would have been much easier, as well as more pleasant, to gloss over the negative aspects. If I am often critical of the current show scene as it affects Arabians and other breeds, that should not be taken to mean that I am against showing. On the contrary, it is precisely because I enjoy going to shows that I care so much about the less pleasant things I see and hear about in showing. Shows can be a great forum for breeders, owners and exhibitors, as well as those who simply admire the horses, to get together and talk about their chosen breed or discipline. They can be a way of assessing the excellence (or otherwise) of one's own stock or of evaluating the level and correctness of a horse's training. The important thing is that they should be *fun* for both horses and humans. It is because I see so much of this element of fun lacking that I have been so outspoken.

I also care very much about the future of the Arabian horse. Showing dominates the Arabian horse world to the extent that one would sometimes think it was the only suitable activity for an Arabian. More and more people are beginning to realise that this is not so and as a result there is a growing gap between the 'show Arab' people and the rest. I cannot believe that this is good, either for the breed or for the individual horses and people concerned.

Shows can be fun: the author with Zareeba, Northern Group Arab Horse Society Show, 1992

I have no axe to grind, other than love of the Arabian horse. I am not a large-scale breeder or a professional showman whose livelihood depends on his or her ability to 'deliver the goods'. Nor do I believe that I have somehow reached a pinnacle of perfection from which I may look down on others and pontificate. On the contrary, I am painfully aware of my own shortcomings, both as a rider and as a general horsewoman. I hope that, by studying, learning, and listening to my horses, I may one day be worthy of their generosity. One of the greatest horsemen of this or any other century, the late Portuguese *maestro* Nuno Oliveira, wrote: 'I have made countless errors in the training of literally thousands of horses . . . I know that I still have much to learn, and will go on learning until my dying day'[1].

My main hope is that this book will encourage other people to go on learning, and that it will make them aware of the pitfalls of taking showing – and any other form of competition involving animals – too seriously and help them to avoid those pitfalls. Although it is devoted to the Arabian horse, perhaps it will help lovers of other breeds to realise that those breeds can also suffer from the same short-sightedness in breeding and from some of the excessive showing practices to be found in the Arabian horse world. Maybe it will spur them to take action before it is too late.

If, in the end, what I have written causes people who show and breed Arabians to stop for a moment and think deeply about what they are doing with their horses; if it makes even a few of those with influence and standing in the Arab horse world decide that it is time to take action to stop the rot, then this book will have fulfilled its purpose. Who knows? Along the way it may even enable more Arabians and their owners to have fun.

Notes

1 Oliveira, Nuno, *Reflections on Equestrian Art*, J. A. Allen 1976, p.30

Chapter 1

THE EARLY SHOWS

'. . . in spite of disadvantages, Shows are a necessity in any country where horses are bred. There is no better method of comparison within the breed.'

MARGARET GREELY

HORSE SHOWS! Where would we be without them? Whether your interest lies in showjumping, dressage, showing classes, driving, heavy horses or whatever, there can be few horse lovers who do not take some pleasure in a good, well-run show. Indeed, for many, as we shall see, shows are their *raison d'être*, by which I mean that their lives consist of breeding, raising and producing horses solely for the purpose of exhibiting them at shows. When we consider breed shows, there are probably more shows specifically for Arabian horses than there are for all the other breeds combined. Yet, in terms of people's association with horses, this is a relatively recent phenomenon. It is only since the end of the Second World War that there has been such a boom in showing, and the expansion of interest in Arabian horses is of even more recent date than that. It comes as something of a shock to realise that until the Arab Horse Society was formed in 1918 there were hardly any breed classes specifically for Arabians, let alone entire shows devoted to the breed.

Horse shows evolved out of the old-style country fairs which themselves dated back to the Middle Ages. To begin with, these country fairs and, as they later became, agricultural shows were not concerned with horses except those of the agricultural and general transport variety. Horses purely for riding were too expensive for the people who generally frequented such fairs and shows; the only people who could afford horses for leisure activities were the landed gentry and the aristocracy who either bred their own horses or bought them from agents, professional nagsmen or friends. By the eighteenth century, when the old country fairs were starting to develop into something more like agricultural shows as we know them, those who did keep horses for leisure were almost exclusively concerned with the chase or with the racecourse. They might keep hacks in the countryside but mostly they drove wherever they wanted to go and in town they rode, if they rode at all, in Hyde Park or in Rotten Row.

The early agricultural shows were, therefore, mainly for cattle, sheep and pigs but gradually horses began to make their way on to the scene. It must be remembered that in those days there were no equestrian competitions as such, other than racing. The nearest Britain came to such competitions were the informal steeplechases (from which was derived our point-to-point racing and, ultimately, National Hunt racing). Britain had little need for large numbers of cavalry so, by and large, there was no necessity to test troops either in the *manège* or over obstacles. On the continent, where cavalry was still a vital part of the armed forces and where there was a greater necessity for standing armies to be kept in readiness for war, there were some such tests which later evolved into the military forerunners of three-day events.

It was not until the mid-nineteenth century that this situation began to alter. Immense social changes – comparable to those experienced in the mid-twentieth century – meant that increasing numbers of people now kept horses for recreation. The great popularity of English horses (as Thoroughbreds were then known in Europe) and light horses of similar type, and the decline of many of the great academies of equitation, meant that *manège* riding for its own sake no longer held the appeal it once had for the aspiring horseman. What was required was something altogether more in keeping with this thrusting new age. 'Leaping' competitions, the forerunners of modern showjumping, were held in France, Russia and Germany. It was not long before Britain and Ireland caught on. Such competitions were held at the Royal Dublin Society's Show in 1865, followed by more 'leaping' competitions at British agricultural shows. By now the horse was firmly established as part of the show scene and, increasingly, breeders and dealers used shows as a 'shop window' where they could display their wares. Special classes were introduced for stock either too young, or considered unsuitable, for riding, such as broodmares and stallions. Stallions were rarely ridden in Britain at that time and it is only relatively recently that this prejudice has, to some extent, been overcome (though all the original Crabbet horses were ridden, including broodmares, and while in Lady Wentworth's day Crabbet was not a 'riding' stud as such, her horses, including the stallions, were still ridden at home). Classes for specific breeds became common. However, there were still no classes for Arabians.

This is hardly surprising. In spite of numerous imports (usually gifts from Eastern rulers), Arabian horses were still relatively scarce in Britain. They were little known and even less understood, being regarded by many as either an undersized horse or an overgrown pony and, in any case, of very little interest to the true sporting horseman. There were also other reasons for this prejudice, as we shall see in Chapter 5, but while in Europe Arabians were highly regarded, especially as light cavalry horses or for the improvement of native stock, British suspicion of the breed scarcely abated even when Captain Roger Upton, and later the Blunts, brought their first acquisitions home from Syria and Arabia.

There were, in fact, general classes for 'Eastern' or 'Oriental' horses at some shows. These might include anything from Barbs to 'Turkoman' horses, which, in practice, could cover almost anything from the Near and Middle East. The Blunts themselves, although they did enter their horses at such shows as had classes for them, were never very enthusiastic about the idea of showing. They believed that a horse's value as breeding stock lay not in the number of prizes won at shows but in the excellence of his or her progeny. It was left to the eccentric but highly enthusiastic Miss Etheldred Dillon to badger the various show organisers into providing classes for Arabian horses. By offering prizes, she managed to have such classes put on at the Hackney Show in 1884, at Bath from 1887, at Oxford in 1890 and at Crystal Palace between 1896 and 1898, but once she gave up her stud in 1898 these classes were largely dropped. However, the idea had been planted, and Miss Dillon's enthusiasm contributed to the eventual formation of the Arab Horse Society. Whatever her faults (for comment on her foibles and eccentricities see Lady Anne Blunt's *Journals*), there is no doubt that the Arabian horse world owes Miss Dillon a debt of gratitude for her persistence and passionate faith in the breed.

It is also apparent from Lady Anne's journals that these early shows were as plagued by favouritism and biased or ignorant judging as any modern show. Lady Anne wrote of the Ranelagh Show in 1895 that 'the prizes went to underbred or inferior animals. We left in disgust and drove to London . . . one judge wanted to give Safran something but the other refused.'[1] Of the 1897 Crystal Palace Show, Lady Anne commented on the fact that the Reverend Vidal was to judge the class: 'This seemed incredible not only because Vidal's character is known to Vero Shaw the manager but because Vidal is an exhibitor'.[2]

In her journal for 6 June 1900, Lady Anne records that she had received a telegram saying that Mesaoud had been placed fourth after three of the Sultan's horses at the International Exhibition in Paris, where there was a class for Arabians. This result, she felt, was as good as nowhere. '*I* ought not to mind as I knew beforehand nothing would be awarded and had I cherished the least doubt it would have vanished when I saw that among judges of *Arabs* two *English* people were admitted. Between the Sultan and our compatriots *pas de chance*.'[3] However, Lady Anne, who had been against sending any horses to the exhibition, consoled herself with the thought that 'Possibly *any* notice ought to be taken as a confession of great merit! For W's [Wilfrid Blunt] unpopularity must count as something – there is no disguising the fact that he does get "people" in general against him.'[4]

Lady Anne's complete honesty and objectivity make it impossible that such comments should stem from 'sour grapes'. That was not her way. In spite of these disappointments, they did have some success at shows. Her journal for 14 July 1896 records a first place for Mesaoud and second for Mejliss, with Rosemary commended 'In Reserve' at Crystal Palace Show; in 1897 at Crystal Palace Mesaoud again came first, with Bozra third and Ahmar commended; in 1898, again at Crystal Palace, Mesaoud gained a first place yet again, while Safran was second and Rosemary and Bint Nura, respectively, first and second in their classes.

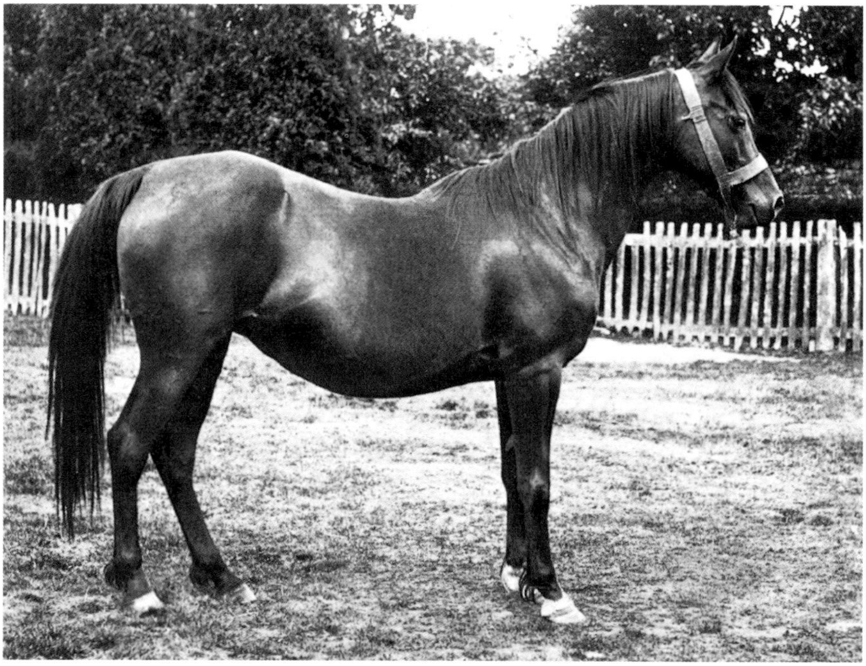

Rosemary (Rosemary Archer)

In general, however, there was no great interest in providing breed classes for Arabians. With Miss Dillon no longer on the scene, and the Blunts not particularly enamoured of the idea of showing, it was not until the formation of the Arab Horse Society in 1918 that the number of shows providing classes for Arabians started to increase, with classes being put on at shows such as Newmarket and Richmond as well as Ranelagh, although, as Margaret Greely points out in *Arabian Exodus*, at these early shows the breed might be represented by as few as nine individuals.[5] None the less, with the foundation of the Arab Horse Society, interest in the breed continued to increase. The Second World War halted many equestrian activities and even meant the complete closure of a number of studs, but in 1946 the first all-Arabian horse shows were held: a spring and a summer show. Margaret Greely recalls the occasion:

> 'People who knew little about Arabs, came out of curiosity to see either "something out of a picture-box" or an undersized "pony-type" horse, and though the classes were by no means big it was impressive enough as a spectacle to bring such a large crowd to the Summer Show that the printed Schedules fell short of the number required, and the ring was too small to accommodate the crowd of spectators round it. Though several Studs were represented, the winning horses with four exceptions came from either Crabbet or the Hanstead Studs.'[6]

In the USA, as in Britain, it was not until the 1940s that the first all-Arabian shows were held (although the Americans, as we shall see, were very much quicker to recognise the Arabian's capabilities in performance classes). Until then, it was only the occasional fair and horse show that, in the words of Gladys Brown Edwards, 'condescended to include classes for Arabians either in hand or performance.'[7]

When the first show of the newly formed Arabian Horse Breeders Society of Southern California was held in 1945, the judge selected was actually a dog judge specialising in terriers. There were 63 entries in the 17 classes, only four of which were performance classes; there was no championship for mares, the idea apparently being to promote stallions. The second show, held the following year, had many more entries and the success of these shows ensured their continuation. It was at these early shows that some of the curious terms sometimes used at American Arabian shows originated, such as 'underyearling' (described by Gladys Brown Edwards as 'idiotic') for foals. Edwards recalls a number of howlers from the programmes of some of these shows, such as referring to two-year-old colts as stallions, or to all foals, regardless of sex, as 'colts'; for example, 'the howler of the lot . . . the class for hermaphrodites, apparently, since it was labeled, "filly colts" . . . To be equally colloquial, "Them animals just ain't." '[8]

At many of these early shows there was a considerable number of special classes and attractions: pig-sticking, running races, trotting races, stock horse classes, dressage exhibitions, and many more. The immense success of these shows quickly led to all-Arabian shows being held elsewhere. The Arabian Horse Breeders Society of Southern California joined the American Horse Shows Association, the body which governs all affiliated horse shows in the USA. This had the beneficial effect of introducing uniformity of rules for judging, where previously there had been no such uniformity and even, in some cases, no rules at all! Other Arabian associations were founded and more and more shows were being held in various parts of the USA. Soon there were so many shows on the west coast that it was decided to hold a Pacific Coast Championship which, in turn, triggered the idea of holding Regional Championships. Ultimately, of course, this led to the creation of the National Shows; there had been 'Nationals' before this, but they were not held on a continuing basis to begin with. This was a completely different situation from that of Arabian shows in Britain, where the opposite had been the case. There, the National shows had been the nucleus from which the regional Arabian shows developed.

In Britain, after the Second World War, the showing of Arabians blossomed as it had in the USA, although never on the same scale because of the sheer difference in size of the respective countries.

Although the format was basically the same in principle, these early shows were very different in many respects from what we see now. The atmosphere was very much more formal, with grooms and handlers expected to conform rigidly with regard to dress and conduct in the ring. In photographs of early shows the handlers are all male, as one might expect in that era. They are, without exception, smartly dressed, accordingly to the prevailing ideas of smartness, in either jacket and trousers with a bowler hat, or tweed jacket, breeches, gaiters and a cloth cap. This was the universal stud groom's dress and it was a cause for comment if a handler appeared in the showring in unorthodox dress. Fred Rice, who worked at Crabbet for most of his life, and who was, for a number of years, the head showman there, recalled one year at the Windsor Show when, for some reason, he had been wearing Oxford bags which flapped about in the wind. Lady Wentworth was not amused. On Fred's return to Crabbet she waved a photograph at him, saying, 'Lovely photo, but look

Islington Show – one of the early shows (Rosemary Archer)

at YOU!' She made him go and get measured up for some proper, well-fitting breeches, saying, 'Don't ever let me see you in the ring again in those abominations; you're not tall enough.' Ever after that, Fred wore the standard jacket and breeches.[9] One wonders what Lady Wentworth's reaction would be to some of the more *outré* fashions now seen at Arab shows.

This sartorial severity applied to the horses, too. While they were beautifully turned out, there was little or none of the artificial presentation so common nowadays. Their show bridles and halters were of the simple, workmanlike type now more often used for Welsh cobs. At most they might sport brass rosettes decorating the ends of the browband. They were expected to be well behaved, to stand quietly in line and to stand up for the judge in as natural and relaxed a pose as possible. Bad manners were definitely frowned upon and judges had no hesitation in sending a badly behaved horse out of the ring.

But if the in-hand classes were generally rather more decorous than is often the case these days, the same cannot be said of the ridden classes. If Lady Wentworth's comments, recorded on a programme of the 1948 Arab Horse Society Show at Roehampton, are an accurate record, the ridden classes must (in the words of Gladys Brown Edwards) 'have been in the nature of a refined rodeo.'[10] Rithan, wrote Lady Wentworth, could not be mounted, and was sent out, while, 'Boaz was unmanageable – threw his rider and was sent out'; Indian Jewel 'attacks other horses and should never win' (apparently he didn't); Haji was 'riotous and badly ridden'; while Star Diamond 'stood first but got upset and was sent out.'[11] None of this can have helped the public image of the Arabian as a riding horse!

By modern standards it might all seem rather dull, and so perhaps it was, except to the real enthusiasts (apart from the high jinks referred to above, which must have enlivened the proceedings considerably). On the other hand, it did enable lovers of the Arabian horse to see it at its best without too many disguising frills and overt showmanship. Showmanship there was, certainly. Fred Rice tells how the Crabbet grooms, instead of waiting at the ringside as others did, walking their charges around until the next class was due to go in, always took their horses straight out of the loose box to the showring, so that they were still full of bounce and so showed themselves off better than the other horses which had grown stale from waiting.[12]

One of the early shows. Skowronek is on the extreme right (Rosemary Archer)

In general, though, such tricks of the trade as there were seem mild in comparison with what goes on behind the scenes and in the showring these days. Fred Rice recalls that Lady Wentworth did not believe in oiling the horses' hooves as she said it wasn't natural. So Fred used to get up early, muck his horse out, put down fresh straw, then take his charge for a walk in the long grass. Then he would bring the horse back into the clean straw, '. . . and they always used to say, "How the hell do you get their hooves like that?" Our ladyship, she never believed in polishing them, reckoned that wasn't natural. But that's the way I always used to do it.'[13]

In those days, of course, a show groom's life was much harder than it is now – and few people would call it a cushy number even now. Before the Second World War there were few motorised horse boxes. At Crabbet they used to walk the horses to Three Bridges and load them on to a train. A cart horse would take the show equipment to the station separately. Horses travelled in strong, well-padded boxes and porters and station-masters proved very helpful with the loading and unloading. Cecil Covey, who was at Crabbet for many years, and who inherited the stud on Lady Wentworth's death, commented in *The Crabbet Arabian Stud* that horses could be sent at any time, day or night, to any part of the British Isles as long as the station had a loading platform. This was how horses in general travelled until well after the Second World War, though, as Cecil Covey recalls, when they went to shows, 'There were often so many horses that the train amounted virtually to a Crabbet Special and until the railways went electric the boxes could be hitched to the back of passenger trains if there were not enough to make a separate train.'[14]

The grooms and horses would go about three days before returning home again. 'You'd go up to London, and then go up to Leicester, all around there.'[15] At all the big shows the grooms and handlers used to 'rough it', sleeping in the hay in extra loose boxes ordered for them. It was not until after the war that horse boxes came into wider use, although some people had them before the war. Lady Wentworth had a big box that even had a dining room at the back of it '. . . we thought we was in heaven when we got that!'[16]

From the reminiscences of Fred Rice and others, it is apparent that, in spite of the hard work, shows were fun – as, indeed, they still are today – for many people. However, listening to people like Fred (who sadly died early in 1995) and George White (who was for many years stud manager at the famous Barton Lodge Stud), one detects a note of wistfulness, a regret at the passing of more carefree days when showing was less of a cut-throat businesss. As Fred Rice said, 'They were good days.'[17]

Sainfoin, Stallion Championship winner seven times between 1927 and 1936 (courtesy of George White)

What partly made the difference was the fact that there were relatively few studs and individuals breeding Arabians so the shows were dominated by a comparatively small nucleus of studs: Crabbet, Hanstead, Courthouse, Barton Lodge, etc. The horses were, in general, rather different in type from those now winning in the showring. If we look at photographs of some of the early show winners, many of them appear quite plain compared to the ultra-refined show horse of today. However, photographic evidence is, at best, unreliable. Lady Wentworth, herself a keen and skilful photographer (although she spoilt many of her photographs by retouching them), stated that: 'The "camera cannot lie" is one of the biggest falsehoods ever uttered. The camera is an arrant fraud. It can distort and caricature horses beyond belief and practically never flatters them.'[18] – although the reverse can also be true, as we shall see.

With regard to the often very unflattering photographs of the early Arabian champions, it must be remembered that these photographs were taken in an era when today's sophisticated presentation techniques, particularly as regards photography, were relatively unknown (Lady Wentworth, for instance, although she always insisted on having her horses properly posed for photographs, used a simple Box Brownie for all her photography; and even her own photographs do not always do her horses justice). In her famous book, *The Authentic Arabian Horse*, she comments that, 'People have sent me pictures of their horses for insertion in this book which did their horses such injustice that I was obliged to omit them in their own interests.'[19] It is scarcely surprising then that so many of those horses do not appear to match up to glowing descriptions of them. Nor does black and white photography flatter horses (unless done in a very 'arty' way); the richest bay and the most glowing chestnut tend to look rather dull beside the gleaming greys. When we consider that, for many years, chestnuts predominated, one can see why in many photographs they do not exactly grip the attention. Without skilful presentation, such as would largely be taken for granted nowadays, brown, bay and chestnut horses can look much less refined than greys when seen in black and white. Muzzles can look larger and 'blockier' than they really are; eyes smaller and less luminous.

There is no real evidence that greys reproduce the more refined Arabian 'type' better than bays, chestnuts or the relatively rare true black, although in some families colour may possibly be linked to the genetic inheritance of certain characteristics (I should be interested to hear about any research done on this subject). Certainly, grey does tend to show up some features better than chestnut or bay, particularly in black and white. Added to this, many chestnuts have extensive white markings and while a narrow blaze may enhance a fine head, a broad blaze can sometimes make a good head appear plain. This seems to have been the case with the famous Crabbet mare Rissla, celebrated as the dam of a number of very fine horses. On some photographic evidence, Rissla appears to have been no beauty, yet her human contemporaries, the most knowledgeable of whom certainly knew a good head when they saw one, were universal in their praise of her classic type.

Some horses, which are in reality quite stunning, can appear very ordinary, or even plain, when photographed in an infelicitous pose or in poor light. Equally, some horses that are flattered by clever photography are disappointing when seen in the flesh. Even film or video, while certainly far more reliable than ordinary photography, cannot capture the full 'essence' of a horse, although if we look at films of Lady Wentworth's famous Crabbet parades, and other films taken a number of years ago, we can see that many of the champions featured in them were far more impressive than their still photographs would suggest; and in some cases their quality and freedom of action has never been surpassed.

What is very evident from many of these photographs and films is that these horses were, by and large, very much more substantial than some of today's show winners. They had their share of faults, certainly, but in gen-

Bahram, Supreme Male Champion 1954 (Rosemary Archer)

eral they looked as if they could have carried a sheikh or a mail-clad Turkish or Persian warrior into battle.

It is only fair to say also that there were certainly plenty of plain or ordinary horses around, some of them actually doing better in the showring than they should have done. In trying to emulate Lady Wentworth by breeding bigger Arabians, some British breeders went too far and started to produce horses that were losing Arabian type and beginning to look more like Thoroughbreds or, at best, Anglo-Arabs. This has led to a certain plainness in some bloodlines that still persists to this day, and it is perhaps from this, more than anything, that English bloodlines have gained a largely undeserved reputation for being strong and workmanlike but lacking in refinement. Here, as everywhere, some very off-type horses have been bred but, among our top show winners of the past, there have also been some horses the like of which are rarely seen these days.

The Crabbet horses were noted for their presence and style, while the Hanstead and Courthouse horses, although they lacked the sheer size and majestic presence of the Crabbet horses, were perhaps more classic in type and could certainly equal the Crabbet stud for quality and action. The names of winners at shows of both pre- and post-war eras have passed into legend: horses such as the fabulous Skowronek whose quality transformed the British Arabian scene. Like all horses, he had his faults; his shoulder was somewhat too upright and his action consequently not of the best. But his good qualities he transmitted in abundance, and of him Fred Rice said simply, 'He was LOVELY.'[20] At Courthouse there was the beautiful Sainfoin who had a show record that must surely be one of the most remarkable in the history of showing. Between 1927 and 1939 he won the Gold Medal for best stallion or colt at the London Show eight times, coming reserve once. Because of the small number of horses competing in ridden classes in those days, there was only one ridden class, open to stallions, mares or geldings. Sainfoin won this class five times, coming second three times and third once. At Hanstead (and later at Crabbet), there was the splendid Raktha, described by Cecil Covey as 'one of the very few perfect types of Arabian stallion'[21], whose majestic bearing made him a star wherever he went.

It was in the post-war years that some of the brightest 'stars' shone. Rosemary Archer recalls the first shows at Roehampton: 'The spacious ground with its back drop of trees, the pleasant garden party atmosphere

Skowronek. Here shown with Lady Wentworth at Richmond Show, 1924 (Rosemary Archer)

and the sight of England's finest Arabian horses, made the Roehampton shows an unforgettable experience.'[22]

There were horses such as Grand Royal who took the Supreme Championship in 1953 and 1956, and Dargee, a small horse with a fine head, noted for his brilliant action, Supreme Champion in 1955 and 1960. Indian Magic 'was undoubtedly one of the most imposing stallions of all time and with his superb style and presence, stood out like a beacon every time he appeared in the show ring.'[23]

Grand Royal, Supreme Male Champion 1953 and 1956 (Rosemary Archer)

It was at the Arab Horse Society's Summer Show in 1946, Margaret Greely recalls, that she first saw 'Grey Royal, that exquisite daughter of Raktha. The entries in the class had been lined up by the judges; a class which included Rubiana, Carlina and Selma II, all beautiful fillies who drew murmurs of admiration from the crowd, and then, suddenly making a late entrance, Grey Royal "floated" in. There was an amazed hush in the crowd. The arch of her neck, the carriage of her tail, and her airy, almost weightless action were incredible. Together with her perfectly dappled

Grey Royal: a prolific winner, she was unbeaten in the showring (Rosemary Archer)

coat, and dark mane and tail, she made a picture that must always live in the memory.'[24] Grey Royal went on to win her class, and although she came up against all the best mares in the country, she was never beaten in the showring.

Many of the best Crabbet horses were never shown – horses such as Naziri, Indian Gold and Silver Gilt – as Lady Wentworth apparently considered them too valuable to risk (in the case of Indian Gold, too uproarious to box). In addition, she shared to some extent her parents' opinion that the real value of a horse lay in its stock. However, she recognised the value to her stud of the prestige and publicity her successes in the showring brought her.

Whether they came from Crabbet, Hanstead, Courthouse, Barton Lodge or from the smaller studs, there were many great horses which went on to prove themselves, not only as show winners but as splendid sires and dams: horses such as Silver Vanity, Blue Domino, Shammar, Bahram, Darjeel, Benjamin, and, of course, one of the most famous stallions of the century, the great Count Dorsaz, later exported to the USA (where he is still known in certain circles simply as 'The Count'). 'Dorsey' twice won the coveted Winston Churchill Cup for the Supreme Riding Horse at the

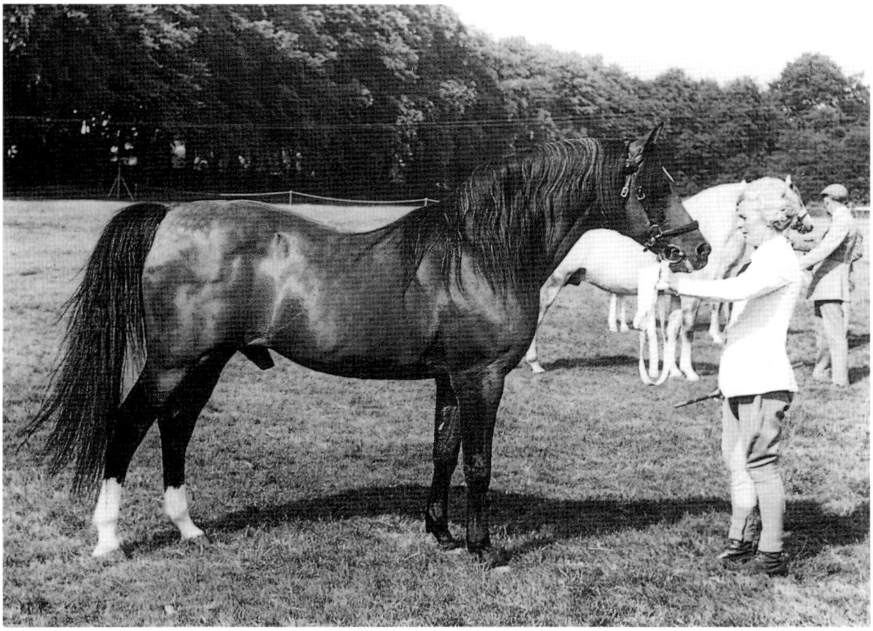

Benjamin, Supreme Male Champion 1963 (Rosemary Archer)

BELOW *Blue Domino (Rosemary Archer)*

Royal International Horse Show. Rosemary Archer remembers: 'It was a memorable sight to watch the beautifully schooled chestnut stallion give his spectacular display at the White City, when as a finale he would race at high speed round the arena and then stop dead in his tracks in a couple of strides, to tremendous applause!'[25]

These are only a few of the outstanding horses of their time; they and the many others not mentioned here would require a whole book to themselves to do them justice.

Many of us are too young to remember, or even to have known, those horses in the bright days of their glory. For the most part we must rely upon photographs for our impressions of these former champions and, as we have seen, photographs can give us only a pallid glimpse of what they once were. Let us allow a true master, Nuno Oliveira, who loved horses – all horses – like life itself, to have the last say on this subject:

> '. . . once the horse is dead, nothing, not even films, can reproduce the sensation felt when the horse is seen in movement . . . After the horse is no more, only those who have admired him keep a remembrance of his quality in their hearts, which is gradually effaced by time, and others who have not seen him know him only by romanticised tales, recounted, and sometimes embroidered, by those who have truly loved him.'[26]

Count Dorsaz, twice winner (and twice Reserve) of the Winston Churchill Cup; shown here, unusually, in-hand (Alexander Heriot)

Notes

1 Blunt, Lady Anne, *Journals and Correspondence 1878–1917*, ed. Rosemary Archer and James Fleming, Alexander Heriot 1986, p.475, note 79
2 Blunt, entry for 5 June 1897, *Journals*, p.261
3 Blunt, *Journals*, p.281
4 Blunt, *Journals*, pp.281–2
5 Greely, Margaret, *Arabian Exodus*, J. A. Allen 1975, p.62
6 Greely, *Arabian Exodus*, p.73
7 Edwards, Gladys Brown, *The Arabian: War Horse to Show Horse*, The Arabian Horse Trust of America 1969, p.173
8 Edwards, *The Arabian*, pp.180–1
9 'An Afternoon with Fred Rice', *Arab Horse Society News*, no. 72, pp.80–1
10 Edwards, *The Arabian*, p.123
11 Edwards, *The Arabian*, pp.122–3
12 Rice, Fred, *Chestnuts, Greys and Rodeo Days*, Oran's Paddock 1993, p.23
13 Rice, *Chestnuts*, p.23
14 Archer, Rosemary, Pearson, Colin, Covey, Cecil and Finke, Betty, *The Crabbet Arabian Stud*, Alexander Heriot, 2nd ed. 1994, p.208
15 Rice, *Chestnuts*, p.80
16 Rice, *Chestnuts*, p.81
17 Rice, *Chestnuts*, p.81
18 Wentworth, Lady, *The Authentic Arabian Horse*, George Allen and Unwin, 2nd ed. 1962, p.277
19 Wentworth, *The Authentic Arabian*, p.275
20 'An Afternoon with Fred Rice', *Arab Horse Society News*, no. 72, p.81
21 Cecil Covey, in Archer, etc. *Crabbet Arabian Stud*, p.220
22 Archer, etc. *Crabbet*, p.191
23 Archer, etc. *Crabbet*, p.191
24 Greely, *Arabian Exodus*, pp.73–4
25 Archer, Rosemary, *The Arabian Horse*, J. A. Allen 1992, p.31
26 Oliveira, Nuno, *Reflections on Equestrian Art*, p.118

Chapter 2

THE MODERN SHOW SCENE

'Neither horse nor man likes anything in the world that is excessive.'

XENOPHON, C. 400 BC

IF A SPECTATOR at one of the early all-Arabian shows could be miraculously transported to an equivalent show in the late twentieth century, what would their first impressions be?

They would probably notice first how big some of the classes are compared with those of the early shows. They would also be somewhat startled by the strange varieties of clothing worn by the handlers, and the fact that so many of the latter are female. This last point would seem particularly strange as, traditionally (and even now, to some extent, in the Thoroughbred racing world), stallion handling was considered to be a man's job.

Next, our time-traveller might be struck by the extreme variations in type to be seen among the horses in almost every class; while at the same time they might shake their head a little at the sight of some of the very fragile-looking (though undeniably attractive) show halters adorning the ultra-refined heads on display.

Finally, our time-traveller would be rather bemused by the bizarre antics of some of the handlers, and by the equally bizarre behaviour of some of the spectators. They might recall the sedate proceedings at Crystal Palace, Richmond or Roehampton, and conclude that 'things are not what they used to be'.

They would, of course, be quite right. The world has not only seemed to shrink during the course of the past century, it is changing at a rate bordering on insanity. Too little change leads to stagnation; too much, and chaos threatens. Such is the stress engendered by so much change in such a short time span that, for many people, their only refuge is participating

The modern show scene is very different

in, or attending as spectators, activities perceived to be 'traditional' and therefore to some extent static and unchanging. After all, what could be more traditional than a good old English country fair or agricultural show? Yet, as our time traveller would observe, even our shows are gradually changing – but is this change for the better?

It was to be expected that the immense social upheavals which followed first the Great War and then the Second World War would affect the showing scene. As personal incomes began to rise, together with the amount of leisure time people had at their disposal, more and more ordinary people began to realise their dream of owning one or more horses. This did not happen overnight, of course; it was a gradual process, and it has been only within the last two decades or so that – in Britain at least – the boom in horse ownership has permeated all levels of society. Nevertheless, the shows that were held following the Second World War slowly began to change in character. They had once been almost purely a showcase for breeders to exhibit their stock (and thereby to attract customers) and in the process they helped to maintain breed standards as judges would, theoretically, be selecting the best from what was then a relatively small pool. Now shows began to be much more of a competition. That is not to say that there had not previously been a competitive element; there was, of course, and it was often a fierce one. It was, however, a different kind of

Ralvon Elijah, Supreme Male Champion 1984 (Sweet)

competition. A handful of breeders held a virtual monopoly over the breeding of Arabian horses in the UK and in other countries; in many cases the owners did not depend on the success or otherwise of the stud for income, so that, while there was rivalry, it was seldom of the cut-throat variety. With the boom in Arabian horse breeding that started in the USA in the 1960s and 1970s, this situation altered.

With more and more studs being run as a business, pressures to exhibit at shows (and of course to win) became much stronger. In addition to this, there arose a relatively new kind of exhibitor: the one- or two-horse owner who exhibited purely for pleasure and recreation. That is not to say they did not take showing seriously; they did, and still do, and while the big studs and professional show producers may appear most prominent, it is, in fact, the small-scale exhibitors who, by and large, keep shows going.

All this led to a change of emphasis away from the idea of a 'showcase'. This concept is still there but it has been relegated more and more to the background, with showing – as with so many other equestrian activities involving competition – now being seen increasingly as an end in itself.

Which of us, particularly those of us who own beautiful Arabian horses, does not, in his or her heart, like to show off? It is true that some wealthy people collect beautiful horses in the same way as they collect art treasures – simply to parade their wealth and pose as persons of aesthetic discernment. However, this is not to say that they cannot appreciate what they have, or that they do not take the same intense pleasure in their ownership as the modest one- or two-horse owner who may have no horse worth more than a couple of thousand pounds but who derives as much enjoyment from them as if they were worth millions.

One of the pleasanter aspects of the great social changes mentioned above is the fact that the attainment of such pleasure is now open to a much wider range of people than ever before. But everything has its price and we must ask whether this boom in the ownership and enjoyment of Arabian horses has necessarily been beneficial, either to showing or to the breed itself?

One aspect which, in the view of many owners and breeders of Arabians (not to mention outside observers) has proved extremely detrimental, is the change in the general tone of in-hand classes and the manner in which the horses are being presented.

Estasan ibn Estopa, World Champion Stallion 1987 (Sweet)

There has been much talk of a 'new and exciting' way of showing Arabians over the last decade or so. Much (though not all) of this new way has been imported from the USA, either directly or via the European shows. As the popularity of the Arabian increased, more countries began to hold shows, or rallies as they were sometimes known. By the 1980s there were not only national and international shows, but European and World Championships. These international shows took on a new kind of character, derived partly from American shows and partly from the character of shows in the host country.

The general tone of these is flamboyant, with almost as much emphasis being placed on the performance of the handlers as on that of the horses. With this style of showing, horses are expected to be very lively and full of presence (although the best horses have always been full of presence). In practice, this often means that they are 'hyped-up' almost to the point of being uncontrollable. Some handlers enact strange ritual dances around their charges in an attempt to attract the horse's attention (cynics might say that, in many cases, this is to attract the judges' and the spectators' attention *away* from the animal's faults); some look as if they would be more at home in the *corrida* than in the showring (again, cynical humorists might liken the showring itself to the *corrida*). There is often much flourishing of whips, much posing of horses (and handlers) in a variety of artificial stances. When trotted up, horses are made to go very fast, so that they produce some spectacular airborne extensions – that is, provided they can retain their balance sufficiently not to fall into a canter. The detrimental effects of this are examined more fully in Chapters 3 and 6, but misgivings about these effects were being heard even before the first international show was held on British soil, at Towerlands, Essex, in 1989.

In that year Jane van Lennep (owner of Triumphal Chant, British National Champion of 1986) visited the Masters Open Championship in Ostend. She was not overimpressed with what she saw. 'The trot was demonstrated at high speed around a triangular course, accompanied by claps, bangs and rattles from the enthusiastic audience. At the corners, the horses were pulled up sharply and wheeled around their leaders before setting off on the next sprint . . . one could not help wincing at the "unhorsyness" of it all."[1]

Fred Rice, for a number of years head showman at Crabbet, was not impressed at all by the American style of showing: '. . . they trot too much in front of them, as though they got dogs, everybody shouting and hollering . . .'[2]. This 'shouting and hollering' is part of a phenomenon which is increasingly to be seen at contemporary shows in Britain, although it has long been a feature of the scene on the continent and in the USA – that of 'audience participation'.

As horse transport has become easier and more comfortable for both horses and their attendants, and more show enthusiasts have attended shows in Europe and elsewhere, it has become fashionable to deride the traditional British attitude to shows; i.e. that audiences, however enthusiastic, should remain quiet and restrained (whether the ringside audience at a Welsh Cob class in Wales could be regarded as 'restrained' is a matter of opinion). Whenever overt enthusiasm is demonstrated, it is generally regarded as *infra dig.* for this to exceed a modest amount of applause. I would go so far as to say that the majority still prefer it this way; it accords well with the generally serene (from a spectator point of view) atmosphere of the typical British showground. This does not mean that people are not enjoying themselves; it is simply that many do not feel that outbursts of noisy enthusiasm are appropriate.

That is not the view of a number of increasingly vociferous showing personalities and spectators. They believe that traditional British shows lack the sparkle and pzazz of their continental counterparts, and that it is

Lilac Shadow, Winner of the Veteran Mare Class, Arab Horse Society Summer Show 1993 (Sweet)

time British audiences were encouraged to express their enthusiasm more openly. This has resulted in some very noisy displays at shows, notably the Arab Horse Society Summer Show at Malvern, and the northern show at Haydock; but most especially at the International Show held at Towerlands. In some cases audience behaviour has degenerated into what appears closely akin to a display of mass hysteria; in others it seems nothing more than an excuse for blatant rowdyism, with spectators screaming and shouting during each class. One does not have to be a 'stuffed shirt', believing that audiences should remain silent at all times, to find this behaviour extremely distasteful. Indeed, it is precisely this hysteria that has led some eminent breeders and exhibitors in the USA to withdraw from showing; one correspondent from the USA remarked in a letter to the *Arab Horse Society News* that this 'is part of a complex of bizarre behaviours that keeps me away from the shows'.[3]

Other letters in the same issue deplored the increase of such noisy 'audience participation'. Marianne Slesinger wrote: 'I do not belong to the group who think we should never clap or show appreciation of a good performance; in fact it is sometimes very difficult not to burst into spontaneous applause if a horse has performed spectacularly, but more often than not we spoil the performance anyway when the horse breaks its rhythm . . . I simply love happy horses and would rather not look around me and hear and see a yelling mob.'[4] Another letter expressed concern at the 'excessive clapping and shouting while the judging of horses was in progress' at the 1994 Summer Show at Malvern. 'It was distressing to see so many horses put off their stride and sometimes upset by those people in the stands that were either politically motivated or just giving way to uncontrolled exuberance.'[5] Barbara Campbell, a noted Arab Horse Society judge and a governor of the Society, was moved to write about the 1994 International Show at Towerlands that '. . . it was with a growing sense of shame that I saw the classes. The undignified and disgraceful behaviour of onlookers at some of the European shows has been taken up at Towerlands and it was with dismay that I heard the announcer actively encouraging the screaming and yelling that accompanied every class. This behaviour denigrates the horses . . . I felt ashamed of the hysteria shown by the majority of the onlookers. Must we continue to behave in a fashion that shames the Arabian horse?'[6] Such displays of rowdyism are spreading to regional and county shows, and it is quite evident from the above and from previous correspondence, as well as from conversations I have had with a large number of showing enthusiasts, that a significant proportion of show supporters find the noise distracting and unpleasant, spoiling the enjoyment of other spectators and, more important, upsetting the horses.

It is the latter aspect which concerns many people the most. I would ask those who advocate (and in some cases actively promote) this kind of 'atmosphere' to consider its effect on highly strung horses. All those who work with, or indeed spend any time around horses – particularly the hot-bloods – cannot fail to realise how very thin is the veneer of 'civilisation' which separates even the best-trained horse from his primitive reactions to sudden movement and loud noises. It is certainly possible – as with cavalry horses and police horses – to train them to ignore these to a great extent, although the 'bomb-proof' horse so often advertised does not exist and never has done. For such working horses as these, tolerance of noise and disturbing situations becomes part of their job; and horses are far better at recognising a worthwhile activity than most humans give them credit for. But what of the highly strung show horse?

It may take months of careful handling to produce calmness and response to the trainer; in the process trust in the handler is (hopefully!) built up and must be maintained if future progress is to be made. Most horses, even the nervous types, will then endure all kinds of potentially threatening or worrying situations, because they trust their handlers sufficiently to believe that the latter will never deliberately put them in danger; many horses also have an uncanny knack of knowing whether the handler's action was deliberate or not.

When a horse enters a showring where there are a number of other horses, he is less likely to feel intimidated by the strangeness of the surroundings because he is in the company of his own kind (he may still become excited by them but that is another story). If the atmosphere in the showring remains calm, there is no reason for the horse to get upset unless something untoward happens.

However, what if a horrendous noise suddenly erupts from the audience? If this happens when the horse is giving his individual walk or trot up for the judge, he is likely to assume – possibly correctly – that all the noise is directed at him personally and even if he does not break out into an open panic, he may still become very upset and unsettled. This is even more likely, of course, with vulnerable youngstock. As any even mildly knowledgeable person will know, horses are extremely sensitive to atmosphere and especially to loud noises. It has been proved that horses respond favourably to subdued music of the classical type, whereas they become very tense, irritable or upset when loud, aggressive rock music is played close by. It must be torture for animals with such sensitive hearing to be subjected, not only to loud music at some shows, but to the yelling and stamping of a crowd of people. It is perfectly true that some horses, such as those of the Royal Horse Artillery, can tolerate very loud noises, but it must be remembered that in these instances the noise is of relatively brief duration and the horses come to regard it as a necessary, if unpleasant, part of their job. In any case these horses are specially chosen for their phlegmatic temperament; 'phlegmatic' is not a word that springs to mind when describing the average Arabian in-hand show horse!

Of course, individual horses vary in their reactions. Some appear to love the atmosphere; some appear indifferent. However, many others are clearly upset by it, which is demonstrated by the number of horses that are put off in mid-stride, breaking the rhythm of the trot because of sudden noises from the audience. It is difficult to believe that some of those bursts of applause or other noises are not a deliberate ploy to put off a rival's horse; in some cases the loud cheering greeting the entry or passage of a particular horse must be a none too subtle attempt to influence the judge. These are tactics which have no place in our showrings, and if they are an attempt to ape what has been happening in the USA and in other countries for years, they will only serve to bring the Arabian still further into disrepute. The Arab Horse Society Show rules recognise this problem, and Rule 17 (Outside Assistance) specifically states that rattling tins and banging on the side of the ring is forbidden. However, it is a pity that the rules do not specifically recognise the disruption and potential danger to the class that unruly ringside behaviour can cause, nor do they provide for the removal of such disrupting influences. The difficulty of implementing such a rule should not be a consideration; there are always ways round such difficulties.

The Arab Horse Society has been trying for some years – with varying degrees of success – to banish the image of the Arabian as a pretty but useless show horse. In spite of this, many serious horse-lovers who are not directly connected to the Arab world, stare with disbelief when they see some of the antics in Arabian in-hand classes, even at regional and county shows. One such observer, watching a regional group in-hand class a year or so ago, remarked to me that she thought the whole thing was 'farcical', and did nothing whatever to enhance the Arabian's reputation. How much more scathing would the pronouncement of this very knowledgeable person have been if she had witnessed what is already happening at the International Show and is starting to happen at shows like the Summer Show at Malvern. If attempts to 'jazz up' the Arabian show scene spread, then I cannot see any end other than the total alienation of the serious, knowledgeable horse-lover.

Part of the problem, I feel, is that, in contrast to the trends of previous eras, too many modern owners of Arabians are not horsemen or women in any real sense of the term. So many appear to regard their horses as living ornaments and bring to their ownership insufficient understanding of the Arabian's physical and mental needs *as a horse*. No matter how beautiful or exotic an Arabian may be – and I would be the first to admit that in certain respects Arabians *are* different – they are still *horses*, and the same principles of horsemanship – whether they relate to the keeping or riding of horses – apply to them as to any other breed. It seems to me that many owners, breeders or exhibitors of Arabians become 'horse-blind' – they can see no virtues in any other breed but their own. This is understandable but it produces a blinkered view which, in the end, does neither them nor their horses any credit.

One rather disturbing trend which has appeared relatively recently at international shows is that of the liberty class. At first it may seem strange that I should call this trend 'disturbing'; after all, surely the sight of horses moving freely about a ring is most enjoyable and exciting? And so it can be *if* it is done correctly. By this I mean that the horse is prepared with as much skill and attention to detail as may be found in the best circus liberty acts, such as those of Mary Chipperfield and Yasmin Smart. In these acts each horse has been thoroughly well educated in what is expected of him, so that when he first appears in the ring in the exciting atmosphere of a public performance the familiarity of the routine and his absolute trust in his handler serve to soothe any fears he may have about the noise and the strangeness, and calm any tendency to overexuberance. When it is handled with the skill and finesse of the trainers referred to above, this kind of liberty act is an absolute joy to watch, expressing perfect harmony between the horses and their handler, in much the same way as a performance by the Spanish Riding School. Jane van Lennep, commenting on the Masters Open Championship at Ostend in 1989, wrote of the liberty act given by Yasmin Smart and Dany César, which involved eight Arabian stallions: 'The grace, harmony and sheer skill displayed were the highlight of the whole show, far more an advertisement for the Arab's grace, beauty and trainability than anything else seen all weekend.'[7] This true type of liberty act bears almost no resemblance, however, to what is currently being seen at some international shows. Following the introduction of such an act to the International Show at Towerlands in 1994, Marianne Slesinger wrote in the *Arab Horse Society News*: 'I cannot see the pleasure of chasing horses round an arena while people clap, scream, whistle and generally behave as in a mindless mass hysteria. Some horses, such as the Maxwells' splendid mare Aliha, seem unconcerned by it all. 'But not all horses are the same and if the "class" is going to grow we shall see a number of horses being totally confused and some very scared.'[8]

With all these developments, what of the horses themselves? I mentioned earlier the variations in type among the horses exhibited as one of the things which our mythical time-traveller might well find startling. They would see a considerable difference between the kind of Arabians they were accustomed to see in the ring and many of the exhibits adorning our showrings nowadays. If they belonged to the heyday of the great studs, such as Crabbet, Hanstead, Courthouse and Barton Lodge, they might be struck by how much 'finer' so many of the modern horses are. They might remark on the preponderance of greys, where once chestnuts predominated. They might well wonder, looking at some of the in-hand winners, whether they would actually like to *ride* such a horse, or whether it would be up to the demands of such hard work as it would have been required to do in the desert. Nevertheless, they would also be taken by the refined beauty apparent in so many of them, although, at the same time, they might question why so many of them seem incapable of behaving well as they had always understood the Arabian's superb temperament to be one of its major assets.

Rostam, Reserve World Champion 1982 (Sweet)

As with everything else in the showing world, the change in the horses' appearance did not come overnight. It has been a gradual process as more and more horses are imported from other countries where popular ideas of how an Arabian should look may differ somewhat from those formerly held in Britain. These changes have accelerated over the last ten years or so as the steady flow of imports changed to a flood, to the extent where it sometimes seems that every other horse seen in the showring is imported. Whether such changes have always been for the better is very much open to question, as we shall see in Chapters 5, 6 and 10.

Fred Rice who, in his day, saw some of the finest Arabians in the world, was critical of some of these imports, particularly the Polish ones: '. . . I thought they was too long in the cannon bone, and I thought they had tremendous long tendons, you know, and sort of funny feet at the end of them'.[9]

Nor was Fred any more impressed by some of the Russian imports: 'One or two came over was pretty good, but they was very coarse, taken for all. I didn't reckon much of them, and I didn't think they reined well'.[10]

Nevertheless, whatever misgivings some Arab enthusiasts may have about the type of horses now winning in our showrings, the past few decades have seen some outstanding horses, both imported and home bred. The grey stallion Roxan (Count Roland x Bint Roxana) was himself highly successful both in the showring and as a TV star (he was the horse in the famous White Horse Whisky advertisement – 'You Can Take a White Horse Anywhere'). However, it is as a sire of show winners that he has proved himself even more successful. One of his sons, Rostron (x Gold Roseifa) has won extensively both in-hand and under saddle, and Rostron's full brother Roseif won the National Futurity Gelding class of the 1989 Arab Horse Society Show. Al Rakka (Roxan x Russalka) was reserve best yearling colt at the 1988 Summer Show, while Roxan's grandson Rusleem (El Saleem x Rullante) took that award in 1990.

Roxan: 'You Can Take a White Horse Anywhere' (Kit Houghton)

Riaz (Darjeel x Razehra), the elegant liver chestnut stallion bred at Barton Lodge by Lady May Abel-Smith, had many show wins to his credit. Another impressive stallion tracing back

Mehzeer, British National Male Champion 1982

to the foundation mare Nuhra is Mehzeer (Mehriz x Alzehra) who, after many wins elsewhere, went on to become British National Champion in 1982.

Two other outstanding stallions who have not only done well in the showring but have gone on to show that they can transmit their qualities to their offspring are Ahmoun (Ludomino x Shtaura) and Golden Cavalier (General Gold x Crystal Gold). The latter's son Imad (x Ivory Wings) has not only proved himself in the showring, but was assessed as Grade 1 by the National Stallion Association and Grade A by the Arab Horse Society in the 1993 Stallion Performance Testing held under the auspices of the National Stallion Association. A very elegant horse, full of type and presence, Imad is, like his sire, proving prepotent and his stock can be seen doing well at a number of shows.

Another outstanding stallion bred from the more traditional bloodlines is Crystal Magician (Crystal King x Sheer Magic), a prolific show winner both in-hand and under saddle. Spearmint (Shammar x Sappho), of classic Courthouse breeding, was British National Junior Male Champion at Ascot in 1985. He, too, has proved a sire of fine horses.

In 1976 the Maxwells of the famous Lodge Farm Arabian Stud visited the Vlimmeren International Show where they saw a yearling who took their eye. They decided to lease him and, within two years, he had won two National and two European Championships. The horse was El Shaklan (Shaker el Masri x Estopa) who proved to be, in the words of Emma Maxwell: '. . . the most popular horse we ever stood at stud and it was with great regret we saw him return to Germany one year ahead of time due to the death of his sire.'[11] After his return to Germany, El Shaklan went on to win the German National Championship, was Senior European Champion and Reserve World Champion. El Shaklan must surely have been one of the most influential sires worldwide and he has stamped his type on the Arabians of several countries. His son Maleik el Kheil (x Muneera) has also been extremely influential in the UK and won not only the World Championship but many other championships and also sired a number of show winners. He was bred to Atlantica (El Shaklan

ABOVE *Spearmint, British National Junior Male Champion 1985 (Sweet)*

Imad (Betty Finke)

x Aliha) (Aliha was World Champion Mare in 1988, and one of the truly outstanding mares of our time), to produce another filly, Ayat (1993) who has since been National Reserve Champion, Nations Cup Reserve Champion, and UK International Champion – underlining Emma Maxwell's comment that: 'El Shaklan is one of the few horses it is possible to inbreed to so closely and produce unflawed results.'[12] Atlantica herself has also been World Champion Mare (in addition to winning many other titles) as well as being successful on the race track!

However, one of the most exceptional horses of the past few decades (although possibly not fully appreciated in Britain) must be Carmargue (White Lightning x Velvet Shadow). His breeder, the late Glyn Greenwood, hit upon one of the often sought after, but seldom found, 'golden crosses' when he put the mare Velvet Shadow (Bey Shadow x Nasim) to White Lightning (Burkan x Latawica). The result was a number of outstanding progeny, such as Rostam (Reserve World Champion in 1982), and the lovely mares Lilac Shadow and Ermine Shadow. Of all of them, however, it was Carmargue who made the most impact. As a yearling he was correct enough but had little about him to suggest that he was

Carmargue, World Champion 1985, Spanish National Champion 1986 (Sweet)

world champion material. However, Alun Prothero, who eventually bought him, recognised his potential, and decided that this was the horse for him. His faith was amply rewarded when Carmargue won the World Championship in 1985 while on lease to Don Diego Mendes in Spain. A couple of years after this triumph, which he followed in 1986 by becoming Spanish National Champion, Carmargue was leased to Jay and Sigi Constanti of the Om el Arab stud in California. He delighted the Constantis in every way, both by his beauty and by his temperament, a legacy from his forebear Bright Shadow who was renowned for his lovely nature. Jay Constanti described Carmargue as 'flawless and wonderfully functional'. Constanti, who has taken part in long-distance rides such as the gruelling 100-mile (160 km) Tevis Cup (over some extremely tough terrain) took the stallion up into the mountains and reported that he was 'absolutely phenomenal on the trails. Nothing rattles him and he is a power machine, moving right along, never breaking. He could do the Tevis over and over again and come back totally fit and sound every time.'[13]

Carmargue's stock are now coming through successfully in the USA, while in Britain we are starting to see more of his offspring doing well in the showring. Several of his sons, such as Djammal (x Bint Jamiellah), W S A Charismma (x Bint Shantu Halima), Sajiid (x Liana el Shaklan), Arazi (x First Blush), H T Nyagra (x Nyarra), and Phoenix Kalibur (x Bur Sable), among others, have come to the fore, with Sajiid Reserve Junior Male Champion at Malvern in 1992, and Arazi Junior Male Champion in 1993. Another son, Ali Khalil (x Liana el Shaklan), is also beginning to make his mark. It is to be hoped that Carmargue proves as prepotent as the ancestor to whom he traces back through several lines, the great Skowronek, and that in putting Carmargue to mares of El Shaklan bloodlines Alun Prothero may have found another 'golden cross'. Only time will tell.

No chapter on modern shows would be complete without a mention of that splendid veteran Hanif (Silver Vanity x Sirella), winner of many awards, who, to the delight of his many fans, won the veteran class at the Arab Horse Society Summer Show at Malvern in 1991 at the grand age of 29. An irrepressible and delightful character, he has sired a number of prolific winners, including Haroun (x Indian Snowflake), who was three times reserve champion, Supreme Champion in 1974, and European Champion in 1980.

Of the many other outstanding show horses of our time, it is impossible to mention more than a few, such as the elegant Mustaphah (Melchior x Crystal Shadow), Senior Male Champion in 1991; the Polish-bred

Hanif, winner of Veteran Class, Arab Horse Society Summer Show 1991 (Sweet)

BELOW *Mustaphah, Senior Male Champion 1991 (Sweet)*

Pilarka (Palas x Pierzga) and Egina (Palas x Estrada), both very stylish mares; and the showy Estasan Ibn Estopa (Ibn Estopa x Bint Estawa), bred in Germany. I have omitted others that undoubtedly deserve a mention simply because the sheer quantity of Arabian horses now being bred and the number of shows at which they can win is so enormous (ridden Arabians are given a mention in Chapter 4).

In some cases these show winners have dazzled briefly, only to plunge into obscurity. Others have impressed in the showring but failed to sustain their promise elsewhere. The dangers of relying on show wins as a criterion of excellence have never been so apparent, as we shall see.

Sadly, there has been a trend in later years for owners whose interests lie primarily in gaining wins in the showring, to import and win rather than breed and win. While this may be highly satisfactory for the parties concerned, it does not make for a very healthy situation as far as consistency of breeding is concerned. Fortunately, some breeders who are dedicated showmen and women, and who have imported quite a number of horses over the past few years, have devised breeding policies based on a mixture of home-bred and imported stock.

Even so, the policy adopted by so many owners, of importing horses specifically to show, rather than showing stock from their own breeding programme, has had a disturbing impact on the breeding of Arabians, not only in the UK but abroad – as we shall see in Chapter 10.

As far as the overall Arabian show scene is concerned, we shall see that all is far from well. At a time when the Arab Horse Society is valiantly trying to promote the image of the Arabian as an all-round riding and performance horse, the image of the Arabian horse in the minds of the general equestrian public is not improving. This is due not only to prejudice against the Arabian itself but to a perception of the Arabian horse world as being rather dotty and full of weird characters and even weirder practices. I suspect that many owners and riders of Arabians are growing tired of having to be somewhat apologetic about the fact that they own and show Arabians. That all this is unfair is not the point. The above perception is based on the strange behaviours (on the part of both horses and handlers) too often seen in the showring; on the fact that so many of the exhibits look as if they would crumple if a saddle were placed on their backs; and on the way in which so many of the horses are presented as lunatics ('good-looking nowts' as one forthright Yorkshireman observed to me). A distorted view? Perhaps; yet that is how the equestrian public at large views us and, as the following pages will show, we, the owners, breeders, exhibitors and judges of Arabians, have only ourselves to blame.

Notes

1 Van Lennep, Jane, 'They Do It Their Way', *Horse and Rider*, April 1989
2 Rice, Fred, *Chestnuts, Greys and Rodeo Days*, p.41
3 Letters, *Arab Horse Society News* no. 84, p.58
4 Letters. *Arab Horse Society News* no. 84, p.58
5 Paine, Beatrice M., Letters, *Arab Horse Society News* no. 84, p.59
6 Letters, *Arab Horse Society News* no. 84, p.58
7 Van Lennep, 'They Do It Their Way'
8 Letters, *Arab Horse Society News* no. 84, p.58
9 Rice, *Chestnuts*, p.77
10 Rice, *Chestnuts*, p.77
11 Maxwell, Emma, 'A Quantum Leap – El Shaklan', *Arab Horse Society News* no. 83, p.51
12 Maxwell, 'A Quantum Leap', p.51
13 Quoted by Gari Dill-Marlow, 'State of the Union', *Arab Horse Society News* no. 72, p.50

Chapter 3

THE IN-HAND ARABIAN

'An Arabian should be judged for his ***natural*** *beauty . . . but this method of assessment presupposes a body of judges who are familiar with the natural beauty of an Arabian in natural surroundings. Such surroundings and such judges are a rarity in any country today. So the art of Showmanship must take the place of Nature.'*

MARGARET GREELY

AMONG ALL the activities in which one may take part with pure-bred Arabians, in-hand showing reigns supreme. It is not that owners of Arabians do not do other things with their horses; they do, but their efforts go largely unsung except in the fields of racing and endurance riding. Whether this is because of a reluctance to publicise their activities or whether these activities are not widely reported because they do not come directly under the aegis of the Arab Horse Society it is difficult to determine, but a glance at the twice-yearly *Arab Horse Society News* serves to confirm the disproportionate amount of weight given to in-hand showing.

For instance, one recent issue devoted three pages to endurance riding, three pages to Arab racing, and no less than four pages to reports of in-hand shows (this is apart from reports of in-hand shows in other counries). Just one and a half pages are given to ridden classes, while reports of the other activities were (perhaps understandably) confined to snippets of news sent in by members of the Arab Horse Society. This implies no criticism of the editor and contributors to the *AHS News*; it is simply a reflection of the way things are in the Arab horse world.

Whether this overconcentration on in-hand showing is healthy for the breed is another matter. The whole purpose of in-hand classes was originally to show breeding stock which was not normally used for riding, such as broodmares, foals, youngstock too immature to be ridden, and serving stallions. As we have seen, showing has now become an end in itself, with all that this implies for the wellbeing of the horses.

Showmanship has taken over from the simple presentation of a horse to the extent that the original purpose of these classes – to set standards of conformation and type and to give breeders something to aim towards – is in danger of being forgotten. With the immense importance being attached to in-hand classes, it should also be remembered that success in these classes is not – and should never be – the sole criterion of excellence. It is merely a starting point from which to begin assessment of that excellence which can only be decided by reference to many other factors impossible to determine within the limitations of the showring.

An in-hand class (or 'halter' class as they are known in the USA and Australia) is basically a very simple affair: all the horse is required to do is to walk round the ring in company with the other horses, stand up to be individually examined by the judge, who will assess conformation and type, and to walk and trot up so that the judge may gauge the straightness and quality of the gaits. Such a limited test of the horse's qualities and ability can, at best, give only a sketchy idea of its true value as breeding stock. It cannot, for example, give any real indication of the horse's temperament, although a horse which is well mannered (without any signs of having been intimidated) may well have a more equable temperament than a horse which misbehaves (although this is not always a reliable indicator). Nor can it, on its own, give any idea of the horse's ability to pass on its own good qualities to its stock, although there are various Sire Produce and Family Group classes which can, to some extent, supply this deficiency but only in a limited fashion. The danger, too, is that in concentrating, as so many judges do, solely on the quality of the trot, the other gaits may be disregarded. A horse may trot spectacularly but have a very moderate, or even poor, walk and canter; yet it can still win a championship. As the canter is not (for obvious reasons) seen in an in-hand class (except where the horse breaks gait) it is in danger of being forgotten, although the walk can often give a reliable indication of what the canter will be like. A horse that has only one or two good gaits is a very much poorer specimen than one which has three good, even if not spectacular, ones.

With these caveats in minds, there is no doubt that, done well, the showing of a beautiful horse in-hand can provide a very pleasing, enjoy-

Sire Produce Group (Monitor) Arab Horse Society Summer Show 1994 (Pleasure Prints Area D)

able sight. The fact that it is simple does not mean that it is easy; indeed, few things to do with the training and handling of horses can be said to be easy. It takes a great deal of patience and tact to persuade an exuberant colt, a high-spirited stallion or a fidgety mare to stand still long enough to be examined by a judge and, at the same time, to show itself to best advantage. It is even more difficult to walk and trot the horse up in-hand in such a way as to display its gaits while also retaining its manners – the showring can be a very exciting place, especially for youngstock. It takes hours of patient practice at home and, even then, with such high-spirited creatures as Arabians, the lessons in deportment so carefully imparted at home can easily be temporarily forgotten. Foals, too, can be very unpredictable. One can only sympathise with those whose foals behave like angels at home, only to turn into little monsters in the electrifying atmosphere of the showring; and this can happen to even the most experienced exhibitors. The answer lies partly, of course, in experience and preparation; the more shows a horse attends, the more settled and well behaved he or she is likely to be (although care must be taken not to overdo the showing; this brings its own problems, as well as being most unfair to the horse). All credit, then, to those exhibitors who manage to show beautifully turned out, well-mannered horses in a simple, natural manner, yet still retain their horses' presence and sparkle.

Having said all this, one should not *over*-estimate the amount of skill required to show a horse in-hand or to train it for these classes. After all, what is the horse required to do? To stand still when asked to do so; to walk and trot in such a manner,, that the judge can adequately assess its movement. It is something that any truly competent handler should be able to do. Certainly, presentation plays a part but should only be the icing on the cake, as it were.

Here is the nub of the matter. The distinction between 'presentation' – the showing of the horse so that it appears at its best, without disguise or artificial enhancement – and 'showmanship' – which is all about maximising a horse's best points and minimising its bad ones – has become blurred. Very often 'showmanship' involves the disguising of defects, whether by artificial means or by clever presentation. 'Good judges', says Sharon Byford, in *The Arabian: A Guide for Owners*, 'aren't easily fooled by tricks of showmanship. They can spot a faulty Arabian even when it is shown cleverly, and they recognise a good Arabian even when it is poorly shown.'[1] In an ideal world this would indeed be so but all the evidence points the other way. Time and again I have seen an Arabian of superior type, conformation and movement, not to mention presence and manners, end up down the line, whereas an inferior specimen, shown in a flamboyant or 'artful' manner has ended up the winner. This has hap-

Standing the horse up for the judge

pened even when the judge is a person of many years' experience. Whether they have been influenced by the fact that the handler and/or the horse is well known, or by the style of showing, is not, of course, something that the spectator can know; all that is apparent is that the judge has, for whatever reason, been taken in.

There are many ways in which 'showmanship' can disguise faults. Byford says, 'When trotting or walking toward or away from the judge, move in a straight line. If the horse wings or paddles, it can be led at a slight angle toward or away from the judge to partly conceal its faulty action.'[2] The point here is that no horse with faulty action should be placed high in a breed class; judges should be alert to attempts to disguise such a fault and should insist on the horse being walked or trotted up straight. An exhibit which refuses or is unable to do this should be marked down. Yet how often does this happen? Very rarely, if one considers some of the faulty action allowed to go unpenalised. I have a videotape of one show where the judge is not even looking at some of the highest placed exhibits to see if they move straight!

Apart from the cosmetic abuses discussed in Chapter 9, perhaps the most controversial aspect of this 'showmanship' is the posing of the horse in an unnatural, stretched position. In this, the horse is made to stand with its head elevated much higher than it would normally be carried, with the neck stretched until it resembles a giraffe; the forelegs are sometimes (though not always) slightly advanced, while the hind legs are stretched well behind a vertical line dropped from the point of the buttock to the ground. The thinking behind this is that the length of the neck and the topline (currently of paramount importance in the USA, almost to the exclusion of all other characteristics) are thereby accentuated, while any hind-leg faults are minimised. In this way a great many conformational faults can be disguised. The arch of the horse's neck, and the manner in which its head is set on, cannot be properly seen; while the topline and the straightness or otherwise of the limbs cannot be fairly judged.

Hazel Moss, in her report on the 1994 Northern Arab Show at Haydock, comments that to the observer this pose does have its disadvantages, 'the main one being that it draws attention to limb faults'[3]. I must disagree that it accentuates leg faults; on the contrary, if anything it serves to disguise them. With the hind legs stretched behind the body, it is very difficult to assess the correctness of the limbs. Sickle hocks, or a too-straight hock, can be very neatly hidden. Nor can any lack of muscle on the quarters or gaskins be readily detected. In any case, it would surely be a good thing if leg faults *were* accentuated; it would at least then be possible for serious faults to be marked down, as they should be. I should say, too, that for the horse this pose has very many more disadvantages than it does for the observer. To begin with, it is highly unnatural – horses at liberty never assume a stance like this unless, exceptionally, they are reaching up to take a succulent piece from a tree. They will not do this if there is better food to be found at a more comfortable height, nor do they remain in that stance for more than a very short time. To ask a horse to stand like this for even the short time it is in the showring is to place an unacceptable degree of stress on its musculo-skeletal system; while during the training necessary to get the horse to assume this pose, the degree of strain imposed is enormous. For a horse to be trained in this manner and then at a later date asked to carry its head in the position necessary for it to work efficiently under saddle, is not only mentally confusing but may result in actual physical damage. Others may disagree but I maintain that the weight of evidence is against them. In Chapter 5 I describe how the horse's back functions somewhat like a suspension bridge, and how the long back muscles lengthen and simultanesously contract isometrically (i.e. without shortening) when the horse is moving correctly. When the horse is made to stand 'stretched' with its head in the air, not only does this hollow its back, it forces the long back muscles to contract *isotonically* (just as a person's arm muscles contract isotonically to flex the elbow joint), bringing the neck and the croup closer together along the topline. This not only inhibits the free transmission of power from the hind legs, it eventually stiffens the back muscles almost permanently, requiring lengthy retraining to correct. In some cases the damage may, indeed, be permanent. Of course, in the USA, where a champion Arab is scarcely required to *move*, this hardly matters (except to the horse) but it is one reason why we see so much peculiar movement in Europe.

Relatively few people seem to understand the mechanism of a horse's back. Reading Sharon Byford's generally excellent book (referred to above) I was astounded to find the following statement regarding the conditioning of halter horses: 'Driving . . . helps level the topline, whereas riding has the opposite effect by lowering the horse's back.'[4] I cannot emphasise too strongly that *if the horse is correctly ridden*, its back should most certainly *not* be lowered; in fact the opposite should be the case. Correct ridden work – with the horse's back lifted and rounded – should, as with proper lungeing, serve to strengthen and improve the horse's topline. Riding that does the opposite is, at best, poor and unbalanced and, at worst, downright abusive. Bad driving can similarly affect the horse's back; in fact, it is even more likely to do so if the horse is driven with its back hollowed. (For further discussion of the horse's back mechanism and how it can be affected, see Chapter 5, also Chapters 4, 6, 9 and 10 *passim*).

To return to the 'stretched' pose, not only is this exaggerated pose potentially harmful to the horse, it does not (contrary to the belief of those who practise it) enhance the horse's appearance. It is not only forced and unnatural, it is downright ugly and it does absolutely nothing to improve the image of the Arabian in the eyes of horse-lovers in general. As one renowned and very much respected teacher and trainer (who herself owns a part-bred Arab – in fact, a Luso-Arab) wrote in a letter to the author, '. . . isn't it sad the judges are going for such a weedy type and also encouraging them to stand up in such an unnatural way. People's ignorance causes so much unhappiness to horses.'[5]

How much better it would be if all exhibitors held to Lady Wentworth's maxim that: 'When showing a horse he must stand square on his legs.'[6] Standing a horse up for a judge is not at all the same as posing it for a photograph. The camera can see only one angle at a time; the judge can walk round the horse, therefore there is no reason to pose it with one or both hind legs stuck out behind it although some horses stand like this naturally. The horse should be alert, with his head and neck raised no higher than they would be held naturally when the horse has seen something which captures his interest. Fortunately, there is a chink of light: some judges are now beginning to insist on horses being shown in a more natural stance, and many more exhibitors are showing their horses in a much more relaxed, natural way. At a big northern show recently, I was encouraged to see that in a large class only one horse was shown in a stretched pose; it was clear from the handler's mode of dress that someone had been to an international show and had modelled their showing methods on what they had seen there. For once, they were the ones out of step! However, many of the top exhibitors, both professional and amateur, are sticking to the 'stretched' pose, perhaps (and this is taking the charitable view) feeling that they will be at a disadvantage at international shows if they do not. If, as many people believe, continental exhibitors look to Britain to set the tone at such shows, perhaps we should be setting an example by being courageous enough to insist on natural poses at international shows too.

Hazel Moss feels that: 'The vogue for showing horses "stretched" is one that is likely to stay with us.'[7] One hopes, for the sake of the horses, that she is wrong.

There are of course numerous other ways in which 'showmanship' can have a negative effect. Some practices even come under the heading of

Alert yet natural: Triumphal Chant, British National Champion 1986 (Sweet)

abuse (these are discussed further in Chapter 9). For the present, however, we shall look at the effects of 'showmanship' on movement.

One of the things which most readily strikes the impartial observer is how few of the horses seen in in-hand classes – particularly colts and stallions – walk or trot freely, without tensing, jogging, dancing around or, in some cases, rearing up or even pulling away from the handler. In the walk, few overtrack as an Arabian is supposed to, either because the gait is faulty or undeveloped, or because the horse is so tense that it cannot step out freely. In some cases horses may be seen to be pacing, that is the hind and foreleg on each side are lifted and set down simultaneously, resulting in a two-beat footfall instead of the four beats we should expect. This is a very serious fault which I have never seen marked down by a judge, even though the quality of the walk – the 'mother of gaits', as the great French trainer Baucher put it – is the basis for that of the other gaits. Yet an Arabian with a true, free-moving walk is a delight, especially under saddle; the pace has a lovely, flowing quality, almost like that of a cat stalking along and putting its feet down precisely and delicately as it does so.

Then there is the trot, which many people mistakenly believe is the Arabian's natural gait. This is not so: if the breed can be said to have a natural gait, it is the canter which, like the walk, should have a smooth, flowing quality, enabling the rider to stay as if glued to the saddle. The trot is certainly a brilliant affair but, as we shall see in the chapter on movement, what is too often exhibited is either a heavy, if superficially extravagant, movement, or a stiff, daisy-cutting effort; in either case the forelegs shoot out in eye-catching extension but the hind legs are inactive, resulting in a stilted, 'proppy' action, or a wild scrambling of the hind legs as they attempt to catch up with the front. The gait should have rhythm and cadence, which requires a proper flexion of all the joints.

Of course, it would be ridiculous to suppose that so many horses truly have such poor action. Some do, of course, and unfortunately some of these are seen winning at a high level; but many more have a perfectly good action which is restricted by the manner in which the horse is handled.

There is no great mystique about training a horse for an in-hand show. It is all about common sense, an understanding of the horse's nature, time and patience. The best professionals and amateurs know how to teach the horse to lead calmly and straight, to trot up on a loose rein and to stand up for the judge or in line without fidgeting. Whether they always choose to show the horse like this is another matter. As with the 'stretched' pose, a multitude of faults can be concealed by – as Sharon Byford says – walking or trotting the horse at an angle to the handler. If a horse jogs or refuses to trot up sensibly; if it will not stand still when being presented to the judge; if, in fact, it is so hyped-up that it *cannot* do any of these things, then any deficiencies of action are nicely disguised, as are faults of conformation. That it is almost impossible to judge such a horse fairly does not deter some judges from awarding such horses high places.

Not that 'showmanship' (or perhaps it should be called 'gamesmanship') is the sole cause of some of the erratic equine behaviour seen. A great number of people in the Arabian horse world seem to believe that a horse – particularly a colt or a stallion as it is most often among these that extreme behaviour is seen – can only have 'presence' when it is indulging in 'high jinks' or overtly spirited behaviour. In the words of Owen MacSwiney, Marquis of Mashanaglass (who spent many years training horses in-hand): 'They feel that an animal that is nervy and agitated at the end of a lead rein is exhibiting some of the fire that is within. Some show judges are impressed by this kind of behaviour, so that one is advised to increase the oats before presenting the animal in-hand'.[8] This is a situation that has become so well established that to many observers it is the norm. Watching a video of a C class show recently, I was struck by the fact that in the Three Year Old Colt class not one of the exhibits displayed good manners. All of them jogged; none of them walked out freely, while two were quite clearly pacing; and although some of them stood up for the judge quite nicely (that is, apart from being presented 'stretched'), as soon as they were asked to trot they started rearing and plunging, and in no instance did a horse trot round without breaking into a canter or leaping around, in one case threatening to trample the handler.

I am as well aware as any of the difficulties a high-spirited colt can present, especially in such a highly charged atmosphere as that of a showground. However, there is simply no need for some of the excesses we see in these and the stallion classes and most of it can be put down to poor preparation and ignorance. Take the business of feeding horses up before shows, to give them 'sparkle'. To stuff an animal, well known for its frugality, full of high energy food before a show is courting disaster, not only because of the uncontrollable behaviour that often results, but because it places a considerable strain on the horse's metabolism, not to mention its mental equilibrium. To my mind it is not far short of abuse to get a horse so 'hyped up' that it is incapable of standing still, let alone behaving itself. (When this same condition is achieved by use of the whip or drugs, then, of course, it *is* abuse – see Chapter 9). Such a horse is in a permanent state of near panic and therefore a danger not only to itself but to its handler and anyone unfortunate enough to get in its way. As the Arabian has always been famous for his superb temperament, this is hardly going to convince the general equestrian public that this 'superb temperament' is not simply a myth. It should be obvious that, quite apart from any danger, this is a highly undesirable state of affairs but, incredibly, there are still those who seem to believe that a horse that is nearly unmanageable makes a fine spectacle. It may look impressive to the ignorant; one wonders, would they be so impressed if such a horse broke loose and killed someone?

It is even more disgraceful to see some handlers deliberately inducing a horse to rear. Again, a horse which rears on cue may look very impressive to those ignorant of horse behaviour but, quite apart from the obvious danger to the handler and to bystanders, what is it doing to the horse? Colts and stallions rear in play, certainly, but these play-fights are merely 'practising' for the time when they may have to defend either their mares or their position in the herd; rearing is therefore part of the stallion's armoury of defence or attack. The highly skilled trainers of the circus, and of certain centres of equestrian excellence such as the Cadre Noir at Saumur, will teach a horse to rear on cue, but it is not the uncontrolled rear that we see in the showring. Their horses are kept very calm, and only those with a very steady temperament will be taught something so potentially lethal. Nor can the *levade* of the High School, as seen in the Spanish Riding School, be compared with what we see in these highly charged show horses. Certainly, there are exceptions to be seen in the showring, such as the Maxwells' highly talented mare Aliha (see illustration) performing her 'party piece' with Emma Maxwell. However, Emma Maxwell possesses a talent for handling horses that is shared by relatively few exhibitors of Arabian horses, and Aliha is an exceptional mare. As Sylvia Stanier (who has a vast amount of experience of training horses in High School work) points out in *Classical Circus Equitation*: '. . . you should not teach your horse to rear just for the fun of it. It is a movement which horses will use against you, especially stallions, if they feel like it.'[9] A stallion that has been taught to rear is potentially dangerous under saddle, and

An exceptional mare: Aliha, World Champion Mare 1988 (Sweet)

even more so in-hand, unless ridden or handled by very skilled people who know exactly what will 'cue' a rear, and who can keep the horse calm and steady. 'Calm and steady' are not words that can be readily applied to many of the Arabian show horses we see leaping around the ring.

Not long ago I witnessed such an exhibition on the part of an Arabian stallion. It was a beautiful horse which undoubtedly deserved to win its class without any vulgar 'showmanship' but the enjoyment was ruined for me (and, to judge from the disgusted comments of spectators, for a good many other people besides) by the sight of this horse continually rearing and walking towards the handler on its hind legs, lashing out with its forefeet as it did so. This was not impressive, it was simply downright dangerous. Yet not only did the horse win its class, the judge made no comment on such behaviour.

The Arab Horse Society Show rules are quite clear on this. Rule No. 3 states: 'Exhibitors will not encourage their horses or ponies in any sort of dangerous behaviour.' Some judges seem incapable of recognising dangerous behaviour even when – as in the above case – it is right under their noses. It is surely time the Arab Horse Society started to enforce this rule more stringently, before a real tragedy occurs and either they or some unfortunate show organisers end up with a messy lawsuit and claims for damages on their hands.

George White, former stud manager at the famous Barton Lodge Stud and a veteran of many years' experience in the showring, comments that bad-mannered horses used to be sent out of the ring. 'We need a few more today like good old Glenda Spooner . . . she'd soon send them out.'[10]

Fortunately, as with the abuses discussed in Chapter 9, it is a minority who deliberately descend to such methods of 'showmanship'. Most other instances of bad behaviour are either a temporary lapse on the part of an otherwise well-behaved animal (which can, of course, be forgiven as horses are not machines) or are due to lack of knowledge or experience on the part of the handler. Similarly, some undesirable practices are caused by a lack of understanding of the horse's mechanics of movement, a prime example of this being the controversial method of turning the horse when it is trotted up in-hand.

When trotting up for the judge, at some point the handler is going to have to turn the horse if he is not to come to an abrupt and unsightly halt after trotting in a straight line. To keep going, preferably in as wide an arc as possible, gives the judge a better chance of observing the trot, since some of the more extravagant movers do not get going properly until a considerable distance has been covered. Most handlers continue the trot around the back of the line-up, where – if they are lucky - the judge may still be watching and a horse which has failed to trot up well initially may be given a chance to redeem itself.

The safest way to turn a horse is always away from the handler; this minimises the risk of being trampled should the horse misbehave or shy. I know this from bitter experience – it is not until something like this happens to you that you realise the wisdom of such advice. Many professional handlers, however, and some amateurs, prefer to turn the horse around them, particularly as they are often moving at such speed that it is almost impossible to turn the horse away from them when meeting the turn. Some people maintain that as they are trotting their horses fast on a long rein, this makes it easier for the handler to turn the horse around themself, and that it is difficult to push the horse away from you when going so fast. It is, of course, entirely up to these handlers whether they want to run the risk of being barged or trampled on. However, it is not so simple for the horse.

An Arabian at liberty will frequently gallop up to a fence or other obstacle, stop dead, spin round on its hocks and dart off again. It will rarely, however, perform the same action at a trot, because the diagonal pattern of steps makes it very difficult for the horse to turn in a small circle. Too sharp a turn may cause strain to the horse's back and hind leg muscles, ligaments and tendons, besides putting the bones of its legs under stress. It is for this reason that the lungeing of horses under two years old is not recommended and that the smallest circle in trot demanded, even at Prix St Georges level dressage, is one with a diameter of 8 metres (26 ft) – and horses taking part in these tests are very well-balanced, supple horses. Yet the circle being demanded by handlers who insist on turning their in-hand horses around them is, even on a loose rein, very much less than 8 metres. It is really most unfair, as well as potentially damaging, to ask such a movement of in-hand horses which are, for the most part, nowhere near as supple and agile as a highly trained dressage horse; and even more unfair to demand it of immature youngsters whose growing musculo-skeletal system is very vulnerable to damage.

It would be much better to halt the horse, turn it around the handler at a walk, then set off again at a trot but this, of course, will result in a 'break' which may cause the judge to lose interest. It would, in fact, be far better to trot the horse up at the correct speed for it to maintain its balance going round the corner. It is certainly more difficult to turn the horse away from you when it is really powering along but it can be done with practice.

The real reason why so many handlers find it difficult is, of course,that current fashion dictates (under the guise of making showing more exciting) that horses are trotted up far too fast. Some can cope with this, but the majority find it difficult to keep their balance at a flat-out trot and so, instead of a true, active trot in which all the horse's leg joints are flexed, we see instead a 'running' trot of the kind commented on earlier in this chapter. It is often this excessive speed that causes the horse to lose its balance and, in order to compensate, break into canter. The handlers who practise this fast trot may think it looks wonderful but, in fact, it does their horses' gaits no good whatsoever. It would be a very poor rider who compelled their horse to trot like this under saddle, so why on earth should we inflict it on the horse in-hand? How much nicer it would be for the observer, and more pleasant for the horse, if the latter were simply allowed to trot out at a natural, balanced speed, active and forward going, certainly, but comfortable for the horse. One must ask, do the people who advocate trotting up fast (and, indeed, some of the other questionable aspects of in-hand showing) ever stop to consider the effects of what they are doing on the horse? Do they possess sufficient knowledge to be aware of those effects? Do they care? At times, one must certainly doubt all of this very much.

However, there is one thing practised by the advocates of more 'exciting' showing which can only be for the good: that is walking and trotting the horse on a long rein. It is, in fact, the length of rein which can cause all manner of problems in walk and trot. Far too many horses are held on much too tight a rein. I used to be guilty of just this error; I always felt that my exuberant youngster would get away from me and tank out of the ring with me dangling helplessly behind (as indeed he almost did during our trot up the first time he went to the Great Yorkshire Showground). Then I realised that not only was I restricting his stride, I actually had *less* control than if I held him on a relatively long, loose rein. Owen MacSwiney points out that: 'It is a psychological fact that horses do not like to be led short . . . A horse that is led short puts up an automatic defence against the leading hand. This is most probably due to the fact that a short-held rein restricts the natural balance and pendulum action of the head and neck, so essential to comfortable movement. Remember that a horse is constantly changing its centre of gravity as it moves, while balancing itself with its head and neck'[11]. He goes on: 'I contend that most leading faults are due to this simple root, believing that the majority of problems may be overcome by simply giving the horse more rein, because, believe it or not, you have more *control* through a longer rein.'[12]

Leading too short causes the horse to move crookedly. The author with Zareeba

Leading short creates the problem of horses bending towards the handler, which, because the body then angles away from the handler, leaves the horse no alternative but to walk or trot sideways. Other leading problems can also result, such as jogging. If the handler lengthens the rein and drops back to the level of the shoulders, the horse will usually walk or trot in a straight line; if it does not, then the whip can be used as an extension of the hand to push the horse gently away. If the horse attempts to get ahead of the handler in the trot, or to rush, it can be restrained, not by jerking on the lead rein, as is so often seen, but by a gentle tap on the chest with the whip. Once the horse gets the message, the same degree of restraint can often be gained by simply holding the whip horizontally in front of the chest (long lead rein in the left hand, whip in the right hand). All this training should be done at home, but if the horse does get exuberant in the ring, the whip is there as a reminder – not to punish, but to explain. As MacSwiney says, 'The whip is merely an extension of the tutor's hand.'[13]

There is, therefore, simply no need for any excesses in the showring. It is perfectly possible to have horses that are full of presence and sparkle – the *brio escondido*, the hidden fire of the Spaniards, so prized in their own horses which are also well mannered and docile. This combination of fire and docility, of spirit and gentleness, has always been one of the Arabian's great virtues. Indeed, to knowledgeable and educated observers, a colt or stallion that is well behaved is far more impressive than one that is allowed to be ill mannered under the pretext that it is showy or brilliant. Owen MacSwiney says, 'I shall never forget the outstanding stallion Romadour II who stood for half an hour, half in, half out of his open box at the Westphalian National Stud, Warendorf, while I modelled his head and neck. It has to be pointed out that a very wide stable passage was in front of him and that fully occupied boxes of other stallions were to the right, the left and in front of him. He had simply been told to stand, and stand he did, his only movement during the whole session being to reach over and sniff at the model of himself on the modelling stand.'[14]

Lest anyone is tempted to say, 'Ah yes, but that was a warmblood, and they are much more "laid back" than Arabians', let them consider the comments which follow the above, about '. . . the splendid colt at Mr Pitt-Rivers's Tollard Arabian Stud, who stood without moving, framed by the open door of his box, while mares and geldings were led past him.'[15] My own pure-bred gelding will, if told to 'stand up' when a rider dismounts from his back, stand like a statue while his saddle and bridle are removed and placed on the fence some distance away. He will do this whether in the middle of the schooling arena or in the yard facing his own box. His playmate, a pure-bred colt, will also stand like a rock in his stable. If my husband or I leave the stable, the colt will only move when called to the door. I have to say that he was a very boisterous foal and his early manners in the showring were appalling; he still has plenty of spirit and fire about him but there is no reason why, with time and patience, he should not be as well mannered in the ring as he is at home.

If a horse shows a lack of presence or sparkle in the showring when it normally displays these qualities at home (and if it does not then perhaps it should not be in the showring), the temptation to overfeed it in order to induce artificial sparkle should be resisted, as should the temptation to resort to some of the abusive practices designed to 'hype up' a horse for the showring. Instead, it should be considered whether the horse is simply bored by the whole procedure. Even the most ardent devotee of in-hand showing must admit, if they are truly honest, that there is not a great deal of scope for a horse to use its intelligence in an in-hand class (although there are still some people who consider the horse to be a rather stupid animal. This will be considered in greater detail in the Conclusion).

My pure-bred gelding is a case in point. He did very well during his first season of showing; his lowest place was fourth, his highest first at the Northern Group Arab Horse Society Annual Show. The following year, however, he lost his showring sparkle. It was all just 'old hat' to him, and tedious old hat at that. He would come out of his box at a show snorting and prancing like a stallion but as soon as we got into the ring he simply swtiched off and I could almost hear him thinking, 'Oh God, not *this* again!' When standing up for the judge he would sabotage the whole performance by resting one foot and all but nodding off. I realised that he was just fed up with the whole business and so have not shown him in-hand again. Not that he dislikes shows; on the contrary, he and his part-bred half-brother adore going to shows and can hardly wait to install themselves in the wagon. But they have to be the right kind of shows, which means ridden classes. Even here, we have to be careful not to take them to so many that this, too, becomes boring. The right balance can be difficult to find and it is all a matter of knowing your horse. Even where the prestige of a stud depends on the showring success of its stallions, broodmares and youngstock, the thoughtful and intelligent manager will be very selective with showing, taking particular care not to overshow the youngstock. Unfortunately for the horses, some stud owners/managers are not so thoughtful and too often we see the same foals, yearlings, two and three year olds trotted out at show after show, with no thought for the physical and mental wellbeing of the creatures thus treated as so many living assets.

If a horse does show signs of 'ring fatigue', surely it would be better to give it a complete rest. Or, if mature enough, it could be brought out under saddle as most Arabians find this much more rewarding. Some horses may solve the problem themselves. Garda Langley tells the delightful story of an Arabian stallion who thought that being led around the showring at the end of a lead rope was simply *infra dig.*; he would grab the cuff of his owner's coat in his teeth and lead her round the ring instead![16]

So far we have concentrated on the horses but what about the handlers? Some, whether professional or amateur, are really good and manage to show their charges to advantage simply, naturally and without having to resort to 'showmanship'. Others are a disaster and some so disgraceful (such as those who deliberately incite their horses to bad behaviour or indulge in what I call 'passive whip abuse') that they bring the breed into disrepute. Although of late there has been more moderation in handlers' behaviour, there are still those who appear to believe they are participating in a circus act, wearing bizarre items of clothing, enacting strange ritual dances and waving whips to attract their horses' attention. If I want to watch a circus act then I shall go to the circus; indeed, at the circus the training and handling of the horses is generally of a far superior standard to what is normally seen in our showrings. I come to a horse show to watch the horses, not to watch handlers cavorting around and whipping up artificial excitement.

Shows can be part of a youngster's education

By all means let us enjoy our in-hand shows. They can be tremendous fun if approached in the right frame of mind; and in moderation they can be good for young horses in particular. As shows give trainers something to aim for, the good behaviour of horses in the showring can be the goal which makes all the patience and tact required in teaching these good manners seem worthwhile. Youngsters learn to accept new sights and the company of different horses, which is a valuable part of their education. Let us not, however, be continually seduced into taking these classes too seriously or according them a greater emphasis than they rightly deserve. As Betty Finke remarked in 'Malvern 1991: A Visitor's Impression' (*AHS News*): 'If the Arabian is to gain broader acceptance as a horse, it is time to get rid of exaggerated show fads and to demonstrate that there is more one can do with an Arabian than put a pretty halter on it and stand it at the end of a lead rein.'[17]

Notes

1 Byford, Sharon, *The Arabian: A Guide for Owners*, Alpine Publications Inc. USA 1987, p.290
2 Byford, *The Arabian*, p.291
3 *Arab Horse Society News* no. 83, p.35
4 Byford, *The Arabian*, p.271
5 Sylvia Loch in a letter to the author, June 1994
6 Wentworth, Lady, *The Authentic Arabian Horse*, p.275
7 *Arab Horse Society News*, no. 83, p.35
8 The Marquis MacSwiney of Mashanaglass, *Training from the Ground*, J.A.Allen 1987, p.127–8
9 Lijsen, Henrik Jan and Stanier, Sylvia, *Classical Circus Equitation*, J.A.Allen 1992, p.16
10 *Arab Horse Society News*, no. 74, p.70
11 The Marquis MacSwiney of Mashanaglass, *Training*, pp.130–31
12 The Marquis MacSwiney of Mashanaglass, *Training*, p.131
13 The Marquis MacSwiney of Mashanaglass, *Training*, p.154
14 The Marquis MacSwiney of Mashanaglass, *Training*, p.140
15 The Marquis MacSwiney of Mashanaglass, *Training*, p.140
16 Langley, Garda, *Understanding Horses*, David and Charles 1989, p.98
17 *Arab Horse Society News*, no. 77, p.42

Chapter 4

THE RIDDEN ARABIAN

'Practice without true principles is nothing other than routine, the fruit of which is a strained and unsure execution.'

FRANÇOIS ROBICHON DE LA GUÉRINIÈRE, 1733

IN THE OPINION of many show producers, the supreme accolade is the coveted Winston Churchill Cup for the Supreme Riding Horse, awarded at the Royal International Show. It has been won by several Arabians: by Astran (Rithan x Astrab); twice by Count Dorsaz (Rissalix x Shamnar); once by his son Count Orlando (x Umatella); twice by Ludo (Blue Domino x Rithyana); by Dadia (Darjeel x Arcadia) and by Carrik Crystif (Crystal King x Nazif). It is fashionable these days to imagine that it is only in recent years that there has been any real appreciation of the Arabian as a ridden and performance horse but, as the above record shows, this is wide of the mark. When the Blunts imported their desert horses to Crabbet in the last century, these were all ridden or driven, whether out hunting, as a means of transport or simply for pleasure. Countless breeders and enthusiasts have, since then, appreciated the Arabian's outstanding qualities as a riding horse, some in a quiet, private manner (for example at Mr and Mrs Kydd's famous Cruglas Stud where the horses were ridden in work on the farm); or in a more flamboyant manner such as winning the Winston Churchill Cup.

Certainly there were fewer opportunities in those days as far as showing was concerned. There was – then as now – a great deal of prejudice against the Arabian and the late Glenda Spooner, doyenne of the showring, put the boot in as far as the Arabian was concerned by damning it with faint praise.[1] Where obvious opportunity was lacking, however, some determined souls made their own opportunities. Mrs Valerie Mallender of

Ludo, twice winner of the Winston Churchill Cup for the Supreme Riding Horse (Rosemary Archer)

the Meadowbrook Stud in Yorkshire, who has produced many in-hand and ridden show winners, wanted to show her pure-bred gelding, Sahla, under saddle. In the late 1950s there were virtually no ridden Arab classes in which she could enter him so she plaited him up and showed him at county level in show hack and small hunter classes, where he always gave the judge a good ride. Later on she hunted him, and comments that: '. . . no day was too long nor jump too high for him and he hacked to and from the meet each time.'[2]

In spite of the present-day success of such outstanding ridden Arabians as the splendid mare Liquidambar (Indian Diadem x Bright Reflexion), the geldings, Berobrien Pharami (Pharis x Fine Fare) and Trevelte (Keemah x Mindela) and the stallion Crystal Magician (Crystal King x Sheer Magic), to name but a few, the number of riders prepared to make the kind of effort shown by Mrs Mallender and others like her is relatively few and this is reflected in the overall standards. In its efforts to combat prejudice against the breed, the Arab Horse Society is constantly reminding the equestrian-minded public of its qualities as a riding horse. A casual observer might ask, 'Then why is so little support given to Arab ridden classes at shows and why are these so often hidden away in remote, minor rings far from the main public eye?'

Crystal Magician, a prolific winner in-hand and under saddle (Sweet)

This may have its roots in our culture. In the USA, perhaps because of the traditional need for fast, agile, handy horses for cattle herding, there has been far less prejudice against smaller breeds, and there have always been greater opportunities for ridden Arabs than in Britain. In Europe there has, until recently, been even less emphasis on ridden classes. Some European shows are now beginning to incorporate more of these but this is very sporadic and the results have sometimes been less than happy. During the second half of the twentieth century, the pre-eminence of the large warmbloods for general riding may go some way towards explaining this lack of enthusiasm for the ridden Arabian as former appreciation of the breed for cavalry purposes has been largely forgotten. Riders who are carried away by the sheer size and power of some of the German and other continental breeds may well fail to recognise that the Arabian can give a much bigger ride than its size would suggest. In Britain, the almost universal obsession with jumping and cross country riding, and a tendency to regard the Thoroughbred and the hunter types as the only 'proper'

Liquidambar, ridden multi-champion with Caroline Nelson (Sweet)

horses, has also led many people to overlook the excellence of other breeds, in particular the true 'hotbloods', i.e. the Arabian and the Iberian horses (which include the Andalusian, or pure-bred Spanish horse, and the Lusitano).

However, it seems to me that there are deeper-rooted reasons than this. It is not as though a showing class demands anything extraordinary in the way of complicated movements. It is, in fact, relatively simple. All the horses are expected to do is to show obedience, manners and good paces in all gaits, on both reins; depending on the show and the judge, to give a short individual show; and to give the judge a pleasant, comfortable, well-mannered ride. Of course, in reality there is much more to it than that.

Recently, watching a video recording of a ridden class at a regional show, I was struck by the fact that, although the horses being ridden were all beautiful animals, of excellent conformation and gaits, none of them appeared to be using themselves properly. In every instance the walk – the mother of gaits, as I have already remarked – was lazy, with the hind legs not coming under the horse sufficiently even to step into the hoofprint left by the forefoot, let alone overtrack by the required six or more inches (15 cm). In most cases the trot appeared comfortable but not really going anywhere; there was none of the real 'lift' and sparkle for which Arabians are famed. Furthermore, obeying the principle that faults in the slower gaits are magnified in the faster ones, the canter in every case was a rather perfunctory affair.

The overall impression was, in fact, rather dull: well-mannered horses, certainly, but lacking any spark, any desire to go forward, or to do anything more than the bare minimum required of them. Indeed, there was evidence in some cases of considerable resistance: tightness in the neck and withers, a hollowing of the back. There was nothing here to convert the anti-Arabian rider, nothing to confirm the Arabian as a superb riding horse; on the contrary, it all served to reinforce the more commonly held prejudices against Arabians. I must emphasise, too, that although this was only one show out of many that season, it was by no means unique; in spite of some improvement in recent years, such sights are all too common at Arab shows.

There are, of course, a number of riders, both professional and amateur, who go to immense trouble in producing their horses and who almost invariably give a superb ridden show. As I write I have in front of me a photograph of Caroline Nelson riding the very talented mare, Liquidambar. It is a picture of classical beauty: horse and rider in harmony and balance, bounding forward in a joyous canter which expresses perfectly the partnership of horse and rider. Sadly, such sights are all too rare; too many riders seem to think that if a horse is well behaved and going in a pleasant, safe manner, then this is all that is required. It seems, sometimes, that some judges too are ready to accept this mediocrity. To those who know what Arabians are capable of achieving, this is very frustrating. It is as though the very people who have the means to combat prejudice against the breed are, in fact, busy confirming that prejudice.

What is the reason behind this? I suspect that it is grounded in that good old British characteristic, intellectual laziness. This manifests itself in a reluctance to indulge in any form of equestrian activity which involves mental as well as physical effort (although,of course, at higher levels at least, *all* forms of equestrian activity require mental effort). Witness our habitual denigration (in spite of the surge of interest of the past few years) of dressage. 'Oh, boring old dressage,' is the parrot cry still often heard. Yet, leaving aside the competition aspect, dressage is nothing more or less than the systematic training of the horse, by means of suppling and gymnastic exercises (which need not be boring at all, but a stimulating challenge), to carry himself and his rider with the same balance and ease as he carries himself when riderless and at liberty. Basic dressage – the 'dressing', or training of the horse – is the foundation of every branch of equestrian discipline; the neglect of this foundation is the reason why the majority of horses ridden in the UK spend all their lives bumbling along on their forehands, often being blamed for being 'spooky', 'scatty', 'a lunatic', when, in fact, if they had been properly 'dressed' or schooled, they would be a much safer, pleasanter and more comfortable ride. A horse that is truly 'on the aids' or 'on the bridle' and listening to its rider, is much less likely to spook and cause an accident than one which is trundling along on its forehand, not working from behind, and not really paying much attention to what is being asked of it.

I am not exaggerating when I say that the majority of horses ridden in Britain are not truly working properly. I am not, of course, referring to the properly schooled dressage horse or well-produced show horse, but to the average horse ridden by the average rider. Many riders fondly imagine their horses are on the bridle because they have their heads tucked in and appear to be going in a nice outline. Closer examination shows that the horse's hocks are in the next county, as the saying is, and it is not really using itself behind. This is too often seen with show ponies, many of which arch their necks and point their toes prettily, but whose hind legs are not really going anywhere. The point I am making here is that to train a horse to use itself properly in a supple, gymnastic and responsive manner is extremely hard work, both physical and mental; it is intellectually demanding because it requires knowledge, dedication, patience and discipline, which the average British rider seems to lack, because they only want to do the 'exciting stuff'. The result is that horses are forced into an outline either by heavy, unyielding hands at the other end of a Pelham or a double bridle (both excellent in educated hands) which the rider does not understand how to use, or by means of gadgets such as draw reins or running reins (which both have their place in the scheme of things, but *only* as a remedial tool in extremely expert hands as their potential for damage is so great) and they never, ever learn to use themselves properly.

It is a depressing thought that equestrianism has declined so much in this land of horse-lovers that dressage is still thought of to a large extent as a somewhat arcane pursuit beyond the reach of ordinary riders. Yet in the seventeenth century one of the greatest exponents of the equestrian art (which in those days meant High School) was William Cavendish, Duke of Newcastle; and in the seventeenth and early eighteenth centuries no horse was considered fit for a gentleman or a lady to ride unless it was schooled to a very high level. The Duke of Newcastle and his successors, the eighteenth-century masters such as the Earl of Pembroke, would be unable to understand how in this century we can put up with so many poorly trained horses. It is not beyond the reach of the average rider to attain a reasonably high degree of schooling. It takes determination, patience and, perhaps above all, understanding but the results, in terms of benefit to both horse and rider, make all the hard work infinitely worthwhile.

Ah, yes, one might think, but what has dressage to do with showing? After all, we are constantly being told that the two are very different. The question is often asked, what should be the difference between the way of going of a show horse and that of a dressage horse? The answer is, there should be *no* difference; in the dressage horse as in the show horse, lightness, expression and brilliance of the gaits should never be sacrificed to mere mechanical accuracy.

The amusing (and rather sad) thing is that a number of top showing people seem to look down slightly on the idea of dressage because they imagine that a dressage horse is invariably held in a heavy contact in a stiff outline and they would not want their show horses to go like that. It is unfortunately true that a large number of dressage judges do still seem to reward a heavy-handed style of dressage, so we see all too many dressage horses, even at the highest international level, ridden on a strong contact with harsh aids. None of this is necessary; as the classical riders of Portugal and Spain and of the Spanish Riding School have shown time and again, a properly trained horse can be ridden in all the High School movements on the lightest of contacts and with the lightest of aids.

What the show people who appear to dislike dressage don't seem to realise is that when the best of them produce superbly schooled horses in a light and responsive manner, what they are doing *is* dressage! Molly Sivewright, whose books *Thinking Riding* should be compulsory reading for every riding instructor and pupil, tells an amusing story about an occasion on which she was asked to give a commentary to the Riding Clubs at an open day at one of the leading showing establishments. After giving a most polished performance on two beautiful horses, the lady who owned the yard halted, dropped the reins, looked Mrs Sivewright straight in the eye and said, 'One thing I would *never* do with my horses is – dressage!'

Mrs Sivewright, stunned, said, 'But that is just what you *have* been doing, quite superbly . . .'.

It was the showing lady's turn to look puzzled. 'But', she said, 'my horses are not on their forehands, leaning on my hands – I like them to be light and to have presence.'

'Exactly so,' said Mrs Sivewright.[3]

Unfortunately, the number of riders capable of producing such lightness, responsiveness and sparkle is relatively small. I believe that the biggest cause of this ineffective riding is the lack, in Britain, of any continuous tradition of classical riding, such as can be found in many other countries of Europe, particularly Spain, Portugal, France, those countries formerly belonging to the old Austro-Hungarian Empire, and Germany and Russia. There are many reasons for this and for a fuller understanding lengthy discussion is required, such as can be found in Sylvia Loch's inspiring book, *Dressage: The Art of Classical Riding*. It is enough to say that the craze for hunting and cross-country riding which developed in the eighteenth century led the British to abandon the principles of *manège* riding as irrelevant to their outdoor pursuits. While this was to some extent understandable, the effects on riding standards were lamentable.

The saddles used for hunting were designed with the laudable aim of encouraging an early version of the modern 'forward seat', with the stirrup bars much too far forward. Unfortunately, few riders were capable of adapting to a light, forward seat across country, and what emerged was the notorious English 'hunting seat'. The buttocks were pushed to the back of the saddle by the forward placed stirrup, which, in turn, meant that the legs were placed too far forward. The only way to achieve security in such a position is to adopt a fairly short stirrup, thrust the lower leg forward and press on the stirrup. The rider was thus perched almost on the loins of the horse, the most vulnerable part of its back. Lieutenant-Colonel M. F. McTaggart wrote, '. . . the shorter the stirrup, the more it throws back the weight on to the horse's loins at the walk and stand, and the more cramped the rider becomes.'[4] Not only is this seat inelegant, it makes the leg insensitive because of the muscular tension involved, particularly as, in the interests of security, the heel is often forced downwards, which serves to tighten the calf muscles, rendering the leg incapable of acting subtly. In addition, the horse's back is vulnerable to damage from the pressure near the sensitive loins. It was, in fact, the antithesis of the classical, balanced seat of the High School rider, in which the rider sits forward in the dip of the saddle so that the horse carries the weight on the strongest part of his back, just behind the withers. McTaggart says of the English hunting seat,

'. . . in which the body was back and the feet forward at the canter . . . however pleasurable to the rider, it is very much the reverse to the horse. It is in fact a travesty of riding, it is not horsemanship.'[5]

I realise that this may offend a number of people who are, or have been, involved in showing and riding Arabians, particularly as photographs of ridden Arabians of even relatively recent years show the riders almost universally adopting this seat, while today it may still sometimes be seen in some cob and hunter classes. They may understandably object that their horses went well for them when they rode in that manner, or that so-and-so always gets a stunning performance out of his heavy hunter, or whatever. This may be so; I would suggest, however, that the success of so many of these riders has been due to their natural skill and talent which have enabled them to overcome the limitations imposed by the 'English' seat. It is a testament to the excellence and forbearance of so many horses that they have indeed gone well for riders adopting this harsh, heavy seat; but how much better might they have gone, and how much more pleasurable it would have been for them if their riders had only possessed the knowledge to enable them to ride in a lighter, more balanced manner.

This situation has not been helped by the type of saddle generally used. As stated above, the traditional hunting saddle had the stirrup bars much too far forward for anyone riding in anything other than the modern, balanced, forward jumping or cross-country seat. This stricture also applies to most showing saddles and even to the majority of general purpose saddles (some very good showing saddles are now being made which are a great improvement on the old ones; for a discussion of these and other saddles, see Appendix I). Not only this: it used to be the fashion in the showring (and still is, to some extent) to set the saddle as far back as possible in order to show off the horse's front. This is bad news for the horse who must then not only struggle with the weight of a rider whose seat is by its very nature unbalanced (for a truly well-balanced seat is a rarity indeed), it must also carry this weight on the most vulnerable part of its back. Moreover it is a complete fallacy that sitting further back helps the horse to come off its forehand. It does nothing of the sort; it simply overburdens its hindquarters (for a fuller discussion of the biomechanics of this, and of the equally fallacious idea that raising the forehand involves the use of the rider's hands, see Mary Wanless, *Ride With Your Mind Masterclass* p. 230 *et seq.*, and Paul Belasik, *Riding Towards the Light*, p. 44).

The type of saddle, its position, and the unbalanced 'chair' seat have also played a leading role in a style of riding that is extremely popular in the USA, and which is (unfortunately) gaining popularity in the UK in some breed classes. I am referring, of course, to the American Park horse. Park horse classes are considered the epitome of equestrianism at many shows (including all-Arabian shows) in the USA, and the horses are indeed very showy, with their very high-stepping trot similar to that of a Hackney. I am assured by American show enthusiasts that it takes a great deal of skill to produce a Park horse properly; I can well believe it, but I also know that many of the training methods often used are dubious in the extreme. To me there are few equestrian sights as strained and artificial as that of the Park horse, with its head held high at an angle which actually works against the horse's own biomechanical system, and its unnaturally long toes, weighted by heavy shoes to exaggerate the high knee action. The seat adopted by the riders of Park horses is the epitome of all that is bad in riding. It does not even have the saving grace of being elegant; many of the riders practically stand up in the saddle, with their hands held so high that it is physically impossible for them to have a sensitive contact with the horse's mouth – yet the type of curb bits used, with their ferociously long shanks, cry out for the softest, most sensitive hands possible!

Sylvia Loch describes the evolution of this seat which was originally designed to be easy on both horse and rider:

> 'Initially, park riding was developed from a semi-classical, upright seat, the nineteenth century park saddle being close to a modern straight-cut dressage saddle . . . Gradually however . . . Anglomania took over and as breeders selectively bred for more extravagant pacing action and developed four and five gaited horses, a seat which was based on what was now being referred to as "English style" took over at the big shows of Kentucky or New York. This was a bastardised seat since all that was bad in the old English hunting seat was converted for the riding of gaited horses. Riders, unable to maintain a proper balance, began to slip behind the horse's centre of balance, pressing uncomfortably close to the loins. . . To complement this latest style, lengthened flat-seated, low-cantled show saddles were designed with cut-away heads. It was thought that by sitting further back, the front of the horse would be more exposed and impressive. Riders compensated for this unnatural balance by pushing their legs forward against the stirrup, and holding the hands unnecessarily high, a style still in vogue today in certain showing classes.'[6]

Jeanne Melling, in *The Complete Morgan Horse* (1986), says that this seat, originally designed for English Pleasure classes, was 'developed first for the

American saddle horse to accommodate his regally high head carriage'; she goes on to say that it 'allows for greater freedom of motion in the fore-hand'[7]. However, Sylvia Loch points out that this also has the disadvantage of restricting the rounding of the horse's back, and with a heavy, unbalanced rider could seriously hamper the action of the hind legs. 'Nevertheless,' she says, 'because this flattening effect often causes a more exaggerated use of the horse's front legs to compensate for the problems behind and under saddle, the park saddle seat has remained immensely popular.'[8] It would be interesting to know the proportionate number of horses ridden in such a manner that suffer from severe back problems. It is difficult to see how these could not arise as a consequence of the horse being asked to carry himself in such an unnatural manner, with so much pressure on the vulnerable loins from a rider who, no matter how skilled they may be in the art of presenting horses, can never be in a balanced position.

These critical comments may cause offence, particularly to American readers. However, it was, after all, an American, Colonel T. A. Dodge, who, in the nineteenth century, warned against this departure from true American riding, saying, 'We may love our British cousin and yet not adopt his style.'[9]

This question of the rider's position in the saddle is not merely one of elegance or of some pernickety insistence on 'correctness'; it is a matter of biomechanics. Brigadier-General Kurt Albrecht, former director of the Spanish Riding School, wrote in *Principles of Dressage* that, 'Firmness and effectiveness of seat are not dependent on force of grip or tension of reins but entirely on a correctly balanced position of the rider. A correctly balanced posture is the indispensable foundation of a 'deep' seat; every rider should understand that establishing this posture is a paramount necessity.'[10] There are some very talented riders who have taken the trouble to acquire a correct position and technique, while others have so much natural talent that they manage almost by instinct to apply the classical principles. However, there are far more riders who simply do not know how to sit correctly on a horse and are not even aware of how much they are hindering the horse's progress by this lack of knowledge. Even when the rider is, theoretically, in a balanced position, what we see all too frequently is a tendency for riders to slump in the saddle, with rounded shoulders and collapsed back and waist. They sit like this in the mistaken belief that they are sitting in a relaxed manner; however, there is a vast difference between a body relaxed and free of *excess* tension, and a slack body free of *any* tension! The latter would simply fall over as it is some degree of tension which keeps us (and horses) upright. What is required is the correct amount of muscle tone in the right places. Loose, sloppy riders lead to loose, sloppy horses – not what we want to see in the showring!

Brigadier-General Albrecht states further that: 'It is the quality of a rider's seat that determines whether riding is horsemanship or merely the burdening of a horse with a cumbersome load which he has to transport as best he can.'[11]

Even among riders who have adopted the 'hunting seat' previously described, there have always been those with good hands; indeed, at one time no greater compliment could be paid to a horseman than to say, 'he has good hands'. Unfortunately, this also reflects the British tendency to ride with the hands rather than the seat, abdomen, back and legs. Far too many British riders, even a good number of those competing at the highest levels, have harsh, backward-pulling hands. The stiff 'pram-pushing' hand position, derisively known on the continent as 'English' hands, often goes with arms held rigidly away from the body. It is virtually impossible, with such an arm/hand position, to achieve any kind of sensitive contact with the horse's mouth. When the arms are held in front of the body in this manner, the whole weight of the rider's shoulders tends to bear down on the hands, causing a harsh, unyielding contact and stiffness and fatigue in both horse and rider. In addition to this, the hands are frequently held far too low and wide apart; or, in a misguided attempt to 'follow' the movement of the horse's head, the rider moves the hands back and forth in a kind of 'rowing' action, resulting in an unsteady contact and unintentional pulling back.

Again we must heed the wisdom of Brigadier-General Albrecht:

> 'If the arms are not allowed to fall loosely to the vertical from the shoulder joint, the elbows also are stiffened, precluding both sensitive contact with the horse's mouth, and effective resistance should he endeavour to escape control. Whenever the sensitive elastic contact with the mouth through relaxed arms and forearms has to be transformed into steely resistance, the arms have to be immovably fixed to the chest, and the effectiveness of resistance depends entirely upon the firmness of the whole seat. An incorrect posture of the rider is the root cause of innumerable difficulties in controlling direction and also of faulty carriage of the horse.'[12]

In November 1994 the great Dr Reiner Klimke conducted the Association of British Riding Schools 40th Anniversary Masterclass at

Towerlands in Essex. He was asked what he would most like to see change about British riding. He replied without hesitation, 'Your positions, your hands in particular, and the application of the aids.'

If all this seems rather harsh and critical, it is because I believe that one of the main reasons why so many ridden Arabians fail to fulfil their potential is that they are hindered by ineffective or even harmful riding. Riders in Britain have got away with a great deal because of the immensely tolerant nature of our native ponies, cobs and crossbred hunters and riding horses. The best of these horses will adapt themselves to whatever is going on in the saddle, adjusting their balance as best they can to compensate for the unbalanced weight on their backs. Some of them, including the Thoroughbred, are less forgiving, which is one reason why we have so many horses branded as difficult, or even as lunatics. With the sensitive, hot-blooded Arabian things are apt to be equally uncomfortable. Some Arabians, of course, are extremely laid back; but even these types can be easily upset if they are subjected to harsh riding or contradictory aids. Some react violently; others take refuge in a kind of sullen lack of co-operation, or simply 'switch off', producing at best an uninspired and uninspiring performance. Reporting on standards in the pure-bred stallion ridden classes at Malvern in 1992, Barbara Cary said, 'The purebred stallions . . . were particularly disappointing – with one or two notable exceptions few showed style, manners or exceptional paces. I always think they should be the "Rolls-Royce" of the horse world and to have the privilege of riding them should be something to look forward to.'[13]

I think that, apart from the deficiencies in riding referred to above, one of the main reasons why general standards (in spite of some recent improvements) continue to be so low in the purebred classes is because riders (and this includes even some top showing people) have been seduced by the persistent idea that Arabians dislike being schooled and made to go 'in an outline'. Quite apart from the fact that *no* horse should be 'made' to go in an outline (as the horse makes his own 'outline' as a result of correct training and riding), this simply is not true. Certainly, if the average Arabian is drilled in the manner that some people regard as 'dressage' training (i.e. endless trotting in circles), he will quickly lose interest and 'switch off'. Who can blame him?

Besides, endless trotting in circles without purpose is not dressage. The key to suppleness, engagement of the hindquarters and, in the process, maintaining the horse's interest, lies in transitions, bends, circles and loops, voltes, quarter-turns and progressive lateral work. As the horse gains in suppleness and gymnastic ability, he will delight in learning to use himself properly; the kind of delight an athlete takes in the exercise of a well-trained body. As his schooling progresses, if it is correct, the horse will take ever greater joy in expressing himself through disciplined movement. With horses trained in the classical manner (which incorporates the wisdom of great masters throughout the ages and has been preserved in all its purity by the Spanish Riding School), their training works in harmony with their nature and enables them to express that nature in movement. Thus it is not regimented, repressive training, for that would produce mere mechanical obedience, which is not what we see in classically trained horses. Nor can such performance possibly be obtained by coercion, for any trainer worth the name would agree with Xenophon that: '. . . what the horse does under compulsion . . . is done without understanding; and there is no beauty in it either, any more than if one should whip and spur a dancer. There would be a great deal more ungracefulness than beauty in a horse or a man that was so treated.'[14] On the contrary, it is the result of inviting the horse to do what he takes pleasure in, and enabling him to do this in a balanced, athletic manner.

Certainly, the very fire and sensitivity of the Arabian presents a challenge and perhaps it is the rigour of this challenge which leads so many riders to seize happily on the excuse provided by what I call the 'Great Arabian Myth'.

Some prominent showing people maintain that it is not easy to get Arabians to come 'on the bit' because their conformation makes this difficult for them. There is also a widespread belief that Arabians cannot 'do' dressage. Even those who concede that Anglos and part-breds might excel at this discipline seem reluctant to accept that the pure-bred Arabian is capable of the gymnastic athleticism required of the advanced dressage horse. Rosemary Archer, in her excellent book *The Arabian Horse* (in J. A. Allen's Breed Series) says, 'Some dressage experts complain that the Arabian's short back and general conformation make it unsuitable for this particular discipline. It tends to be less supple than some other horses.'[15] This, I may add, is not Mrs Archer's own view; she is merely quoting the opinions of others and, in fact, believes, as I do, that such opinions stem from prejudice.

I believe this prejudice is the result of a basic lack of understanding, both of Arabians and of the mechanics of conformation in dressage. First, let us consider the 'short back'. Far from being a drawback, this can actually be a bonus when it comes to the highly collected work that is the basis of advanced dressage. The Iberian breeds most commonly used in High School dressage – the Lipizzaner in the Spanish Riding School and

Red House Ziona, a prolific winner under saddle (Sweet)

the Andalusian and Lusitano in Spain and Portugal – have even shorter backs than the Arabian. Indeed it is this short back, with its wide, powerful loins and muscular quarters, which gives the Lipizzaner the athleticism and power necessary to perform the celebrated 'airs above the ground', while the same characteristics enable the Lusitano to perform its incredibly agile manoeuvres in the fiercely exacting mounted *corrida*. As the short-backed Iberian breeds are clearly supremely suited to this highly collected work, how contradictory it is to object to the Arabian's short back as being unsuitable for dressage! Indeed, the only true objection to the short back (so long as it is not excessively short, which would make for an uncomfortable ride) is that it can restrict speed and the length of stride, making real extension difficult. As neither of these restrictions applies to the Arabian the shortness of its back causes a problem only to those who do not know the true purpose and meaning of dressage.

Nor is it clear what other aspects of the Arabian's conformation could render it objectionable (except for the 'flat-back' syndrome which I shall discuss in Chapter 5). The Arabian shares with the Iberian breeds a naturally high head carriage. In *The Classic Arab Horse* Peter Upton says, 'The hocks are engaged well under the horse so providing great impulsion and suppleness. The hind legs should track up well . . . This and the high carriage of the head and forehand tends to place the centre of gravity further back than is generally found in other breeds of horse.'[16] So far from the Arabian being unsuitable for dressage, the picture emerging is that of an ideal dressage horse!

Of course, the problem is that the dressage arena, like the showring, suffers from fads of fashion, and currently the warmblood rules the dressage world. The Arabian's comparative lack of size is also a disadvantage as judges like to see a horse that 'fills' the arena. This, however, is a purely cosmetic objection.

As regards the supposed difficulty of getting the Arabian to come 'on the bit', there is no physiological reason whatsoever why this should be so. Indeed, if the hind legs are properly engaged as they should be, the cleanness of the Arabian's gullet, and the natural arch of the neck, should make it easy for the horse to 'bridle'. However, many show producers like their horses to carry their heads in a position that is often really too advanced for their level of muscular development; and where some other, less-sensitive breeds may tolerate the discomfort this causes, the Arabian may well put up considerable resistance.

Or it may simply be that the rider is sitting in a manner that is heavy and/or out of balance, as all too many riders do. If the rider's and the horse's centres of gravity are maximally out of line with each other, and if the rider is not balanced over their base of support (i.e. the feet), then the horse will find it almost physically impossible to work truly 'on the bit'. Some horses may be able and willing to compensate, adopting a superficially pleasing 'outline', but their whole carriage will be incorrect. Others which are more sensitive (and most Arabs come into this category) have no option but to raise the head and hollow the back and, as we have seen in Chapter 3, and as I shall explain further in Chapter 5, this is biomechanically inefficient and potentially damaging. (For a detailed description of exactly what being 'on the bit' entails and the effects of unbalanced riding, see Mary Wanless, *Ride With Your Mind*, Chapter 6, and *Ride With Your Mind Masterclass*, p. 104 *et seq.*; see also Mary Bromiley, *Natural Methods for Equine Health*, p. 171. Saddle fit is also a factor and is always worth checking first.)

Some problems in this respect are psychological rather than physical.

Arabians are very inquisitive, not to say nosy, and some are very easily distracted by what goes on around them. They like to put their heads up so that they can see what is happening, and sometimes this lack of attention can be extreme and very frustrating for the rider. In addition to this, Dr Marthe Kiley-Worthington has made an interesting observation. She writes: '. . . it must never be forgotten that the horse's peripheral field of vision is very large and, in some horses at any rate, if the horse puts his head up he will be able to see the rider on his back. No wonder a young horse is often hollowbacked and carries his head perpetually high, particularly if he is a sensitive reactive animal such as a Thoroughbred or an Arab.'[17] It is therefore up to the trainer/rider to understand the reasons for the horse's distraction and to work through it with patience and sensitivity, but at the same time firmness.

A large number of people believe that horses basically dislike work and that being ridden is for them, at best, a chore for which their sole reward is their dinner bucket. I believe that to start training a horse in this frame of mind is an almost certain recipe for mediocre results. It is as if a teacher, lacking the conviction that pupils can find the learning process stimulating and the pursuit of knowledge fascinating, sets out to teach with the basic attitude of: 'Well, I know you're not going to enjoy this which means it's going to be hard work for me, but we both have to do it anyway so let's just get on with it.' Such a teacher – and there are all too many of them – is hardly likely to inspire anything but the very boredom he or she fears. So it is with horses. Like people, they can vary in their response to work and to training.

Arabians can be particularly rewarding in this respect as their intelligence and natural curiosity about the world, affinity with humans and general willingness to go forward can combine in them to create a positive response to the idea of work. It is essential to make the schooling sessions as interesting as possible. As classical trainer Erik F. Herbermann has observed, 'Contrary to popular belief, horses do not get bored with basic work. If the rider demands exact responses, paying close attention to detail and quality, neither horse nor rider will have time to get bored, rather, a true sense of accomplishment will be gained.'[18] As Arabians are so intelligent and sensitive, they need constant stimulation in order to work well. Thus they certainly present a challenge to the trainer/rider, but the extra effort will be more than rewarded when the horse responds. As trainer Vicki Hearne points out, 'Good trainers ride all horses as though they were potentially world-class; that's the only way you end up with world-class horses.'[19]

There is nothing in the classical schooling of a horse which demands any movement the Arabian does not perform at liberty. True, he may not perform these movements in as polished a manner as the trained horse under saddle, but he performs them nevertheless. The Arabian stallion showing off to mares arches his neck, shortens his whole frame and prances in a wonderful, elevated, collected *passage*. I have on four separate occasions seen my pure-bred Arabian mare perform a *courbette* that would not disgrace the Spanish Riding School. My pure-bred gelding, escaping the boisterous attentions of the pure-bred colt to whom he acts as 'uncle', will perform a perfect canter pirouette; while the colt, son of the above-mentioned mare, shows an amazing agility in performing all manner of classical 'airs' and collected movements from sheer *joie de vivre*.

The Premium stallion Pharis (Fari II x Elmira) (sadly, no longer with us) sire of National and International Ridden Champion Berobrien Pharami, was used by Baron Hans von Blixen-Finecke to demonstrate *piaffe*. When Pharis was about five years old, his then owner (and breeder), Stella Barclay, took him on a two-week dressage course with Baron von

Pharis, Premium Stallion (Sweet)

Blixen-Finecke. The Baron was no Arab-lover, but when he rode Pharis he was astonished by his responsiveness. He said that Pharis had natural, perfect balance and found it easy to perform various manoeuvres. The Baron was amazed at the stallion's natural ability and aptitude for dressage. In fact, he enjoyed riding Pharis so much that he proceeded to demonstrate pirouettes, *piaffe* and various other movements on him, all of which Pharis did with apparent ease. Detractors of the Arabian could point out that Pharis was an exceptional horse (as indeed he was), but one may counter this by saying that he was also a very good example of an Arabian, and that what one good Arabian can do, so can another, to a greater or lesser extent according to individual ability. The point is that it is impossible for a horse to perform these movements well unless it is truly 'on the bit'; if the Arabian's conformation really made it difficult for them to come 'on the bit', then Pharis – an Arabian of good conformation – could never have performed these movements with such ease.

One might legitimately ask at this point what all this has to do with showing. As horses in showing classes are not required to perform the movements of Grand Prix dressage, does it really matter whether Arabians can perform *piaffe* or *passage* or not? I believe it does matter. The point I am trying to illustrate is that we must not allow ourselves to be hoodwinked into accepting artificial limitations for our horses. Certainly, with the exception of endurance riding, some limitations must be accepted in most equestrian disciplines. It is unlikely that pure-bred Arabians will be able to race successfully against Thoroughbreds over the short distances usual in flat racing. It would be unreasonable and unfair to expect the average pure-bred to compete over cross-country courses designed for horses of 16 h.h. and over, or to jump a Grand Prix showjumping course. But there is absolutely no reason, other than prejudice, why pure-bred Arabians cannot compete on equal terms in dressage up to the very highest levels. Indeed some are doing just that in Australia and the USA, and very successfully. If we recognise this, we can also recognise that pure-bred Arabians can achieve so much more in the showring than most of them do at present. The higher the level to which we 'dress' our horses according to classical principles, the greater the degree of presence, sparkle and beauty they will be able to display in the showring.

Finally, I leave you with a quote from one of the greatest equestrian masters of all time, Sieur de la Guérinière:

> '. . . many people who affect an air of expertise . . . say that the *manège* is of no value, that it exhausts and ruins horses, and that it serves to

Beni Zain, Reserve British National Champion under saddle 1985; also proving that Arabs can do dressage (Kandice Trusler)

teach them nothing but to leap and to dance; which consequently renders them unfit for ordinary use. This false notion is the reason that an infinite number of people neglect an exercise so noble and so useful, the sole aim of which is to render the horse supple, even-tempered and obedient, and to have its weight on its haunches, without which no horse, be it for war, for the hunt or for the *manège*, can be agreeable in its movements or comfortable for the rider. Since the opinion of those who speak in such a manner is thus without foundation, it would be pointless to refute opinions which sufficiently bring about their own negation.'[20]

Notes

1 See her comments in Spooner, Glenda, *The Handbook of Showing* (rev. ed.) J. A. Allen 1990, Chapter 3 on 'Quality'

2 Valerie Mallender, 'Expert Opinions' quoted by Stuart Hollings, *Successful Showing*, Crowood 1991, P.182

3 Sivewright, Molly, *Thinking Riding Book 2*, J. A. Allen 1984, pp. 177–8

4 McTaggart, quoted by Sylvia Loch, *Dressage: The Art of Classical Riding*, Sportsman's Press 1990, p.133
5 McTaggart, quoted by Sylvia Loch, *Dressage*, p.91
6 Loch, *Dressage*, p.124
7 Melling, Jeanne, *The Complete Morgan Horse*, quoted by Sylvia Loch, *Dressage*, p.124
8 Loch, *Dressage*, p.124
9 Dodge, Colonel T. A. quoted by Sylvia Loch, *Dressage*, p.124
10 Brigadier-General Kurt Albrecht, *Principles of Dressage*, J. A. Allen 1987, p.30
11 Albrecht, *Principles*, p.30
12 Albrecht, *Principles*, p.31
13 *Arab Horse Society News* no.77, p.47
14 Xenophon, *The Art of Horsemanship* (trans. M. H. Morgan) J. A. Allen 1962, p. 62
15 Archer, Rosemary, *The Arabian Horse*, pp.93–4
16 Upton, R., *The Classic Arabian Horse*, The Arab Horse Society, p.33
17 Kiley-Worthington, Marthe, *The Behaviour of Horses*, J. A. Allen 1987, pp.30–31
18 Herbermann, Erik F., *Dressage Formula* 2nd ed., J. A. Allen 1989, p.6
19 Hearne, Vicki, *Adam's Task: Calling Animals by Name*, Heinemann 1987, p.146
20 Guérinière, François Robichon de la, *The School of Horsemanship* tr. by Tracy Boucher, J. A. Allen 1994 (originally published as *L'Ecole de la Cavalerie* in 1733), p.79

Chapter 5

TYPE AND CONFORMATION

> *'They were all bright bays, unspotted, perfectly matched, and so proportioned as to seem less than they really were. Delicate ears, pointed small heads; the faces were broad and full between the eyes; the nostrils in expansion discolosed membrane so deeply red as to suggest the flashing of flame; the necks were arches, overlaid with fine mane so abundant as to drape the shoulders and breast, while in happy consonance the forelocks were like ravellings of silken veils; between the knees and the fetlocks the legs were flat as an open hand, but above the knees they were rounded with mighty muscles, needful to upbear the shapely close-knit bodies; the hoofs were like cups of polished agate; and in rearing and plunging they whipped the air, and sometimes the earth, with tails glossy-black, and thick, and long. The sheik spoke of them as the priceless, and it was a good saying.'*
>
> LEW WALLACE, *BEN-HUR*

A CONSIDERABLE amount of time spent hanging around ringsides at shows, or gossiping with exhibitors in the horse lines, has revealed to me one universal gripe of exhibitors and spectators alike, particularly after a disappointing or controversial result: 'What on earth are the judges *looking* for?' What, indeed?

One, rather unsympathetic, response to this might be: read books about the Arabian horse that specify the ideal Arabian type, conformation and movement. There are a number of such books available (see Appendix II). However, while most of these books agree on all the basic points, there is no guarantee that judges are actually looking for the same things. As we shall see in Chapter 7, judges may be influenced in a multitude of ways, not all of them desirable.

Another answer might be to attend an elementary judging course, where type, conformation and judging methods are explained. However, this option is not open to every exhibitor as time, distance and availability of places on these courses may prove prohibitive for all but those who are seriously considering becoming judges. Although the Arab Horse Society encourages members to attend these courses for educational purposes, it could be argued that it is unfair for too many people to take up places without any intention of becoming judges.

In any case, I think there is always room for an analytical appraisal of what constitutes the ideal (bear in mind that word, 'ideal') Arabian horse. So what I have attempted to do here is to provide such an appraisal. It does not include an exhaustive discussion of points of conformation, except where these relate specifically to Arabians or to particular aspects of function. There are many excellent books which describe the finer points of general equine conformation in greater detail (see Appendix II). What I have tried to do is to examine what constitutes the ideal Arabian horse.

First I think we must address the problem of what is more important: type or conformation.

What is meant by 'type'? The word is defined in my Collins dictionary as 'a kind, class or category, the constituents of which share similar characteristics' or 'the general form, plan or design distinguishing a particular group'. In other words 'type' relates to those specific characteristics of a breed which distinguish it from other breeds. The Arabian's most distinctive external characteristics are the beauty of the head and the tail carriage. However, these are only the most immediately obvious characteristics: there are others which are inseparable from conformation, which is why I think it is dangerous to try to separate type and conformation. I shall explore this in greater depth in Chapter 10, Breeding for Showing, but it will become evident during the course of the present chapter that 'type' consists of much more than just one or two characteristics. An Arabian may have good conformation without being a good Arabian; it cannot be a good Arabian without good conformation. Therefore I believe that good conformation – i.e. *Arabian conformation* – should be a *sine qua non* of Arabian type.

Judith Forbis, in *The Classic Arabian Horse*, says, 'No Arabian can be a good Arabian without being a good horse; he must be sound in all respects. However, being a good horse is not sufficient. A horse cannot qualify as a first class or "classic" Arabian without having the distinctive characteristics of the breed.'[1] Peter Upton, in *The Classic Arab Horse*, says, 'Although type is essential and the definition of type should be standard, it can be "all things to all men", so variation in type is inevitable. But those variations must fall within the same broad concept of what constitutes the ideal.'[2] American judge Don Burt says, 'There should be emphasis placed on type, but I relate it more to breed characteristics, rather than just saying "type" (which is really only a matter of semantics).'[3] Burt goes on to say, 'Type is the inherent characteristic that separates the Arabian from other breeds of horse. It is considered to be foremost in the selection criteria for Arabian breeding stock, for if we lose type, we lose the Arabian.'[4] He continues: 'The overall "essence" of the horse is the first impression of type: balance, harmony of composition, grace and spirit.'[5]

I would go further than this. If we accept the dictionary definitions of

Balance, harmony, grace and spirit: Arazi, Junior Male Champion, UK International Show 1994 (Sweet)

'type' given above, we can see that it has a much wider meaning, over and above breed characteristics. In this wide sense, it refers also to function; and it is with regard to this that we must consider how type, conformation and function are inextricably bound together.

It is common (in Britain at any rate) to consider all riding horses from the point of view of an ideal conformation. The reference point for this ideal is (again, in Britain; it may vary in other countries) usually the hunter type, without regard to individual breed characteristics related to function. Some of the better books on conformation do address this issue properly, but these tend to be exceptions. However, while some points of conformation (principally those relating to potential sites of unsoundness) may be common to all riding breeds, others depend much on breed characteristics which, as I have said, relate closely to function.

For example, a British native pony's body might be judged too long and deep in proportion to its legs and height when considered alongside a riding pony or a Thoroughbred. This is because the native pony has a larger than average gut, to enable it to cope with the extremely fibrous nature of the food available in its native habitat. This aspect of the native pony's conformation is therefore a breed characteristic, and is bound up with its function and its native habitat. You might not, for example, consider some of the mountain and moorland breeds, with their short, often bouncy strides, ideal riding types; but if you were crossing, say, Dartmoor or Exmoor, you might well be glad of the sure-footedness of these breeds in an extremely unforgiving, often boggy terrain. In addition, the long back assists with the traditional role of some native breeds as pack ponies – a role for which they are still in demand in some parts of the British Isles. Again, this conformational point is a breed characteristic which relates to function.

On the other hand, the Cleveland Bay, also once a pack animal, was traditionally used to transport a different kind of load, and so a shorter back is more correct for the Cleveland. The hard 'blue' feet – another breed characteristic of the Cleveland – were necessary when traversing the steep, hard causeways of the Cleveland Hills – another example of type allied closely to function.

So if we accept that breed characteristics (or 'type') and conformation are both closely bound up with function, how do we define the Arabian's function and, therefore, what his true type and conformation should be?

To do this, I think we must go back in time and consider how popular conceptions (or misconceptions) of the Arabian's origins and function have influenced images of how the ideal Arabian should look.

Numerous books dealing with the various breeds of horse have laid emphasis on the Arabian's contribution to the creation of the Thoroughbred as being its greatest achievement. This is highly contentious, to say the least, for it not only ignores the Arabian's excellence as a cavalry horse, particularly in Eastern Europe, the Middle East and India, it ignores the breed's vast contribution to the blood of countless other breeds of light horse and pony. This insistence on the Arabian's role as the main progenitor of the Thoroughbred, and as the source of all speed (again, contentious to a degree) has even, paradoxically, been detrimental both to the pure-bred's reputation and to an understanding of the Arabian's function (and therefore of its true type).

On the continent, in particular Central and Eastern Europe, closer contact with the Near and Middle East (often *via* the numerous Turkish incursions into Europe) meant that the Arabian had long been well known and valued for its qualities as a cavalry horse. In Britain, however, the lack of necessity (except in India) to produce large numbers of horses for military purposes meant that attention to matters equestrian was fixed on carriage horses, hunters and racehorses. As we saw in Chapter 4, by the time the Thoroughbred had become a fixed type, the British had long since lost interest in the *manège*, so without the counterbalancing influence of cavalry requirements such as might be found in Austria, Prussia or Russia, the only criteria by which horses were judged were those of the hunting field or the racetrack. James Fleming, in his introduction to *The Crabbet Arabian Stud*, describes this situation neatly. After mentioning the evolution of the Thoroughbred from indigenous mares crossed with imported Arabian stallions, he goes on to say, 'Whether the enormous increase in speed that resulted was in fact due to the Arabian influence is a matter of conjecture. What is important is that breeders thought that it might have been.'[6] When later crosses to Arabians failed to increase the speed still further, the blame was laid on the Arabian, the argument being that if it could not continue to increase the speed of the Thoroughbred, it must therefore be inferior. As James Fleming comments, 'The falseness of a proposition that looked for the one quality in the Arabian that it has never possessed was not apparent to people who had never had the opportunity to observe at first hand its real attributes.'[7]

Of course, the mud stuck. Not all Englishmen, however, shared this prejudice against the Arabian or the near-universal passion for the Thoroughbred. As James Fleming notes: 'Opposition to the primacy of the Thoroughbred became explicit when in 1854 the Crimean War demonstrated that British horse-breeding was not the unqualified success that its admirers claimed for it.'[8] One of the strongest critics was Captain Lew Nolan, the brilliant cavalryman (and one of the foremost horsemen of his day) who carried the fatal message setting in motion the infamous charge of the Light Brigade at Balaklava. Nolan wrote, 'Our cavalry horses are feeble . . . the blood they require is not that of the weedy race horse (an animal more akin to the greyhound and bred for speed alone) but it is the blood of the Arab and Persian, to give them that compact form and wiry limb in which they are wanting.'[9]

However, Nolan and those who agreed with him were very much in the minority, accurate though their observations were. Throughout the rest of the nineteenth and most of the twentieth centuries, prejudice against the Arabian has remained strong. Even when some of its good qualities have been appreciated, it has too often been regarded as a kind of smaller, inferior Thoroughbred, whose qualities (other than its obvious physical beauty) consisted principally of the ability to upgrade other breeds (although how could it be expected to do this if it was, itself, 'inferior'?), and of speed and endurance over long distances. Glenda Spooner, a great admirer of the Thoroughbred, classes 'Arab' quality as inferior to what she called 'true' quality – the latter not stated, but implied, as being that of the Thoroughbred. She regretted the fact that: 'Fanatical breeders are apt to resent the fact that Arabs sometimes have to stand down to the very thing they themselves created. To me it is like a beautiful mother being jealous of an even more beautiful daughter'[10] – words that would have elicited a few raised eyebrows from authorities such as Captain Roger Upton and Count Stroganov. It was consistent with the British closed mind about virtually all riding horses other than hunters and race-horses (an attitude which persists even today in some circles) that Lady Wentworth found it necessary to be so insistent on the Arabian being the fount of all excellence in the Thoroughbred (see especially her panegyrics in *The Authentic Arabian Horse*, *Thoroughbred Racing Stock*, *The Swift Runner*, and *The World's Best Horse*) and her passionate declarations on this point leave a distinct impression of the lady protesting too much.

Still others, less concerned with the Thoroughbred, have been equally insistent on the Arabian's qualities as primarily a speed-merchant. There is a persistent vision of the Arabian sheikh on his fiery steed, galloping flat out over vast level plains of sand. But the land in which the Arabian was formed is not composed of vast level plains; quite the reverse. The deserts where the principal horse-breeding tribes of the *bedu* roamed (and it must be remembered that the Shammar and the Anazeh did not migrate to Mesopotamia until the seventeenth and eighteenth centuries), contain some of the roughest terrain in the world. In general, the country is hilly, sometimes composed of rocky, low-lying mountains. Even where there are completely flat areas, the ground is usually broken and very rocky. In the vast stony desert called the Harra, for instance, the ground is so strewn with boulders and stones that the narrowness and intricacy of the paths winding in and out of the boulders made travelling across it with camels very difficult. Even in the Nefûds, where the tribes of Nejd would send their mares to take advantage of the grass that grew throughout the year, the surface of the plain is covered with *fuljes*, huge horseshoe-shaped hills in the sand. Count Stroganov, who travelled among the tribes at the end of the nineteenth century, writes, 'The ground in Arabia is not only strewn with stones and pebbles but is so pitted with the holes of rodents that one wonders how it avoids them even at a walk; but the Arabian horse not only boldly gallops over them but also just as boldly descends steep, rocky slopes.'[11]

Finally, as Stroganov says, 'Though they, too, appreciate speed greatly, the Arabs do not seek to enhance this factor artificially. They devote more attention to nimbleness and agility, which qualities they inculcate from a horse's earliest age . . . only rarely are Arabian horses allowed to gallop at full speed needlessly and even then only over short distances.'[12] Wilfrid Blunt comments that: 'Even in war it is rather a question of endurance, than of speed, which is the better animal; and, where a real flight and a real pursuit take place, the course is so seldom a straight one, that it is as often that the best trained or the best ridden mare gets the advantage, as the one which really has the speed. A mare, celebrated for speed in the desert, is as often as not merely a very well-broken charger . . . They [the Bedouin] must be very hard pressed indeed, if they keep on at a steady gallop for more than a mile or two together. Their parties and expeditions, even where haste is necessary, are constantly interrupted by halts and dismountings; and a steady pace all day long is a thing not to be thought of.'[14]

The reality, then, is far different from the popular idea which has served for so long, in English-speaking countries at any rate, to obscure the Arabian's true qualities. Let us look at the Arabian's true function, which has determined his breed characteristics and conformation.

If we discount the idea of the Arabian springing from the desert fully formed as he is now, like Athena from the brain of Zeus, we must recognise that he has been selectively bred for several thousand years for one purpose only: that of war.

The warfare of the *bedu* was very much of the 'hit-and-run' variety; surprise and speed of attack were of the essence, while the nature of their hand-to-hand combats meant that their horses required great agility and handiness. Lady Wentworth, who was herself adept at handling the long *bedawin* lance, writes:

> 'In fighting with the fifteen to twenty foot lance a rider's life depends on his horse's quickness. It must be able to gallop full tilt at a blank wall, and stop dead in its stride. It must be able to spin round on its hocks and start away again like a rocket to a turn of the wrist, for the rider has no second hand to spare. An awkward change of leg may cost him his life. That the Arabian horse does not break down under this training is the greatest tribute to its soundness. The wonderful breaking of the horses in doubling and turning has been commented on with amazement by every traveller.'[14]

The Arabian's agility and handiness have been praised by poets and warriors for thousands of years, starting with the pre-Islamic poets of ancient Arabia. Palgrave, who travelled to Nejd in 1862–3, confirms them in describing the horses he saw there:

> '. . . they have a delicacy, I cannot say of mouth, for it is common to ride them without bit or bridle, but of feeling and obedience to the knee and thigh, to the slightest check of the halter and the voice of the rider, far surpassing whatever the most elaborate *manège* gives a European horse, though furnished with snaffle, curb, and all. I often mounted them at the invitation of their owners and without saddle, rein or stirrup, set them off at full gallop, wheeled them round, brought them up in mid career at a dead halt, and that without the least difficulty or the smallest want of correspondence between the horse's movements and my own will; the rider on their back really feels himself the man-half of a centaur, not a distinct being. This is in great part owing to the Arab system of breaking in, much preferable to the European in conferring pliance and perfect tractability. Nor is mere speed much valued in a horse unless it be united with the above qualities, since whether in the contest of an Arab race, or in the pursuit and flight of war, "doubling" is far more the rule than "going ahead", at least for any distance.'[15]

Indeed, the Arabian of true type is remarkable for precisely these qualities of agility and an amazing ability to stop from a full gallop, which seldom results in damage to the horse (a) because of its ability to flex its back, loin and lumbosacral joint when galloping, and (b) its ability to brake using the hind legs rather than the forelegs, by means of this flexibility in the back. Lady Wentworth and many others write of the Arabian's incredible braking system and I have on countless occasions seen Arabians, including my own, gallop the full length of a large field at a flat out racing speed, then suddenly slam the brakes on using the powerful hind legs, stop in their own length, spin round on their hocks and shoot off again.

Thus, the Arabian's whole conformation and the bulk of its breed characteristics are related to its function in war. What we have is a horse of great power, speed and agility; small but not weedy; rounded and compact, not angular, long and horizontal like the Thoroughbred, but rather what my facetious grandfather would call 'square-y-cum-roundy'. Some authorities maintain – and I would agree with them – that the body and legs, if viewed from the side, should (metaphorically speaking) fit inside a square – in other words, that the length of the body from point of shoulder to point of buttock should roughly equal the height from withers to ground; and I think this is a good way to judge the proportions of the Arabian. Further, the depth of the body through the girth should roughly equal (as the legs should not be disproportionately long) the distance from the elbow to the ground. Finally, for perfect symmetry of proportion, the body may be divided into thirds, with the forehand, back and quarters each occupying approximately one third of the horse's length. Lady Wentworth deplored such attempts to reduce a living creature to a matter of squares and measurements, and one can see her point; nevertheless, pro-

Silver Vanity, Supreme Male Champion 1958 and 1962 (Rosemary Archer)

vided it is not taken to literal extremes, this is a very useful way of assessing the horse's proportions.

After all, this is surely the quality which stands out above all others – more even than the beauty of the head and the tail carriage – the Arabian's superbly well-proportioned, harmonious, well-balanced form. In 1756 the great veterinary surgeon William Osmer said, 'If I were asked, what is so beautiful about a horse? I would reply: the harmony of all parts of its body. What is the strength of a horse? Again, that same harmony.'[16] Count Stroganov says, '. . . the Arabian horse is extremely harmonious and the various parts of its body are admirably proportioned. This, indeed, is its main virtue because it is to this that it owes all its other qualities, including its beauty.'[17] Captain Roger Upton remarks, 'Whether we look at the Arabian as a whole, or analyse his points one by one, you can arrive at no other conclusion than that he is an animal of perfect form.'[18]

Let us now attempt to analyse the most characteristic points of this 'animal of perfect form'.

All authorities are agreed that the Arabian's head must show refinement and quality. I think few would quibble with Lady Wentworth's requirements that the head 'should be small and tapering, but deep in the jowl and very broad in the forehead and the eyes set low in the head, a long way from the ears . . . the eye should be extremely large and dark . . . a large blunted oval. . . There should be a depression in the line of the profile, the forehead prominent and dipping to a concave curve just below the eyes',[19] although it is worth noting that Roger Upton (the twentieth-century Upton, not the author of *Newmarket and Arabia*) says that the characteristic absent from *bedawin* lists of parts of the horse, and which is nowadays perhaps given too much emphasis in the West, is the *afnas* or dished profile, though, as Upton points out, this has always occurred in Arabians.[20] Lady Wentworth adds that: 'A straight profile should not be a defect if the forehead is very broad, the eyes placed low and very large, and the muzzle small and tapering to a fine point.'[21] She goes on to say, 'The nostrils, which are very large and finely curved, lie almost parallel with the line of the muzzle when in repose . . . Stallions often have an almost flat but very broad forehead . . . the curve being extremely subtle.'[22]

Some breeders like a head with the eyes, *afnas* and tapering muzzle somewhat exaggerated and there is nothing wrong with this, *provided* they remember that an excessively dished profile may inhibit effective breathing, and that the other breed characteristics and points of conformation are not neglected. For if they are, what you end up with is, in the words of another writer, a 'bug-eyed, banana-faced neddy'.

The manner in which the head is set on is all-important, not only from an aesthetic but from a practical point of view. It must not be set on at an acute angle; the *mitbah*, the curve of the throat, must be clearly delineated. This gives the throat its cleanness, and the head and neck their balance. I feel certain that this is one aspect of the Arabian's conformation which leads some people to say that as a breed their conformation makes it difficult for them to come 'on the bridle'; these people assume that the depth of the jowl must interfere with the salivary glands. In fact the width between the jaw branches and the curve of the *mitbah* ensure that this does not happen. 'The neck is a model of strength and grandeur, of which he can make a perfect arch' (R. Upton).[23]

Peter Upton writes, 'Length of neck is important but Arabians generally are not so long in the neck as the Thoroughbred, although its flexibility, high carriage, natural curve and fine throat give an appearance of length.'[24]

The length of neck must be in proportion to the rest of the horse: too short and it will appear thick and coarse; too long and it will look unbalanced and destroy the symmetry of form. The neck is set on high, unlike the Thoroughbred's; this makes it easier for the horse to collect itself and raise the forehand.

'The shoulder is well laid back, long and clearly defined at the withers – which are usually less prominent than the Thoroughbred's.'[25]

The withers themselves run well down into the back, making it easier to fix the position of the saddle.

The Arabian is, according to Palgrave, 'A little saddle-backed, just the curve that indicates springiness without weakness.'[26] 'Back short, loins of immense power' (R Upton).[27] Wilfrid Blunt says, 'The back is shorter than in our thoroughbreds and the barrel rounder.'[28] 'The back is quite short and strong though often somewhat longer in a mare. A slight, concave line is desirable between the well-defined withers and the loins which spring strongly in a curve to the quarters. Being a riding horse there must be a place for the saddle' (Peter Upton).[29]

The topline, i.e. the shape of the Arabian's back and croup, has caused much controversy in recent years, particularly since an exaggeratedly level topline became the vogue in the USA and elsewhere. Because this has had such a profound effect on the type of Arabians being bred, I make no apology for discussing it in great detail both here and in Chapter 10 (where the effects of such breeding are examined).

Lady Wentworth and Judith Forbis are two of the authorities most frequently quoted to support the contention that a very level topline – the

Raktha (Rosemary Archer)

'table-top' line, as it is often called – is correct for the Arabian. Unfortunately, while both Lady Wentworth and Mrs Forbis are being very specific, their specifications are also ambiguous. This is a prime example of how lack of precision in language and pictures leads to confusion. Lady Wentworth says, 'The ideal back is perfectly level and carried on by the level line of loins and quarters, which should be broad and flat and well filled up'.[30] Now, 'perfectly' means (according to my dictionary) 'completely, utterly or absolutely' (*Collins English Dictionary*). This certainly makes it seem as if Lady Wentworth is advocating a table-top line to the back. However, if we look at her own line illustration of the relationship of the back and the withers (*The Authentic Arabian Horse*, p. 226), the horse depicted does not have a 'perfectly level' back. Nor did her own horses exhibit such a peculiar conformation. Indeed, some of them were quite definitely 'a little, a very little saddle-backed', as Palgrave would say, as were the horses she herself selected as examples of good Arabian type – horses such as Shahwan, Skowronek, Raktha, Nasik, Naziri, Indian Gold and Indian Magic.

The same criticism applies to Judith Forbis's description. In her book, *The Classic Arabian Horse* – rightly considered a major contribution to Arabian lore – she states that the croup should be 'long, level, same height as withers'.[31] However, her illustration shows a 'table-top' type of back, with no discernible curve behind the withers. By no stretch of the imagination could the croup in this illustration be said to be the same height as the withers! This back does, indeed, appear 'perfectly level' but where would one put a saddle? Behind the withers, yes; but there is no shape further back to help to hold it in place. It is interesting that here, too, the horses Mrs Forbis selects as being of classic Arabian type do *not* have this 'table-top' back. One such horse is Dahman, one of the horses of Abbas Pasha, depicted in an engraving by Adam (reproduced on p. 230 of *The Classic Arabian Horse* by J. Forbis). It would be difficult to quibble with this choice: Dahman was indeed, if the engraving is an accurate representation, an Arabian of 'classic type', but he most definitely *did not* have a 'table-top' back.

So how on earth do we decide which is correct?

If we look at the drawings and paintings which have been used as examples of the 'classic' Arabian horse, we shall see that these horses (including those depicted in Egyptian bas-reliefs and frescoes, which are of definite Arabian type) do not exhibit a 'perfectly level' back. The backs are *relatively* level, as are the croups; *relatively* being the key word. A relatively level back is certainly desirable in a riding horse, although, as Lady Wentworth herself pointed out, even a pronounced saddle-back (such as may often be seen in mares that have had foals) need not be weak, provided the loin area is strong. On the contrary, such a horse may actually be stronger in the back than a horse with a more level back but with poorly developed loins and quarters. Cecil Covey described both Naseem and his full brother Naziri – both horses that certainly did not have 'table-top' lines – as having exceptionally strong backs.[32]

Indeed, a too-level back can be a much graver conformational fault than a slightly deep back. Contrary to what some people would have us believe, the back and the croup should *not* be absolutely level with each other. Sharon Byford, in *The Arabian – a Guide for Owners*, says that if a too-level croup is echoed by a hip (actually the pelvis) that is too level –

i.e. the 'table-top' back – the horse is faulty.[33] This is not a matter of opinion but of biomechanics.

When the back and the croup are perfectly level, the reason is frequently that the pelvis is too horizontal. This almost invariably opens up the angle between the pelvis and the femur (see the chapter on Movement) and places the hind legs too far back. This shortens the hind leg stride and makes it extremely difficult for the horse to engage its hind legs (which will then, of course, tend to trail).

Furthermore, a too-level loin and croup area imposes severe restrictions on the flexibility of the back. Indeed, it is the lumbosacral joint (together with the sacroiliac joint, where the pelvis joins the lumbar and sacral vertebrae), that is the key point in transmitting the 'drive' from the hind legs. Any excessive lumbar length – now frequently seen in some show Arabians – will increase the stress to this area because of the added lever action of the joint. Some authorities (notably in *Horse Structure and Movement*, Smythe/Goody, rev. Gray, J. A. Allen 1993) maintain that lum-

Kazmierek, Supreme Ridden Championship 1993 (Sweet)

bosacral flexion is of limited importance; however this is contradicted by current biomechanical research. Hodges and Pilliner, in *The Equine Athlete*, point out that: 'Even though the lumbo-sacral joint has limited action, the ability of the horse to move well is dependent on this joint's full function.' They state further: 'Its flexibility, although limited, allows the pelvis and the hindquarters to rotate forwards beneath the horse's body when moving at the gallop and at the canter, when jumping, and when engaging the hindquarters to raise the back.'[34] Susan E. Harris, in her very detailed and useful book, *Horse Gaits, Balance and Movement*, writes, 'The horse's loin flexes most at the gallop, when engaging the hind legs for a major effort such as a jump or buck and when he "works off his hindquarters" in collected gaits, sliding stops or transitions . . . A horse that moves with a stiff back, with little flexion in the lumbosacral joint, is handicapped in his ability to move powerfully and to shift his balance.'[35] These statements are borne out by careful monitoring of the horse's movement by sophisticated electronic devices, as well as by close observation of slow-motion film.

Paul Belasik, in *Exploring Dressage Technique*, and Mary Wanless, in *Ride with your Mind Masterclass*, give two of the fullest and clearest explanations I have ever read of the way in which the horse's 'ring of muscles' – i.e. the long back muscles, the muscles attached to his ribs and vertebrae, and the abdominal muscles – act when he is working in correct carriage. The effects of this can be seen at their most extreme when the horse makes a dropping; then you can see how the abdominal muscles contract, raising the belly, and at the same time the back lifts. The sensation given to the rider who is on board when the horse does a dropping – this 'lift' and expansion of the horse's whole back and thorax – is an exaggerated version of what the rider feels when the horse is using his back correctly.

This 'lifting' of the back is brought about (a) by the contraction of the abdominal muscles and the psoas group of muscles lying under the lumbar vertabrae; (b) the simultaneous lengthening and isometric contraction of the long back muscles; and (c) the stretching of the ligament system of the back and neck over the spines of the vertebrae.

This ligament system extends the full length of the horse, beginning with the dorsal ligament of the neck, attached to the front of the poll. As the horse lowers his head, this ligament pulls on the spines of the vertebrae forming the withers; these, in turn, pull on the spines of the thoracic vertebrae. The dorsal ligament is continued by the supraspinous ligament, which extends backwards over the croup and sacrum. When the horse flexes the lumbosacral joint at the croup, and lowers his haunches, the supraspinous ligament pulls on the spines of the vertebrae in the centre of the back. The effect of these ligaments effectively pulling the spine in opposite directions is to raise the centre of the back. Thus the withers and the lumbosacral joint act like the stanchions of a suspension bridge (see diagram). This lifting and 'arching' of the horse's back is the only way he can work efficiently, especially with a rider on his back. This is why well-defined withers have always been essential for the riding horse; but the action of the ligaments and of the lumbosacral joint has often been overlooked.

As we have said, a pelvis that is too horizontal will considerably reduce the amount of flexion in the lumbosacral joint (as will its opposite, a too-upright pelvis, resulting in a 'goose-rump'). From this we can see that not only will the horse's ability to engage its hind legs be severely compromised, it will also be very much more difficult for the back to lift in the middle, the weakest part – effectively, one of the stanchions of the suspension bridge will be missing. So the excessively flat back, far from being a stronger structure as many people claim, is in fact very much weaker. Not only this, but the horse with such a conformation is going to find it

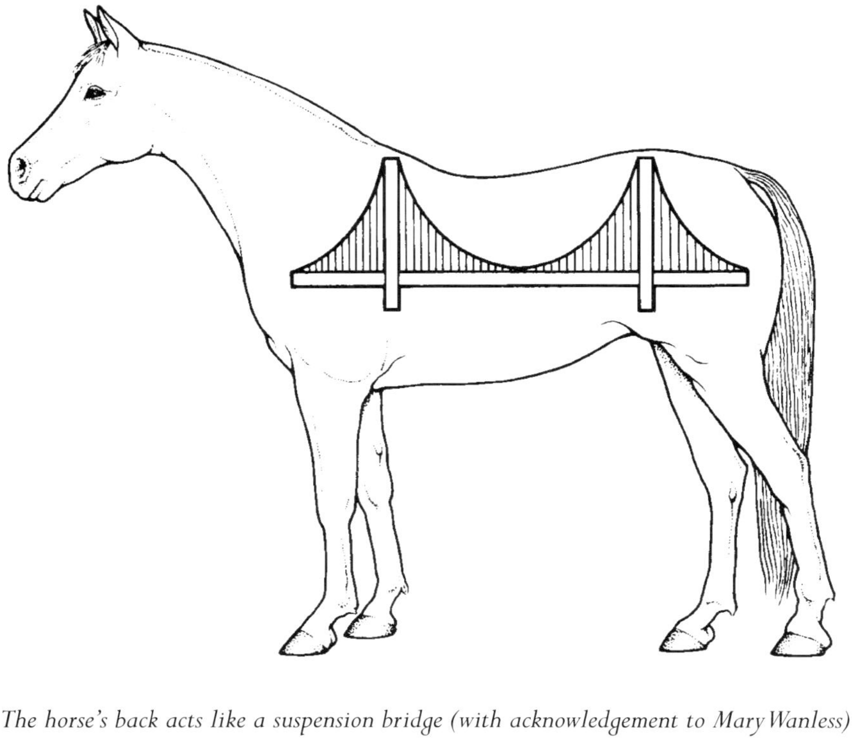

The horse's back acts like a suspension bridge (with acknowledgement to Mary Wanless)

very much more difficult to develop athletically than the horse with a slightly concave back (Palgrave's 'just the curve that indicates springiness without weakness'. The Blunts maintained that Palgrave was no horseman, but here at least he showed more understanding than many people with greater pretensions to horsemanship).

The kind of agility demanded of the *bedawin* war horse – particularly the sudden halts and spins on the hocks – requires considerable flexion of the lumbosacral joint. I have a photograph of an Arabian galloping – an Arabian, I might add, with a 'normal', slightly concave back – and the flexion of the lumbosacral joint is such that the hind legs are actually fractionally in front of the forelegs – few breeds of horse can achieve that kind of flexion! I would argue, therefore, that the completely flat back with the too-level pelvis is totally incorrect for an Arabian horse, and that such a horse is not, and cannot be, of true Arabian type. If a horse cannot do the job the breed was originally developed for – regardless of whether the requirements of that job still exist – then it is not a good representative of that breed. This should not be taken to mean that I am advocating a 'dipped back'. Not at all; I am simply pointing out the dangers of forgetting that 'relatively level' means just that – *relatively*, not literally!

Moreover, we must not forget that an extremely level croup is only a fault if it is accompanied by the too-horizontal pelvis referred to above. The two often do go together, but this is not always the case, and one must be careful to judge whether the croup is so level because the pelvis is too level, or whether it is the result of the set of the tail vertebrae and/or the muscles of the quarters (which is as it should be). If the former, then it can often be determined by the position of the point of buttock. It is worth remembering, too, when looking at youngstock, that very young horses frequently appear slightly peaky in the croup area. This will often resolve itself as the muscles and ligaments in the croup area develop and strengthen, raising the tail vertebrae and improving the line of the croup and tail carriage, often beyond all recognition.

The body itself is quite wide and deep, with well-sprung ribs. 'There is no weediness in the Arab; his splendid barrel will at once convince a judge of his wonderful constitution, and gives the expanse necessary for the play of heart and lungs; great power and ability to carry weight. Stand in front of him, you will see the swell and barrel of chest expanding far beyond his shoulders and width of breast. Look at him from behind; his great back ribs extend far beyond his haunches on either side' (R. Upton)[36]. 'The chest broad and muscular, girth deep, ribs and barrel rounded' (Lady Wentworth).[37] Elsewhere Lady Wentworth remarked that the chest cannot be too wide; but of course it can, resulting in a rolling, uneven gait. On the other hand, narrowness in the chest and barrel is a very severe fault, affecting stamina, soundness and weight-carrying capacity. It must be remembered that in the Near and Middle East warriors often wore chain mail until well into the nineteenth century. The Blunts brought back with them from Nejd a fine example of this mail, which weighed some 80 lb (36 kg). Added to the weight of even a lightweight *bedawin* warrior, it amounts to a considerable burden which could scarcely be borne by a narrow, slab-sided weed (although, as always, there have been exceptions).

Peter Upton goes on to say, 'Although the back is short, the well laid shoulder gives a long underline so that the horse stands over a lot of ground.'[38]

'The point of croup must not be higher than the withers and the line of the quarters should be nearly horizontal with the tail appearing as a natural extension to this line' (P. Upton).[39]

The quarters themselves should be powerful. Palgrave, writing of the horses he saw at Riyadh, says they were 'remarkably full in the haunches', and had a 'full rounded haunch'.[40] Roger Upton, comparing the Arabian with the Thoroughbred, says, 'The loins and quarters of the Arabian are more beautiful and far more powerful';[41] Lady Wentworth says the quarters should be 'broad and flat and well filled up and should appear wide and tabular from behind across the hips';[42] Peter Upton says, 'Good length from hip to point of buttock is necessary, and also good width across both hips and thighs when seen from behind'.[43]

With regard to the legs, Roger Upton notes that the arms are 'long, legs short, hard and clean; large tendons and ligaments';[44] Palgrave describes 'legs fore and hind that seemed as if made of hammered iron';[45] Lady Wentworth says that the forelegs should have 'big flat broad knees and flat legs, and an extremely short cannon bone . . . The bone is of ivory density and iron strength, and so long as the back tendons are not tied in under the knee, but absolutely vertical . . . the leg will stand all the work it can be given. These tendons must never look muddled and undefined'.[46] Roger Upton describes the hocks and knees as 'very good and large; these points much larger than seen in the European horse, not only in proportion to length, but often really so'.[47] In comparison with the Thoroughbred, the hocks are 'larger, better let down, and not so straight' (W. Blunt).[48] Lady Wentworth says the hocks should be 'well let down and extra large with the points well developed'.[49]

'The Arabian is "powerful in the gaskins" (R.Upton);[50] "Gaskins and thighs muscular";[51] 'Gaskins must be strong and well muscled-up.'[52]

The pasterns are 'sufficiently long, large, powerful and springy; fetlock joints well developed, affording room for the advantageous attachment of ligaments' (R. Upton).[53] The leg terminates in 'a neat round hoof, just the requisite for hard ground' (Palgrave).[54] 'The hoofs are round and large and very hard' (Blunt).[55] Peter Upton says, 'Fore hoofs are circular in form and open, the hind ones more oval in shape with a smooth surface giving a naturally polished look.'[56]

Finally we come to the tail. However controversial some other points of the Arabian horse may be, all authorities are agreed that perhaps the Arabian's most immediately distinguishing characteristic is the glorious tail carriage which, when the horse is galloping, seems to stream up and behind it like a banner. A somewhat 'peaky' croup may be compensated for by a high-set and well-carried tail; nothing can compensate for a poorly set or poorly carried tail. However, it must be remembered that a horse's tail carriage cannot be properly judged when he is standing still; it has to be seen in motion to be properly assessed. The tail carriage, like the ears, can provide the attentive horseman or woman with a valuable guide to the horse's mood and to the general state of his internal wellbeing.

The *bedu* themselves have been accused of caring nothing for form or conformation, valuing only purity of blood. This may have been true by the time the Blunts travelled into the desert in the late nineteenth century, when the decline in traditional *bedawin* ways meant that they were growing careless in their breeding in every respect except that of purity of blood. But there are countless examples of *bedawin* poetry which illustrate how much they did formerly prize excellence of form; and indeed it is impossible that the Arabian horse should have remained a creature of such overall perfection if they had not. Roger Upton (not the Captain Upton of the nineteenth century, but the brother of Peter) in 'Arab Horses in Saudi Arabia, Part I' (*Arab Horse Society News*, No. 72) quotes the following *bedawin* description of ideal conformation:

> 'Pasterns the length of three fingers laid side by side, no more
> Legs so strong and so upright as the posts supporting the well wheel
> The muscles on the hind legs, hard like those of a camel'[57]

Later on in the same article, Upton quotes another poem:

> 'The quarters of the gazelle,
> The legs of an ostrich
> And a neck like the curve of a fox's leap'[58]

We have spoken of the 'classic' Arabian horse but how do we determine what is truly 'classic' and what is merely personal preference? Numerous people, at various points during the last 200 years, have put forward their version of the 'classic' Arabian horse, which they insist is the true type. Some even go so far as to insist that this true type is mainly or even solely found in certain countries or among particular bloodlines; others speak of 're-creating' the classic type, as if it had disappeared (which it never did); still others speak glibly of a 'new look' to the Arabian (which means whatever they want it to mean). The fact is that the 'classic type' existed in the desert for more than 2,000 years, and has been found in various parts of the Near and Middle East in a more or less pure form throughout that period. During the past 200 years it has been found (and bred) in whatever countries have imported Arabian horses from the desert. No one country, no one group of bloodlines (usually, these days, referred to by their country of origin, e.g. 'English', 'Polish', 'Russian', etc.) has ever held the monopoly on this type, although at certain times and in certain places some such groups may have approached the ideal type more closely as a group than others.

But how can we be sure that what we are describing is the classic type? There are too few horses of note left in the desert, and the *bedu* have moved too far away from the warfare and traditions of their ancestors for them to provide confirmation of this true type. Early photographs are, as we have seen, not a very reliable guide. We must therefore turn to the drawings and paintings of the many artists of the eighteenth and nineteenth centuries, who immortalised the Arabian horses they saw, whether in the desert itself, in the towns and cities of the Near and Middle East, or in the few studs in Europe that imported pure-bred Arabians of undoubted authenticity and high quality. It may be argued that these artists idealised the Arabians they saw; and this may be true to some extent. In general, however, there is no doubt that they drew and painted essentially what they saw, and in spite of some minor variations there is a remarkable uniformity of type. The horses depicted with such brilliance and clarity by artists such as Adam, de Dreux, Delacroix, Frisch, Fromentin, Harrington Bird, Herring, Kossak, Lalaisse, Pater, Turner, Vernet, and many others are in essence of the same type described by Palgrave, Upton, etc.; and in spite of changes in fashion regarding 'type', the horses that have most consistently been held up as examples of 'classic' types are all remarkably similar.

It is interesting that some Arabian horse enthusiasts and breeders still cling stubbornly to the theory of type-related-to-strain. The proponents of this 'theory' numbered among them, initially the Blunts who later discovered their error; Professor Ridgeway whose assertions regarding the Arabian horse are masterpieces of the art of jumping to conclusions based on the flimsiest evidence – or no evidence at all; Dr Edward Skorkowski; and, most famously, Carl Raswan. While this idea of 'strain-type' was enthusiastically taken up by numerous writers, among them the late Erika Schiele, the latter often regretted that she had ever been taken in by Raswan's 'theory' and the whole thing has been comprehensively debunked by various authorities such as Lady Anne Blunt, Lady Wentworth, Peter Upton and Gladys Brown Edwards. The latter wrote in *The Arabian: War Horse to Show Horse* that: 'belief in "strain-type" is little more than a sublime faith in hash.'[59] (For a fuller discussion, see the relevant sections in that book and in Lady Wentworth's *The Authentic Arabian Horse*.)

Even to the untutored eye, the predominant impression gained when one first sees a truly excellent Arabian horse is one of grace, symmetry, and proportion – in other words *balance*. It is neither too long nor too short in proportion to the height; its head and neck are respectively of a size and

Grace, symmetry and proportion: El Shaklan, former Reserve World Champion and one of the most influential sires of all time (Sweet)

length in proportion to its body. This balanced picture is an integral part of the Arabian's beauty; without it the most beautiful head and the most spectacular movement are meaningless.

This, then, is the classic Arabian horse: a compact horse of great power, substance and agility, combining symmetry of form with refinement, lightness, elegance and sparkle. Palgrave's account of his journey to Riyadh has been criticised in many respects, but surely his description of the horses he found there must stand as a classic in its own right, embodying the very essence of the Arabian horse:

> 'Never had I seen or imagined so lovely a collection. Their stature was indeed somewhat low; I do not think that any came fully up to fifteen hands; fourteen appeared to me about their average; but they were so exquisitely well shaped that want of greater size seemed hardly, if at all, a defect. Remarkably full in the haunches, with a shoulder of a slope so elegant as to make one, in the words of an Arab poet, "go raving mad about it"; a little, very little, saddle-backed, just the curve which indicates springiness without any weakness; a head broad above, and tapering down to a nose fine enough to verify the phrase of "drinking from a pint pot", did pint-pots exist in Nejed; a most intelligent and yet a singularly gentle look, full eye, short thornlike little ear, legs fore and hind that seemed as if made of hammered iron, so clean and yet so well twisted with sinew; a neat round hoof, just the requisite for hard ground; the tail set on or rather thrown out at a perfect arch; coats smooth, shining and light; the mane long, but not overgrown nor heavy; and an air and step that seemed to say "look at me, am I not pretty?" their appearance justified all reputation, all value, all poetry. The prevailing colour was chestnut or grey; a light bay, an iron colour, white or black, were less common; full bay, flea-bitten, or piebald, none. But if asked what are, after all, the specially distinctive points of the Nejdee horse, I should reply, the slope of the shoulder, the extreme cleanness of the shank, and the full rounded haunch, though every part too has a perfection and a harmony unwitnessed (at least by my eyes) anywhere else.'[60]

In the end, it is this 'perfection and . . . harmony' that stamp the classic Arabian of true type. Captain Upton writes, 'There is nothing more beautiful to contemplate than the Arabian horse; not only does he exhibit perfect symmetry, but he is a fit emblem of nobility, generosity and courage . . . Nature, the unerring artist, has not made a mistake'.[61]

Notes

1 Forbis, Judith, *The Classic Arabian Horse* Liveright, New York 1976, p.228
2 Upton, Peter, *The Classic Arab Horse*, p.2
3 Burt, Don, *Winning With Arabian Horses*, Prentice Hall Press USA 1990, p.67
4 Burt, *Winning*, p.67
5 Burt, *Winning*, p.67
6 Archer, Rosemary, etc., *The Crabbet Arabian Stud*, p.14
7 Archer, etc., *Crabbet*, p.14
8 Archer, etc., *Crabbet*, p.15
9 Nolan, Lewis Edward (quoted in *The Crabbet Arabian Stud*, p.15)
10 Spooner, Glenda, *The Handbook of Showing*, p.95
11 Stroganov, Count and Prince Scherbatov, *The Arabian Horse*, J. A. Allen 1989, p.17
12 Stroganov, etc., *The Arabian Horse*, p.13
13 Blunt, Lady Anne and Wilfrid, *Bedouin Tribes of the Euphrates*, John Murray 1879, p.260
14 Wentworth, Lady, *The Authentic Arabian Horse*, p.103
15 Palgrave, William, *Narrative of a Year's Journey through Central and Eastern Arabia* vol. 2, London 1865, p.97
16 Quoted in Stroganov, *The Arabian Horse*, p.24
17 Stroganov, *The Arabian Horse*, p.13
18 Upton, Capt. Roger, *Newmarket and Arabia*, Henry S. King 1873, p.139
19 Wentworth, *Authentic Arabian*, pp.221–2
20 Upton, Roger, 'Arab Horses in Saudi Arabia Part 1', *Arab Horse Society News*, No. 2., p.47
21 Wentworth, *Authentic Arabian*, p.228
22 Wentworth, *Authentic Arabian*, p.222
23 Upton, Capt., *Newmarket*, p.137
24 Upton, Peter, *The Classic Arab Horse*, p.17
25 Upton, Peter, *Classic Arab*, p.17
26 Palgrave, *Narrative*, vol. 2, p.93
27 Upton, Capt., *Newmarket*, p.137
28 Blunt, Wilfrid, *Bedouin Tribes*, p.248
29 Upton, Peter, *Classic Arab*, p.21
30 Wentworth, *Authentic Arabian*, p.229
31 Forbis, *Classic Arabian*, p.238
32 Archer, etc., *Crabbet*, pp.219–20
33 Byford, Sharon, *The Arabian: A Guide for Owners*, p.54
34 Hodges, Jo and Sarah Pilliner, *The Equine Athlete*, BSP Professional Books 1991, pp.55–6
35 Harris, Susan E., *Horse Gaits, Balance and Movement*, Howell Book House USA 1993, p.23
36 Upton, Capt., *Newmarket*, p.138
37 Wentworth, *Authentic Arabian*, p.226
38 Upton, Peter, *Classic Arab*, p.21
39 Upton, Peter, *Classic Arab*, p.22

40 Palgrave, *Narrative*, vol. 2, pp.93–4
41 Upton, Capt., *Newmarket*, p.141
42 Wentworth, *Authentic Arabian*, p.224
43 Upton, Peter, *Classic Arab*, p.22
44 Upton, Capt., *Newmarket*, p.138
45 Palgrave, *Narrative*, vol. 2, p.93
46 Wentworth, *Authentic Arabian*, p.224
47 Upton, Capt., *Newmarket*, p.138
48 Blunt, Wilfrid, *Bedouin Tribes*, p.249
49 Wentworth, *Authentic Arabian*, p.227
50 Upton, Capt., *Newmarket*, p.137
51 Wentworth, *Authentic Arabian*, p.227
52 Upton, Peter, *Classic Arab*, p.27
53 Upton, Capt., *Newmarket*, p.138
54 Palgrave, *Narrative*, vol. 2, p.93
55 Blunt, Wilfrid, *Bedouin Tribes*, p.249
56 Upton, Peter, *Classic Arab*, p.27
57 Upton, Roger, 'The Arab Horse in Saudi Arabia', *Arab Horse Society News*, No. 72, p.47
58 Upton, Roger, 'The Arab Horse in Saudi Arabia', p.47
59 Brown, Gladys, *The Arabian: War Horse to Show Horse*, The Arabian Horse Trust of America, p.300
60 Palgrave, *Narrative*, vol. 2, pp.93–4
61 Upton, Capt., *Newmarket*, pp.138–9

Chapter 6

MOVEMENT

'Sometimes he trots, as if he told the steps,
With gentle majesty, and modest pride;
Anon he rears upright, curvets, and leaps,
As who should say, lo! thus my strength is tried'

WILLIAM SHAKESPEARE, *VENUS AND ADONIS*

AT THE TIME of writing, one of the greatest controversies enveloping the Arabian horse world, especially that section of it devoted to the showring, concerns movement: more specifically, the kind of movement that may be considered correct for the Arabian horse.

As we have seen in Chapter 3, in the in-hand classes, movement means the horse's action at the trot and, while somewhat limiting, this is perhaps inevitable, given the restriction imposed by the lead rope, and the dimensions of the showring itself. There is much concern among Arabian horse enthusiasts that some judges, particularly at international shows and increasingly in Britain, are placing too much emphasis on movement that, while superficially spectacular, is both functionally incorrect and inappropriate for an Arabian.

This overemphasis on movement, it is feared, is causing judges to overlook correctness of conformation and type. Conversely, in the USA there is currently very little emphasis on movement of any kind in the in-hand classes. If, as I hope to demonstrate, conformation largely dictates the type of movement, how can horses with incorrect conformation move spectacularly? And how, given the divergence of opinion regarding Arabian movement that is apparent in conflicting definitions of good movement, can we possibly determine what is correct for an Arabian?

Before attempting to answer either of these questions, perhaps we should look at some conceptions of the type of movement proper to

Arabians. Immediately we are faced with difficulties. The *bedu*, who rode without stirrups, generally did not use the trot. It *is* possible to trot for some time without stirrups, but very tiring, and the *bedu* were not concerned with the niceties of equitation but with practicalities. Even among nomads and horse-oriented peoples who *do* use stirrups (the Mongols and the Cossacks are two prime examples) the trot is seldom used for any distance, and then usually with the rider semi-standing in the stirrups. So among the *bedu* the trot was a relatively undeveloped gait, to the extent that when Arabian horses were first imported from the desert (to English-speaking countries at least), they were often described as two-gaited. In fact, Arabians were frequently accused of having bad action generally (apart from the gallop) and of making bad hacks because they stumbled frequently at the walk; but it was hardly surprising if some of the early imports (which had often been bought in the towns, even though they were undoubtedly desert-bred) moved badly, considering the conditions in which they had been kept – shackled, or confined in small stalls, and half-starved in the desert; in the towns overfed and under-exercised. Captain Roger Upton also pointed out that a horse's gaits were very much what a rider made them. 'It is hardly fair', he comments, 'to blame a horse for the very faults man has taught him'[1]; and there is no doubt that the Arabian's early bad reputation with regard to movement was largely due to poor riding or lack of schooling.

On the continent, as we saw in the chapter on type and conformation, the Arabian's qualities were appreciated to a far greater extent than in Britain. The fact that many Arabians came to Central and Eastern Europe *via* the Turks (and while some of these horses were probably not pure-bred Arabians, a high proportion of them undoubtedly were) meant that there was no question of them not being able to trot, as the Turkish cavalry did use stirrups and made use of that gait wherever necessary. Not only that, the Turkish cavalry was renowned for its horsemanship; the Osmanli horsemasters took great care over the schooling of their horses, and also took infinite pains to teach them with gentleness rather than coercion. They also had a tradition of riding that was very similar in many respects to European High School riding (referred to somewhat contemptuously – and ignorantly – by Wilfrid Blunt, as 'such circus tricks as the Turks delight in'[2]) which they may or may not have inherited from the Byzantines. So they were aware of the Arabian's capabilities as a saddle horse, and of how it could move. In fact it was from the Sultan of Turkey that the former US President General Grant received his famous Arabian stallion Leopard as a gift. Randolph Huntingdon wrote of Leopard in

1880: 'the same movements this Arabian went through [at play] would have blemished every leg and joint upon an American trotting horse . . . the knee action was beautiful: not too much, as in the toe-weighted horses, nor stiff and staky, as in the English race horse, but graceful and elastic, beautifully balanced by movement in the hock and stifle.'[3]

However, the majority of Britons (and Americans) had no opportunity of seeing the Arabian in its lands of origin and even when they did, they did not always display much common sense in evaluating its qualities. Major-General Tweedie (so despised by the Blunts and Lady Wentworth) purported to have had many years' experience of the Arabian horse, both during his service in India and in the course of his diplomatic activities in Baghdad. He wrote a book which exerted a great deal of influence around the turn of the last century, but while *The Arabian Horse: His Country and People* occasionally contains the odd nugget of sense (if one can be bothered to look for them in the mass of turgid, pompous prose), for the most part his ramblings make one wonder whether he ever did, in fact, see an authentic Arabian horse. Nevertheless, his book seemed to confirm all the prejudices held by English-speaking people regarding the Arabian's value as a saddle horse, in particular those prejudices regarding movement.

It might be thought that the obvious way to determine the Arabian's action at the trot would be to observe its movement while at liberty, but as Gladys Brown Edwards points out in *The Arabian: War Horse to Show Horse*, 'there are about as many natural-to-each horse ways of going as there are horses in this breed'.[4] This is something of an exaggeration, although one takes her point. However, just as with type, while we can accept some variations in the kind of movement, these variations *must* (again as with type) come within a certain range of definition, otherwise we lose one of the characteristics that make the breed what it is, and we end up with a horse that is not an authentic Arabian, but a horse with some Arabian characteristics. There is a difference.

The difficulty lies, as we have said, in determining what is correct. Each country where Arabians are bred in any numbers appears to have its own idea as to what constitutes correct movement; and this is largely dictated by the kind of horses traditionally bred in those countries and the purposes to which they have been put. We must remember that the breeding of pure-bred Arabians in any numbers outside Arabia and the immediately surrounding countries is a phenomenon of the twentieth century, so that while it may be the oldest pure breed, as a horse bred for its own sake rather than as a cross to other breeds, it is a relative newcomer to a well-established scene.

In the USA, for instance, we find that in performance classes the preference is for a horse with a very high-stepping action, rather similar to the Hackney. This is the desired movement for the Park horse, which we met in Chapter 4. To American Arabian-fanciers, 'action' means only one thing: the high knee action of the Park horse. In Russia, the prevalence of trotting races over ordinary flat racing, even though it is in the latter that Arabians are most usually raced, means that the taste runs to horses with an extravagant extended action at the trot.

In Britain there is, even now, considerable confusion over how an Arabian should move. Initially, many people felt that as the Arabian was the progenitor of the Thoroughbred, then it must move like a Thoroughbred, even though, by the time Arabians of undoubted authenticity were imported in sufficient numbers to make a widespread comparison, the two breeds were very different in character. This has led to absurdities.

In the 1975 edition of *Summerhays' Encyclopedia for Horsemen* the entry on page 86 under 'daisy-cutting' reads: 'Descriptive of the action which is at the walk or trot close to the ground and shows little elevation, e.g., the Arab.' Yet on pages 13 and 14, in the entry under 'The Arabian Horse', Lady Anne Lytton describes the trotting action of the Arabian as 'moving as though floating with extreme grace' and 'Trotting action should be very smart . . . with hocks well lifted, the whole appearance giving a floating, dancing movement, as if on air and springs'. Clearly this implies some considerable degree of elevation as, without it, the horse could hardly be said to 'float', nor could the hocks be 'well lifted'! Yet daisy-cutting implies exactly the opposite and so prevalent has the idea become that this *is* the correct action for the Arabian, that Elwyn Hartley-Edwards, in various books on the different horse breeds, has felt bound to point out that daisy-cutting action is *not* correct for the Arabian.

But how do we determine that it is not correct? How, indeed, do we determine what *is* correct?

To argue, as many do, that because the *bedu* did not use the trot (and often actively discouraged their horses from using this gait) we cannot tell what the Arabian's natural trot should be, is somewhat shaky reasoning. Lady Anne Blunt listed no fewer than 26 words used by the *bedu* either directly describing, or associated with, trotting. These included words describing a slow, collected trot, fast trot, extended trot, etc. and twelve different words describing prancing, including *zail*, 'a prance without rider'. This is rather more than most European languages can manage! (See Lady Wentworth, *The Authentic Arabian Horse*, for Lady Anne's notes.) As we

King Cotton Gold, Supreme Male Champion 1972; one of the greatest movers of our time (Sweet)

have seen, however, other peoples who also used pure-bred Arabians *did* allow them to trot. As the Turks, in particular, bought mainly colts (preferring stallions for warfare), their horses would be less likely to have had their natural trot 'interfered' with as the *bedu* seldom bothered much with colts but sold all except those required for breeding to the towns. The Blunts' diaries for their Arabian journeys show that the mares they purchased and rode on those journeys could and did trot. When the desert acquisitions were brought home to Crabbet Park, it quickly became apparent that, turned loose in the Crabbet paddocks, these horses mostly showed a very good trotting action and there is no reason to believe that what the Blunts saw was not the horses' natural action. While there was, of course, some variation in the quality, the *type* of action appears to have been fairly consistent. Moreover, this action was transmitted to their offspring. Genetic science has shown that acquired characteristics cannot be passed on; and so the fact that some of the early Arabian imports could not trot well because of their desert upbringing would have no effect whatsoever on their offspring's ability to trot.

Some breeders in the UK but mostly in the USA maintain that the very high-stepping action they are attempting to breed into the Arabian is correct for the breed because that is how the 'trotting breeds' (e.g. the Saddlebred) move. However, it is not clear how they have arrived at the idea of the Arabian as a 'trotting' horse. I know that one argument goes thus: some 'trotting' breeds (such as the Orlov) were founded partly on Arabian stock. But if one looks at the evolution of such breeds, one may see that such infusions of Arabian blood as there have been are usually well back in the pedigree, and that in horses such as the Orlov there is a much higher proportion of blood such as that of Dutch carriage-horses. Even allowing for the Arabian's tremendous prepotency as a breed, it is stretching credibility to suppose that the Arabian influence, which was far exceeded by that of the Dutch, Mecklenburg and Danish element, could really have determined the type of movement to such an extent as is claimed by proponents of the 'Arabian-as-trotting-horse' theory. It is far more likely that the Orlov's movement was dictated by the Danish and Dutch carriage horse element. Many of the other 'trotting breeds' have little or no Arab influence (regardless of some of Lady Wentworth's extravagant claims in this respect); many of them are based largely on the old Norfolk Roadster breed, whose blood has contributed to the action of many breeds such as the Hackney, the French Trotter and the Standardbred.

Other arguments in favour of the Saddlebred type of action for the Arabian put forward no tenable case for the Arabian as a 'trotter', and appear to stem from nothing more than the fact that this is the way the 'trotting' breeds move – which is about as logical as arguing that an Andalusian should move like a Thoroughbred because that is how race-horses move. Such an argument says more about the tunnel vision of its proponents than it does about the types of horse under discussion.

Brilliant as Lady Wentworth was, one has to admit that her exaggerated claims in respect of the Arabian have often done the horse no favours. Her assertion that Arabians are fast trotters has often been held up as proof that the Arabian is a 'trotter'. However, this is one of her statements which it would be unwise to accept unconditionally. Some Arabians can indeed trot fast, as I can testify, having more than once been run away with at the trot by a thoroughly overexcited Arabian. However, this is not a true, rhythmical, balanced trot; it is a running trot, extremely tiring for both horse and rider. In general Arabians will, when they reach a certain speed in trot, shift to a higher 'gear' and break into a canter. This is quite natural as they were not designed to travel far at a fast trot and with them, as with most other riding horses, fast trotting is generally a sign that the horse is running away out of balance. Some American trainers complain that, in Park horse classes (where a high-stepping, but fast, brilliant trot is required), Arabians have a tendency to fall out of the gait into a canter. One would think they would realise from this that they are asking the horse to perform something that it finds extremely difficult and basically unnatural, but apparently they do not.

Horses in the wild, or those kept in herds in vast open spaces such as the steppes of Central Asia, are continually on the move, often covering considerable distances in the course of a single day. However, most of this movement is carried out at a rather leisurely walk or sometimes a canter. If danger threatens, they will gallop. The trot is very seldom used as a means of progression, although when horses play they will trot and canter a little, for short distances only. When a horse – usually, though not always, a stallion or a colt – wants to show off, he will spring into the extremely elevated, animated slow trot that, in its refined form, is called a *passage*. These behaviour patterns may equally be seen in a more domesticated setting where only a handful of horses is involved.

Since the trot, then, is not normally used by the horse as a method of getting from A to B, the horse has to be taught, in the words of the distinguished trainer Dr Henri van Schaik, 'to trot in a consistent way, not just to play'.[5]

If we watch Arabians running about in a field – particularly stallions or geldings – they will exhibit several kinds of trot, basically corresponding to those used in dressage. If they see something they think is worth investigating but not at all exciting or alarming, they will trot some distance to have a look, or to greet a human friend; this trot, though rhythmical and ground-covering does not generally involve a great degree of either flexion or extension, and corresponds roughly to the 'working' and 'ordinary' trots. Sometimes, when they think circumstances warrant it, or when they are playing with each other, this trot lengthens into a kind of medium trot; but they will seldom trot any distance like this.

On the other hand, they may see something very exciting or startling, or decide to show off to another horse or to a human. Sometimes when my husband or I appear in the field our pure-bred colt and gelding will compete with each other to see who can display himself more brilliantly in front of us. Then they will collect themselves and perform a marvellous, elevated *passaging* trot, with considerable flexion of all the leg joints. Sometimes they will spring straight from this into a very brilliant extended trot (which, as we shall see, is precisely how a true extended trot should originate) but, again, they will rarely trot like this very far before breaking into a canter or a gallop. Nor are they ever seen to trot *very* fast (at least, not in comparison with the 'trotting' breeds); and the steady, rhythmical nature of their working trot is one of the things which makes Arabians so delightful to ride. In fact, the metronome-like quality of the trot is one reason why they make such comfortable endurance horses. While it is true that they seldom trot for any distance when at liberty, they seem quite happy to trot for hours under saddle – provided, of course, that the rider is well balanced.

So, if the Arabian is *not* one of the 'trotting' breeds, and if we accept that there is no reason why we cannot establish its natural movement, into what category can we place this movement? In her excellent book *Horse Gaits, Balance and Movement*, Susan E. Harris divides the different types of movement into categories:[6]

Long and low	Long, low strides with little flexion in knees and hocks. Typical of Thoroughbreds, hunters and horses of Thoroughbred type.
Short and low	Low, short strides with little flexion at knees and hocks. Typical of Western horses, especially the old-style Quarter Horse.
Round movement giving the impression of a wheel	Rounded stride with flexion at knees and hocks. Not as extreme as high action. Morgans and some other pleasure riding and driving horses.
High action	Action more up and down than forward. Great flexion of knees and hocks. Forearms raised very high, legs folded tightly. Typical of Hackneys, American Saddlebreds and Park horses of other breeds.
Medium movement	Long, ground-covering strides with some arch and elevation. Can show brilliant extension as well as collection. European warmbloods, some Arabians, some Morgans and individuals of other breeds.

Baroque movement High (though not as high as with the Hackney, etc.), round, elastic movement capable of great collection. Typical of seventeenth- and eighteenth-century *manège* horses. Andalusians, Lusitanos, Lipizzaners.

The type of movement desirable for a particular purpose is determined by the job the horse has to do and the most functional and efficient movement for that job. Allowing for the fact that a few Arabians may move with long and low action, and that some have been selectively bred (usually in the USA) for high action from individuals that have shown this type of action, I would go further than Harris and place the majority of Arabians in the 'medium' category. This does not imply that they are in any way lacking the brilliance of the more extreme types of action; on the contrary, they have their own kind of brilliance which shows itself in the unique floating, 'dancing' quality of their movement.

The skeletal structure of the Arabian gives us a clue as to whether classification of the Arabian's movement as generally of the 'medium' variety is correct. Extensive studies, carried out in the USA and elsewhere, into equine locomotion, have shown that the angles of skeletal structures such as those made by the scapula with the humerus and the pelvis with the femur, largely determine the type of movement the horse will make. Of course, this can be affected by other things such as muscle tone, hoof trimming and shoeing, the way the horse is ridden or handled, the type of ground, etc. The basic type of movement, however, is dictated by the skeletal structure; other factors may enhance or detract from that movement, but they cannot alter it beyond its natural limits.

Don Burt, in *Winning with Arabian Horses*, says, 'Angles are the key to a horse's motion. Angles in shoulders, quarters and pasterns greatly determine the horse's action and freedom of motion.'[7] He stresses that, in determining the height of knee action, the length and angle of the humerus is the critical factor. Technically, action is the result of: (1) the rotation of the scapula, or shoulder-blade; (2) the unfolding at the scapulo-humeral joint; and (3) folding at the elbow and knee. Longer scapulas, says Burt, are capable of a greater arc of rotation; where the scapula is sloping, most of that arc will be occupied in raising the scapula. Therefore a lever system is required to increase the range through which the knee joint can be moved. This is provided by the humerus. We may divide the effects of this relationship between scapula and humerus into various categories (assuming in each case that the scapula is of the long, sloping variety requisite for the riding horse):

1. Humerus long and steep	Motion high yet full of scope (i.e. capable of extension, as with the true hackney).
2. Humerus short and steep	Action short and choppy.
3. Humerus long and horizontal	What Burt calls 'mow the grass' type of action, i.e. daisy-cutting.
4. Humerus short and horizontal	Can be taught to fold tightly at the knee, but will be unable to raise the carpus above the level of the elbow.

'Relating this to the Arabian,' says Burt, 'we find that only one in a hundred Arabians has a humerus proportionally as long as the average Thoroughbred or American saddlebred. Most Arabians have a moderately to very steep humerus. Hackney horses and ponies, however, have the longest steep humeri of any breed.'[8]

These conclusions are borne out by observations of Arabians that conform to the breed standard as set out by Peter Upton and others, and comparisons between the skeletons of various breeds of horse; in particular, there is a noticeable difference between the angle of the humerus in Arabians and Thoroughbreds.

The average Arabian would thus appear to have a moderately long, moderately steep humerus – in other words, with individual exceptions, it does not generally go to extremes in any direction. However, this is only part of the story. With all this discussion of the action of the front legs, we must not forget that it is the *hind* legs which provide the impulsion; and for any horse to move correctly and in balance, at the trot as in the other gaits, the degree of flexion of the hind legs must match that of the forelegs.

Here again, angles give us the necessary clues. Burt says, 'Mismatched angles will create conflicting movement and a tendency toward mixed-gaitedness or not being able to maintain form for any length of time'[9] – in other words, the movement will be inefficient and unbalanced. This is where the angle of the pelvis, expounded at length in the previous chapter, is so important. As far as possible the angle of the pelvis should match

Riaz, a multi-champion and a noted sire (Sweet)

that of the shoulder, and that of the femur the angle of the humerus. If the pelvis is too sloping, as with a real goose-rump, this will tend to place the hind legs too far under the horse, inhibiting free forward movement. On the other hand – and this is the fault most likely to be seen – if the pelvis is too horizontal, this will (unless the femur is disproportionately long) place the stifle too far back, making it difficult for the horse to 'reach under' and engage its hind legs. There should also be sufficient angulation in the hocks to allow good flexion (but not too much or the result is camped-out and/or sickle hocks – both a weak conformation).

The Arabian's long line from hip to hock, with the well-let-down hock and short cannon, gives a long, powerful stride; a shorter line from hip to hock, coupled with higher-set hocks and long cannons (as often found in the American Saddlebred) gives a higher, shorter stride. The straighter hock of the Thoroughbred gives low movement with swinging engagement; the hind leg angle of the Arabian brings with it more flexion of the hock and stifle. So what exactly may we infer from all this? I believe it places the Arabian firmly in the 'medium' category of movement.

That describes the type of movement. However, as Susan E. Harris points out, the *type* of movement should not be confused with the *quality* of the movement. 'Any type of movement can be performed well or poorly, and no one type of movement is superior to another. However, a horse that moves with an inappropriate type of movement for the purpose he is used for is handicapped in his performance.'[10]

As with type and conformation, we must return to the function: what type of movement would be desirable in the desert war-horse? As we have seen, the *bedu* did not use the trot; but the type of movement they required was, as with conformation, dictated by their particular kind of warfare, and the terrain they normally covered.

The chapter on type and conformation described the *bedawin* style of warfare and the rough terrain over which it was waged. These would dictate a medium type of movement, neither too low and ground-hugging nor extravagantly high and uneconomical. On the stony, uneven ground of the desert lands, a daisy-cutter would be prone to stumble so, at whatever gait, a horse would need to be able to lift its feet well in order to get over the ground. On the other hand, extremely high action would use up far too much energy, as well as increasing the risk of concussion damage on hard ground. Even show enthusiasts who prefer such action have to acknowledge that it is very tiring for the horse and cannot be kept up for any length of time. So the extravagant gaits of the Saddlebred and the Hackney would scarcely have been of any use to the *bedu*.

The fact that *some* Arabians have shown a tendency towards high action is no proof that this action is either characteristic of, or desirable in, the breed as a whole. As Sharon Byford points out: 'Arabian horses have been bred selectively for high-trotting action only in recent years as they have become more popular as show horses. When Park Horse classes became more popular, the desire for higher trotting action increased.'[11] Those aspects of the Arabian's skeletal structure which determine the type of action have surely established that the Arabian is not naturally either a daisy-cutter or a high-stepper, but that it has its own type of action which is more akin to that of some of the warmbloods than it is to that of either the Thoroughbred or the American Saddlebred. This may seem like a rather odd statement, until we consider that some of the lighter warmbloods have a considerable amount of Arabian blood in their ancestry. Many warmblood foals and youngstock can produce movement exactly like Arabians – that is, light and springy with a floating, 'dancing' quality. When they are fully grown, it is their sheer size and scope and the way in which their gaits are magnified that can make them seem so different from Arabians with regard to movement. It must be remembered, too, that warmbloods are not pure breeds, and that tremendous variations in type

– even within old, established breeds such as the Hannoverian – can and do occur. Unfortunately, in an attempt to increase the scope, many warmbloods are now being bred that are simply too long in the back; this makes collection increasingly difficult for them and greatly restricts their ability to engage the hind legs. This same obsession with magnified movement seems to be afflicting a number of continental breeders of Arabians; many horses imported from Europe are also too long in the back and, together with the 'flat back' syndrome, this again restricts the hind leg action. The fact that extravagant action (in the European, not the American sense) is being rewarded by judges is resulting in some very peculiar kinds of action currently being seen in showrings both in Britain and Europe. The effects of breeding to please show judges are discussed in more detail in Chapter 10; for now it is sufficient to look at what we should be seeing and contrast it with what we are actually seeing.

In his article entitled 'The Arabian' for the *Encyclopedia of Sport, 1900,* Wilfrid Scawen Blunt wrote,

> 'The shoulder should be well sloped, but without the exaggeration of the English hunter's. It should have, however, the freest possible action, and there is no better test of quality than to turn a colt loose in a paddock and take note of how he moves his shoulders and forearms. There should be little high knee action, but the whole limb should be thrown forward and the hoof "dwell" a second in the air before it is put down. This, with corresponding action behind, like that of a deer trotting through fern, is most important in a sire and a great test of quality.'[12]

Lady Wentworth, following her father, says,

> 'Trotting action should be smart and free and darting from the shoulders, the forefeet dwelling a moment before touching the ground with a semi-floating dancing movement, which suggests treading on air and springs and recalls a deer trotting in fern. The hock action powerful, and the hocks well lifted and brought forwards with a swinging stride, going rather wide when seen from behind. The stifle swing should match the shoulder swing . . . The knee action is rather higher perhaps than that of the Thoroughbred, but it is the shoulder action which matters . . . When looked at coming towards you and the horse is trotting full out, part of the inside of the front hoofs can sometimes just be seen as the foot reaches its fullest extension . . .
>
> 'When walking fast the horse should overstep the front hoof marks

Atlantica, World Champion Mare 1990 (Sweet)

with his hind ones a good 12 inches. If his hind feet step into the tracks of his forefeet when walking freely, he is tied in the hind action.

'The galloping action is astonishingly free at the shoulder, covering far more ground at a stride than seems possible for the size of the horse'.[13]

The distinguished American authority, Judith Forbis, writes of the Arabian: 'In action naturally balanced, smart and free with an airy step'[14] and further:

> 'Smart, free, naturally balanced action. A picture of harmony in motion. At the walk, fast and free, hind feet sometimes overstep the front track by 8 to 12 inches. At the trot, action is extremely brilliant almost "floating". The front limbs move with unrestricted shoulder and knee action; the hock action is powerful, hocks moving sufficiently wide apart, well raised and brought forward with a swinging stride. At the canter, action must be smooth and collected, not jerky or stilted. At the gallop, action is very free and light with long, ground-covering strides.'[15]

Peter Upton says,

> 'The action is free and expressive and naturally balanced, so that the horse moves lightly and easily over the ground. There must be a good flexion of all the joints and not a stiff 'daisycutting' action. Therefore the forelegs should move freely with unrestricted shoulder and knee action giving a long stride with the movement generating from the top of the shoulder. The hocks are engaged well under the horse so providing great impulsion and suppleness. . . . The whole action is full of such harmony that the horse appears to float and dance'.[16]

In the trot, all the leg joints should be properly flexed. The author with Zareeba

The action should be absolutely straight in front. However, as Upton points out, if the ribs are well sprung, as they should be, and the horse is tracking up as well as it should, then the horse may – in order that the stifle may move outside the ribs – go slightly wide behind (or, alternatively, slightly close behind). This is not a fault as long as it is not exaggerated; if this were the case the horse would, if moving too wide, give a rolling, uncomfortable ride; and if too close, run the risk of knocking itself.

Sadly, what is often seen in the showring, both in the in-hand classes and in the ridden classes, is a travesty of how an Arabian should move. In the *Arab Horse Society News Letter* for Summer 1995, the eminent and respected Arab Horse Society judge, Barbara Campbell expressed reservations about one type of action often seen. This is characterised, among other things, by 'a pronounced knee action which results in a heaviness of movement. Contrast this with the true Arabian way of going which should flow lightly and smoothly with elevation and natural cadence. The two are quite different but the audience is generally unaware of this difference, and applauds vociferously any extended movement'.[17]

The type of action Mrs Campbell is describing is one that has become all too common over the last few years: it is the kind of trot in which the horse resembles, not an Arabian, but a racing Standardbred. The racing trot is the most extended of all trots, and as one might expect it is very fast indeed but it is not at all like the extended trot required of a riding horse. In this kind of trot there is a very strong hock and knee action, with maximum extension of the forelegs; the gait is executed at such speed that the hind leg of a diagonal pair may be grounded before the foreleg. This break-up of the diagonal would clearly be unacceptable – and inefficient – in a riding horse but is quite acceptable for the racing trotter. The head and neck are carried high and extended in a manner that, again, is unacceptable – because inefficient in that it restricts the movement of the back – for the riding horse. In this kind of trot the propulsive power of the hind legs exceeds their carrying power. It is not, therefore, a suitable trot for the riding horse, in whom carrying power is far more important than propulsive power. It will, therefore, inevitably be heavier than the kind of trot proper to the Arabian, much as a racehorse, galloping flat out on its forehand, will be heavier-footed than a High School horse performing a collected canter. These are extreme examples but they illustrate the idea.

As Mrs Campbell rightly comments, spectators (and, I would add, not a few judges) tend to be impressed by any kind of extended movement, the more extravagant the better; this is hardly surprising when one considers that even FEI dressage judges persistently fall into the same trap. While there is still too much of the stiff 'daisy-cutting' action, some horses move spectacularly in front, really flinging out their front legs in an enormous, forward-reaching stride. But what of the hind legs? Very often these appear to be doing just as much as is necessary to maintain forward motion, no more. This can often be seen when a horse really reaches out with its forelegs, only to have to withdraw the forefoot before it touches the ground because the hind legs have not caught up. This may be caused by several factors. One is faulty conformation. As I mentioned above, horses that are too long in the back will find it very difficult to engage the hind legs, as will those horses whose pelvis is set too horizontally and/or whose hind legs are set too far to the rear. As we have seen, mismatched angles result in mismatched paces. Sometimes the horse cannot move correctly behind because of stiffness or tension in the back (this can also restrict the action of the forelegs, resulting in a stiff, 'proppy' action). This may be caused by the 'flat-back' syndrome; very often – as with the other action faults mentioned above – it is the result of poor handling and/or training. The stupid practice – currently being seen more and more often – of forcing the horse to trot with its nose in the air, cannot help but restrict the horse's movement through its back – remember the analogy of the suspension bridge outlined in the previous chapter. It also puts a tremendous strain on the poor creature's muscles and ligaments. It is surely bad enough that so many horses are put through the torment of having to stand still with their necks stretched and their backs hollowed without torturing them in this fashion as well.

Chapter 3 mentioned the fact that many horses are trotted up far too fast, resulting in a desperate scuttling of the hind legs in order to keep up with the front. Sometimes the hind legs are trailing so far behind that the horse is given a peculiarly unnatural stretched look. This seems to be the result of two fashionable ideas. One is that trotting the horses up fast (like Welsh Cobs) makes for a more exciting way of showing Arabians. Well, perhaps it does, although I doubt if it is the right kind of excitement. The word 'hysteria' comes to mind when one watches some performances. The other appears to be a belief that an extended trot equals speed and that if the unfortunate animal is rushed off its feet it will extend automatically. So it may, but as we saw in Chapter 3 and earlier in this chapter, it is more likely to extend for a few paces and then break into canter. In fact, it hardly has any option as it is running on out of balance. At a C-class show recently, it was heartening to see that a noted judge insisted on one exhibitor trotting his horse up more slowly after the horse had slipped on the hard going. One wishes that more judges would show the same consideration for horses. Unfortunately they, too, often seem mesmerised by the spectacular extensions sometimes seen. True extension, however, has nothing whatsoever to do with speed. It is all about the horse lengthening his stride, while maintaining the same tempo and rhythm, so as to cover more ground with each stride. Unfortunately, even in Grand Prix dressage a true extension is rarely seen. Mostly, the horses extend their forelegs like mad but they are really running on, as the sound of their footfalls testifies. If you can hear them at all (which with an Arabian you should not be able to do), there should actually be *fewer* hoofbeats than there are in a working or an ordinary trot, as the horse is supposed to be covering the ground in fewer strides. In practice, what you usually hear is *thump-thump-thump-thump* down the long side of the arena.

The truth is that unless a horse is sufficiently collected – which means he *must* be in balance – you will never, whether in-hand or under saddle, get a true extended trot. The greatest master of this century, Nuno Oliveira, wrote that: 'The true extended trot is the one which is the result of maximum impulsion in collection.'[18] Watch the Arabian stallion who, while showing off with arched neck, extends his trot immediately out of a collected, elevated *passage*. *That* is true extension.

It is perfectly possible to teach a horse to extend while being trotted up in-hand without rushing him out of balance and while maintaining the same tempo as the normal trot. Not only is it better for the horse, it is infinitely less hard work for the handler!

Sometimes one may see a peculiar kind of action in which the forefeet are flipped up as they reach the maximum extension. It is a kind of 'goose-stepping' action and, as with the horse whose forelegs extend so far that his hind legs cannot keep up, the foreleg must be drawn back again before it is grounded. All the best trainers warn against this kind of false extension. As Susan E. Harris points out: 'While this action is spectacular, it is a sign of tension, constraint and stiffness instead of true extension. The horse "promises more in front than he delivers behind"; the engagement and impulsion from the hind legs are insufficient.'[19]

Admirers of this kind of action maintain that it is correct: (a) because Lady Wentworth said so; and (b) because it is how a deer trots through fern! (see Wilfrid Blunt's description above). The second assertion is quite simply absurd. I do not know of anyone who has ever seen a deer flip its toes up in this manner, whether trotting through fern or not. The first is more problematical as Lady Wentworth did actually say, 'When looked at coming towards you and the horse is trotting full out, part of the inside of the front hoofs can sometimes just be seen as the foot reaches its fullest extension'.[20] I think Lady Wentworth must have had in mind here the moment just before the foot touches the ground; as the heel is grounded first it might sometimes be *just* possible to see the inside of the front hoofs. However, I think she would have done better to leave this out as it can so easily be misinterpreted by those who have taken her every word as gospel. Not every horse that displays this action is a faulty mover; some normally correct movers do it occasionally when they are tired or a little stiff. However, if a horse habitually moves in this manner then it raises a few questions about its general state of wellbeing.

As well as the kind of heavy movement described by Barbara Campbell, there are other kinds which are becoming more common. There is the short, choppy, up-and-down movement which would be better suited to a dray horse than to an Arabian. Then there is a heavy, 'round' kind of movement more appropriate to driving horses. Some horses whose hock joints flex well are given high marks for action even though the hocks are not really coming under the body and the topline of the horse is hollowed. As one former Arab Horse Society judge remarked in a letter to the author, 'The action is reminiscent of a driving cob.'

One cannot help noticing how few of the horses currently being exhibited really move well, with true, balanced, free Arabian action. If matters are bad in the in-hand classes, they are not much better in the ridden classes. Although many of the horses brought out under saddle seem to have quite good natural movement, too often this is stifled by poor or ineffective riding. I have heard the excuse that Arabians under saddle tend not to move as impressively as they do in-hand because they are 'saving their energy' or some such argument. Since the aim of training the riding horse is to improve its natural gaits and make them more beautiful, this is a very poor advertisement for either the trainers or the riders; one recalls Captain Upton's comments that a horse's gaits are very much what the rider makes of them.

In the end, although the Arabian is no longer used for war, we must remember that this is why he was so carefully bred throughout all those centuries. He is not a racing trotter or any other kind of harness horse. Nor is he specifically a racehorse, although he is often used as such. He was not designed to show off unnatural artificial movement, greatly though he enjoys showing off for its own sake. He was bred to do a specific job which he did superlatively well. It is our good fortune that now he is no longer required in war he can still give us such immense pleasure as a riding horse. Before he can do that, however, he must be able to move

Egina, British National Champion Mare, 1994 (Sweet)

correctly and in balance, in a manner that will cause the least possible premature wear and tear. We have the absolute responsibility to ensure, as far as it lies within our power to do so, that we both allow and encourage him to move correctly. This applies even if he will never be ridden as the horse's general wellbeing can be detracted from or enhanced by the way he moves and the manner in which he has been handled and trained. Those people who, whether through ignorance or misguided ambition and blind adherence to fashion, breed into horses faulty action, or try to force the Arabian into a way of going unsuited to him, or who thoughtlessly destroy his natural movement through coercive 'training', unnatural posing and trotting up and/or poor riding, would do well (if they could summon up the humility) to listen to the words of one of the wisest of horsemasters, Franz Mairinger, for many years a *bereiter* at the Spanish Riding School: 'Preserve his natural gaits. Preserve his personality. Preserve his instinct to go forward. Do this and you must be successful because you are respecting nature's wisdom'.[21]

Notes

1 Upton, Captain Roger, *Newmarket and Arabia*, p.148
2 Wentworth, Lady, *The Authentic Arabian Horse*, p.103
3 Edwards, Gladys Brown, *The Arabian: War Horse to Show Horse*, p.244
4 Edwards, *The Arabian*, p.244
5 Schaik, Henri van, *Misconceptions and Simple Truths in Dressage*, J. A. Allen 1979, p.69
6 Harris, Susan E., *Horse Gaits, Balance and Movement*, pp.102–4
7 Burt, Don, *Winning with Arabian Horses*, p.108
8 Burt, *Winning*, p.109
9 Burt, *Winning*, p.108
10 Harris, *Horse Gaits*, p.102
11 Byford, Sharon, *The Arabian: A Guide for Owners*, p.64
12 Blunt, Wilford, 'The Arabian', *Encyclopedia of Sport 1900* (reprinted in *Arabian Exodus* by Margaret Greely, pp.222–31)
13 Wentworth, *Authentic Arabian*, p.227
14 Forbis, Judith, *The Classic Arabian Horse*, p.229
15 Forbis, *Classic Arabian*, p.231
16 Upton, Peter, *The Classic Arab Horse*, pp.33–4
17 Campbell, Barbara, 'Some Thoughts on Judging', *Arab Horse Society Newsletter* Summer 1995, p.1
18 Oliveira, Nuno, *Reflections on Equestrian Art*, p.80
19 Harris, *Horse Gaits*, pp.41–2
20 Wentworth, *Authentic Arabian*, p.227
21 Mairinger, Franz, *Horses are Made to be Horses*, Rigby, Sydney, Australia 1983, p.16

Chapter 7

JUDGES AND JUDGING

'And diff'ring judgements serve but to declare
That truth lies somewhere, if we knew but where'

WILLIAM COWPER

THE NEWCOMER to showing, whether it is the showing of horses, cattle, dogs, cats, cavies, budgerigars, leeks or chrysanthemums, must – on hearing some of the vitriolic comments emanating from the inevitable crowd of ringside 'judges' – frequently wonder just who the real judge is? Who in his or her right mind would willingly expose themselves to such a barrage of criticism and abuse? For while the unwritten law is that judges are always right on the day, as all showring *habitués* know, unless the judge has placed their exhibit exactly where they want it to be, *the judge is never right.*

Of course, this is an exaggeration. Not *all* exhibitors (or spectators) automatically criticise the judge for making a disappointing decision. Any number of people derive such pleasure from showing that they are happy simply to be there in the showring; a rosette is a bonus to such glad souls who, after all, are the backbone of showing. However, there is no doubt that, in general, a judge will find it impossible to please everyone and the judge who attempts to do so will end up by pleasing no one. Besides, the judge is not there to please anyone; he or she is there to decide which animal (or bird, flower or vegetable) is, *according to his or her judgement*, the best put forward on the day.

Judges have an unenviable task in more ways than one. Unless they restrict themselves to judging solely within their home area (which severely limits their opportunities for judging, especially if their field is very specialised), they are condemned to countless weekends (and sometimes weekdays) of early rising, a great deal of tiring travelling, bad or indifferent food (unless they are lucky) or in some cases no food at all; long hours of standing around in the showring, often in adverse weather conditions (which can include blazing sun with no shade as well as the traditional British downpour). If they are judging ridden classes they may, in Britain, have to ride more horses in one day than many of us would ride in the space of several years (or even a lifetime). The late Glenda Spooner expressed her astonishment that so many mature men and women actually sought all this discomfort and inconvenience, particularly as, she said, the judge is inevitably criticised by many of the spectators and, in addition to this, 'every time he comes out of the ring he has made himself unpopular with the majority of the exhibitors and gained only one friend.'[1]

Judging in all kinds of weather

So who actually *wants* to take on this apparently thankless task and why? Firstly, says Mrs Spooner, it is flattering to be asked to judge and most people enjoy flattery. 'Secondly,' she goes on, 'it is a challenge. In some cases it panders to a sort of power complex, because what the judge says goes. This type of person, needless to say, makes a bad judge.'[2] Good judges are dedicated and absorbed in their task. 'Mostly they are people with a life-long love and experience of whatever type of animal they are judging. Some are judges by tradition – their forebears were judging when they themselves were still in the cradle.'[3] If they do not belong to such a tradition, they may be drawn to judging simply by a desire to make use of their expertise in their chosen field and to help to ensure that standards are maintained within the showring and within the breed as a whole.

On the other hand, they may be drawn from the ranks of those who believe that all judges are blind, drunk or corrupt (or most probably all three), and that once they have succeeded in getting on to the judges' panel, they will sweep the board with their reforming zeal and show them all how it should be done. These types of 'wannabees' usually fall by the wayside when they realise just what is involved in judging, although, to be fair, there are many would-be judges whose failing is too much, rather than too little, humility. One such potential judge went through the Arab Horse Society's complete selection procedure for judges only to announce that she did not feel she had the ability or the right to make such judgements. This must have been exasperating for the people who felt she had wasted their time, but at the same time one must respect her decision. She may not have realised it but the fact that she was able to make such a decision is, in itself, evidence of her judgemental ability. She probably had a great deal more of this than many established judges, yet she lacked the confidence to use it.

Such a lack of confidence would, indeed, be a serious drawback in a judge, who must, above all, have the courage of their convictions. Being seen to be hesitant can seriously undermine a judge's authority and it is another unwritten law of the showring that while a judge may not always be right, he or she is *never wrong*.

But is this true? Can a judge – any judge – really never be wrong?

This aspect of judging – whether of the legal or the showring kind – is what many people find difficult to understand and accept: that judgement is just that – the judicial weighing of evidence and the making of a decision based on that evidence. It is not so simple as an opinion, even though it may look like one. An opinion is, according to the dictionary, 'a judgement or belief not founded on certainty or proof' (*Collins English Dictionary*). Judgement, on the other hand, is a much more authoritative matter, being defined as 'the faculty of being able to make critical distinctions and achieve a balanced viewpoint' (*Collins English Dictionary*).

So can a judge – any judge – be wrong? Of course they can. Facts may not all have been taken into account. This is why all good judicial systems have an appeals procedure. The law may have been wrongly applied (though this is fortunately rare); in the case of the showring judge, points of conformation may have been overlooked or insufficiently examined. Due account may not have been taken of lameness, or of positive aspects such as good movement. There are all manner of ways in which judges can, as the saying is, 'make a bish'. They are, after all, human and since we all make errors of judgement, how unreasonable it is to expect so much more of others than we are capable of ourselves. However, a judge must be, by definition, a person of the highest integrity; and it is this quality, as much as the judges' level of knowledge, that is constantly being called into question by those who are unhappy with current standards, whether in Britain, Europe or the USA.

Many judges take this criticism to heart. Whatever their individual failings, in Britain at least, the best of them do recognise what an immense influence they can have for good or bad. Sadly, some international judges, who may perhaps be said to wield more influence than any others, seem reluctant to accept this burden of responsibility. At one of the European International Shows of 1990 a judge was asked how a horse with so many leg faults could have been selected as a champion. The judge replied, 'Type is what everyone wants in showing these days and it could be fully ten years before leg faults are given the attention they deserve – then only out of necessity.' But, the judge was asked, don't judges have an ethical responsibility? The astounding reply was, 'It isn't up to judges, but to the breeders, owners and the organisations representing them.'[4]

Such a staggering abdication of responsibility makes one wonder what is the point of having judges if they are not responsible for the results of their own decisions! Certainly a great part of the responsibility must lie with the other parties concerned but in the end it is the judge who sets the trend. Don Burt says of judges, 'What you do in the arena, no matter what size show, will have a bearing on breeding programs, training methods and the whole spectrum.'[5] In similar vein Dr Mary Bancroft, commenting on the 1991 Arab Horse Society Summer show at Malvern, wrote that: 'Judges have an enormous responsibility for the breed's development, and it is up to them to ensure that our top show horses are also horses that *could* be used for Long Distance, Racing or any one of a mass of different ridden activities, even if they are destined to be used only for showing and breeding.'[6] Sadly, as long as there are judges who disclaim all such responsibility, the judges' reputations and the breed will continue to suffer.

It has to be acknowledged, however, that the system does not always make the judge's job any easier. One of the most controversial aspects of judging in recent years has been the method used. There are several judging systems in general international use throughout the Arab horse world. In the so-called 'comparative' system generally used in Britain, the judge compares each horse they see with the others in the class. Under the various 'points' systems, the judges (for under this system there are usually two or more) compare each horse individually against the breed standard:

different parts of the horse are divided into sections, and points awarded for each section. The best known points systems are:

- The French system: several judges and up to twenty points awarded for each of several sections.
- The Swedish system: three judges and ten points for each section.
- The American system: several judges and ten points awarded.

Whatever the system used – and there are numerous variations – the principle is the same: the horse with the most marks wins. The most popular system is that which divides the horse into five sections:

1. type
2. head and neck
3. body and topline
4. legs
5. movement

Marks are given out of five, ten, or twenty for each of the five sections. There is one system, rather similar to that used in dressage, where some of the marks are multiplied by different factors, placing greater emphasis on type and movement.

Joan Ratcliff, herself an eminent Arab Horse Society judge, pointed out in an article for the *Arab Horse Society News* that, under this kind of system, although there are theoretically three sections devoted to conformation, in reality there are only two and a half as the head is one of the indicators of type and really belongs in that section. This means that, in practice, especially as many judges on the continent and in the USA appear to attach less importance to the limbs than others, the points system is loaded towards type rather than conformation.[7]

There are similar anomalies with regard to movement. Where does faulty action belong? If, for example, a horse dishes but has otherwise moved spectacularly, where does the fault go? Under legs, or movement? It would clearly depend on how bad the fault was, or even whether it could be put down to leg conformation, which is not always the case. In any event, the judge would have to be very knowledgeable indeed to be able to make such a judgement in the small amount of time available. Either way, as Mrs Ratcliff says, the beauty of the movement would dominate the fault. Similarly, because of the bias towards type noted above, a horse of good type would score a high mark which would move the results even further away from conformation.

One of the main disadvantages of the points system is, I feel, that in splitting a horse up into its component parts, so to speak, it is easy to disregard the overall picture. For example, a horse may have a head that is handsome enough but not the most refined, but the overall appearance may be improved by the manner in which the head is set on and the quality of the neck. Or it may have a less than perfect topline, but this may be redeemed by the level at which the tail is set on and its carriage and/or the rest of the body. There may be faults of conformation which, as long as they are not too significant, may be compensated for by other factors – after all no horse is perfect.

However, the points system as it is generally applied makes it difficult for judges to take account of compensating factors. For example, suppose a horse has a perfect topline, but is slab sided and herring gutted. Does the judge award high marks for the topline and ignore the other body faults, or does he/she simply award a lower mark for the whole body? Or, in the case of a horse with a stunning head but a relatively poor neck, which aspect is given priority?

In his book, *Arabian Horse Breeding and the Arabians of America*, Dr Ameen Zaher wrote that: 'Different parts of the Arabian horse should not be judged individually. Every part should have the right proportion in comparison to the other parts of the body. The head may have the dish, the big eyes etc., but it may be big in comparison to other parts. Therefore, the first look should be for the body as a whole and then every part may be examined and proportionally compared to other parts.'[8]

Some judges appear to forget that the old adage, 'no foot, no horse' is simply another step along from 'no leg, no horse'. Perhaps their concentration on matters above the horse's buttocks is a habit of mind adopted from the American show scene, where, as Gladys Brown Edwards tartly remarked, 'standing still and showing off . . . is what makes an Arabian great.'[9]

However, the opposite would be just as disastrous. If all judges concentrated on conformation at the expense of type, we might end up with a lot of very functional horses that did not, however, look like Arabians. This, to me, illustrates the futility of separating type and conformation (see Chapter 5). Balance, as in all things, is essential.

One of the advantages the points system is said to have over the comparative system is that it makes corrupt or biased judging more difficult. The argument runs that a single judge is more open to corruption than a panel, and that the comparative system relies very heavily on the judge's personal taste and even more on their integrity.

However, all is not what it seems with the points systems. Experience has shown that they are just as open to manipulation as the comparative system. Because of the nature of the points systems, it is often difficult for judges to tell which horse they have placed first, and this often means that, to ensure that their choice does actually come first, judges will give scores which, in the words of Betty Finke, 'reflect this intention rather than the horse's true merit (or faults).'[10] Clearly, this manipulation may be motivated by altruistic concerns; as Betty Finke goes on, 'on one occasion, I have known a judge give an extremely typey filly with very bad legs a low score for type, simply to prevent her from coming first. One should always keep such things in mind when evaluating point scores.'[11]

With regard to movement there may arise a similar imbalance. If the scoring system allows only for an overall score for movement, then a horse with a spectacular trot but a very poor walk could score well for movement. Many people would ask, what is wrong with that? My reply would be, as in Chapter 3, that a horse with only one spectacular gait is not, and cannot be, as good an animal as one which may not move extravagantly but shows freedom and balance in *all* gaits. Suppose, instead, that we award ten marks each for walk and trot. Along comes a horse which has a good trot – for which our hypothetical judge awards eight marks. The walk, however, is only average, and so scores five marks, making a total of thirteen out of a possible twenty for movement. Then our judge is faced with another horse which trots superbly. In this case, however, the walk is not even average, it is quite mediocre, bordering on poor. So the horse gets a ten for the trot, but only a three for the walk. Either way, both horses score thirteen for movement. Those judges who are dazzled by spectacular movement might 'fiddle' with the score for the walk so as to raise the overall score for movement, even though a mediocre or poor walk might be a sign of some functional deficiency of conformation (see Chapter 6 – Arabians seen in the showring are often deficient in the walk, even though the breed can have a superb walk).

These quirks of the marking system may help to explain some of the odder results to be found at European shows. A glance at the winners of some European shows reveals, among horses of undoubted excellence, others that are a caricature of what an Arabian should look like. The sinister trend towards weedy animals of dubious type is discussed further in Chapter 10, Breeding for Showing. While it is increasingly clear that this type of horse is becoming ever more fashionable in some quarters, I find it difficult to believe that so many international judges are so ignorant of what an Arabian of true type should look like and must conclude that some, at least, of these results are due to the vagaries of the points system.

It is also clear that panels of judges are no more immune to attempted corruption than single judges. The conduct of some officials and judges at certain international shows has been an open scandal for years but very little action has been taken because of the difficulty, or even impossibility, of proving accusations against them. I am not suggesting that corruption is universal at such shows, but one would have to be very naïve indeed to believe that where horses of such potential value are concerned, there are not going to be shenanigans of one sort or another.

It may be seen from this that the points system is just as open to manipulation in favour of the judge's personal taste (or for purposes of subversion) as the comparative system. This, of course, raises the question of whether judges are always as knowledgeable as they should be – in some countries judges are undoubtedly better educated as regards the Arabian horse than they are in others. Nor is the selection procedure all it could be. Surely it is time the international organisations got their act together and formulated a policy to ensure minimum standards of judge training and competency, together with a points system which actually makes sense in terms of the whole horse. Heaven forbid that individual countries should be compelled to change their system if the system suits them, but surely it is imperative that international shows, at least, should have some kind of rational system which does not require judges to indulge in acrobatic mental arithmetic. For now, however, let us see how the comparative system fares when set beside the points system.

Don Burt maintains, 'It is almost impossible to judge a single horse against an unknown or a set of standards that are not clear; in other words, to put him against the theoretical perfect horse.'[12] He says further that: 'It's much easier to compare what you see with others that you see at the same time, and that is how a class is really judged – on the basis of comparisons. Comparisons, then, become a matter of opinion, good and bad.'[13]

The disadvantages of the comparative system are immediately obvious. It was a system which worked extremely well in the days when classes were relatively small and when there were far fewer shows, which meant there were sufficient experienced, truly knowledgeable judges to go round. It can still work at smaller shows where the entry numbers may remain at a manageable level, *provided* the judge knows their business. However, at larger shows, particularly the national shows, some classes may have upwards of 30 entries, which makes the judge's task under the comparative system a difficult one indeed. To look at so many animals in such a short space of time; to note each one and remember its individual qualities in detail, is surely asking too much of even the most seasoned and knowledgeable judge. The practice adopted by some judges, of making a preliminary selection (to however many places as there are rosettes awarded at that particular show) and then dismissing the rest of the class, is really not fair (though it may be a practical solution to a judge faced with an enormous class and less than twenty minutes to judge it in). It is quite possible for a judge to rearrange the placings dramatically after a really good look at each horse individually. This happened to us at a recent show where our pure-bred colt was lying about eleventh after the preliminary walk round and trot-up (he was being a bit of a prat). He redeemed himself, however, following his individual trot-up, and ended up in third place. As this show was an international qualifier it made quite a difference to us. Had the judge not given each horse the same searching scrutiny that she directed on her initial placings, we would have been deprived of rather more than a pretty rosette. Every entry has a right to the same consideration; even the most experienced, lightning-minded judge can make errors in their initial choices, and the best are not afraid to change their placings accordingly.

This problem of over-filled classes, particularly at the larger shows, could be better addressed by splitting classes (as is often done in any case) or by introducing (possibly for C-class shows and the Nationals) some kind of qualification system. After all, that is the only way some of the really big, non-breed-specific shows can operate!

Added to this, much unease has been expressed about the degree to which a judge's personal preference dictates the eventual winners, plus the fact that judges may either be biased towards certain exhibitors who are

Making comparisons

well known and therefore easily recognised, or may be reluctant to put down another judge who appears in the line-up with their own exhibit.

Apart from the problems already mentioned when the judge is faced with a very large class, the great advantage of the comparative system is that the judge can make an overall assessment of the horse, balancing faults against good points, and, most important, ensuring that certain aspects such as type and movement do not dominate conformation and limbs.

In comparing the two systems, Joan Ratcliff says, 'The result of the points system is that good, free-moving, typey animals come to the fore, but often with faulty conformation.'[14] Mrs Ratcliff goes on to point out that: 'In the comparative system, because the judge has more time and space, he can consider leg and conformation faults more carefully, with the result that they are balanced with type and movement . . . This may mean that the less extreme members of the breed emerge as winners but, overall and over the life of a breed, it produces a sounder and more able horse.'[15]

In theory, at least, this *should* happen; in practice it is not always so. Some judges appear to disregard everything other than extreme type and/or movement. As previously mentioned in Chapter 3, some judges do not even look to see whether the horse is moving straight, or, if they do, it is a very cursory examination (others, on the other hand, are very scrupulous about this). I do not believe this is necessarily the fault of the comparative system *per se*, but rather a reflection of the level of knowledge, experience and integrity of the individual judge.

These are issues which have been raised numerous times in the equestrian press and not only with regard to Arabians. In *Horse and Hound*, September 28 1995, several letters were published which asked such questions. One criticised the judging in classes of Welsh Cobs (Section D); this correspondent had seen horses that were lame placed by judges at two different shows. 'Both classes', the letter goes on, 'contained superb animals which were not judged fairly. This type of judging does nothing to encourage people to show their horses with confidence.'[16]

Quite recently I have heard similar comments from members of the Arab Horse Society. One member expressed the opinion that judges who exhibit should be prohibited from handling the horse personally in the ring, thus eliminating the possibility of influencing the judge by their own presence (the judge might, of course, still recognise the horse). After all, if you are a judge and you see in the line-up a fellow judge who might well be judging your own exhibit in a forthcoming show, are you really going to put that judge's horse down the line, no matter how much it might deserve to be there? This question was recently put to the Judges' Committee of the Arab Horse Society, which replied that such a system of preventing judges from exhibiting in person would be impossible to implement because such restrictions on showing would mean that no one would come forward as a potential judge. This same point was made by Glenda Spooner who emphasised the need for faith in judges' integrity. With all due respect to Mrs Spooner (herself a person of the highest integrity) the fact of a person being a judge does not automatically guarantee their integrity or that they are strong-minded enough to have the courage of their convictions in difficult cases.

This problem has been discussed in letters to various equestrian magazines, and with the various breed societies, for a number of years and matters are certainly not improving generally. In some areas of showing dissatisfaction has reached such a level, with judges blatantly judging faces rather than the horses, that many previously enthusiastic exhibitors are becoming so disgusted that they are withdrawing from showing altogether. As one exhibitor of Welsh ponies said to me: 'I show for the enjoyment of it, not to win cups and rosettes. But having paid an entry fee – usually a large one – not to mention gone to the often considerable expense of travelling and sometimes staying overnight, I do at least feel I am entitled to have my ponies judged. Yet at most of the shows you know who is going to win as soon as you see the catalogue – and it has nothing to do with the quality of the stock. I don't mind someone beating me if they have a better pony – in fact I'm pleased for them when they do – but I *do* object when my pony doesn't even get a second glance, and the judge puts up someone else's pony because of who they are, not because it's a better animal. So this year, I'm staying at home.' This was not sour grapes because this lady has top quality ponies that deserve to do well. She was simply sickened by the obvious bias in judging. And, as she said in the same conversation, the worst aspect of it is that, in the end, it is the breed that suffers if judges persistently put up inferior animals. We are back to the concept of judges' responsibilities.

It must be said that matters in Britain are not yet quite so bad as they are on the continent and in the USA, where at some shows it is obvious even to the casual observer that the judges are very much influenced by the name and prestige of the owner or the handler. However, they are still bad enough to cause a significant number of exhibitors to give up in disgust.

The universal safeguards built into showing – i.e. the rules concerning judges not fraternising with exhibitors or having sight of a catalogue prior to judging – are of no avail when so many of the best-known exhibitors are inevitably people whose faces are well known to the judge. Sometimes they may even be a friend of the judge, though this may, in some cases, lead judges to mark such exhibitors with unnecessary severity. This should not be necessary simply to prove impartiality and it is just as unfair to the exhibitor as it would be to mark them up because of who they are. Yet, sadly, such is the suspicion of judges these days that a judge in this type of situation simply cannot win.

The usual response from the various breed and showing societies and from diehard supporters of the status quo is that such discrepancies and injustices are all part of showing; that with so much potential for human error and divergences of opinion it would be impossible to expect true impartiality; and further that those who can't accept that this is the way things are should abstain from showing.

I disagree. All exhibitors pay the same entry fee and all, regardless of status, have a right to be judged with as much fairness and impartiality as the judge can muster. Why should someone pay upwards of £100 in travel, entry fees and stabling costs, only to be faced by a judge who is more interested in human faces than equine ones? It may be too much to expect the system to be universally fair but those who operate it have a responsibility at least to *try* to ensure fairness. If, instead, we fall into the trap of accepting unfairness and injustice simply because fairness and justice are elusive ideals, then we abandon whatever integrity we have, and the result is a depressing kind of nihilism.

It may be thought that I am hankering after some mythical Golden Age, when judges were unbiased and exhibitors were all perfect gentlemen. It is not as simple as that; there never was a Golden Age, and there have always been biased judges and exhibitors whose behaviour was anything but gentlemanly. Lady Anne Blunt's comments in her journals about the conduct of some of the early Arab classes are ample proof of that. However, I do think it is true to say that changing standards of behaviour within society in general have led to a deterioration in the way in which such matters as judging are conducted. In the past we had judges like Glenda Spooner, for whom honesty and integrity were almost a religion; such people were universally respected, even if they often made others feel uncomfortable. There are certainly still such judges about, but nowadays integrity and honesty are too often seen (in some quarters at least) as quaint, old-fashioned concepts which have no place in a society where the pursuit of personal gain and advantage is frequently regarded as the only worthwhile activity.

Fortunately, not everyone thinks like that, least of all the ordinary Arabian horse enthusiast who simply loves the breed and wants to see justice done to it.

To its immense credit, the Arab Horse Society has at last recognised that a problem exists and that many judges are by no means as knowledgeable as they should be. While in the past there have always been judges whose experience, knowledge and integrity were beyond reproach, there were also far too many who became judges simply because of *who* they knew and because of the prestige it brought them. In 1994 there was a reorganisation of the Judges' Committee, which resulted in it becoming separated from the Show Committee. A new policy was formulated for the selection, training and appointment of judges which is very much more comprehensive than the previous arrangement.

Formerly, all that prospective judges had to do was to attend two seminars, after which they would be invited to become probationer judges. Under the new procedures, prospective judges must attend two or more elementary courses which are educational and open to anyone interested. These courses include lectures of a practical nature, given by senior judges or other similarly knowledgeable persons, on type, conformation and methods of judging.

Once a prospective judge has attended two or more of these courses under different lecturers, those who wish to continue are invited to attend intermediate courses which are very much more comprehensive, including more advanced lectures on type, conformation and judging methods. Would-be judges have to judge a mock class, evaluating and placing horses and giving their reasons in writing. Lectures on faults and defects are also included.

After passing two intermediate courses, again under different lecturers, the prospective judge is then advised by the Judges' Committee that they should apply to be probationer judges at no fewer than two shows under different judges, with the latter to send in reports. Following this probationary period, those who receive good reports from the judges at their probationary shows are then invited by the Judges' Committee to sit the Arab Horse Society judges' examination. This consists of a written and practical section, and includes three classes to be judged by the examinee. The 'judge' is questioned on his or her placings and the reasons for them.

Examinees passed by the Judges' Committee and accepted by Council then become qualified judges. They must then judge at least six affiliated shows before their names are considered for inclusion in the main list of judges by a panel of experienced National Judges (appointed by the

Judges' Committee). They must judge for five years before officiating at the National Show in that capacity.[17]

It is to be hoped that judges will be encouraged to take notes (few at present appear to do so) and to write up reasons for their decisions on the day (in fact, some breed societies, particularly in the canine world, insist that judges justify their decisions in writing). While it is appreciated that this is time consuming, it is no different from what dressage judges do, and a steward could assist with note taking. This would help immensely in cases of dispute, particularly as the new policy provides for the removal of judges from the list (or they may be asked to take a refresher course) in cases of serious complaint. Any such complaint about a judge must be made in writing, supported by a seconder. The Judges' Committee will then write to the judge in question asking for an explanation and, if necessary, issue a warning. Two official warnings will result in action being taken as above so this is not a matter to be taken lightly by either judges or competitors. Judges are always vulnerable to attack by disappointed exhibitors, and if they can produce evidence in the form of notes taken on the spot to back up their decision and/or actions, then this is clearly going to make the Judges' Committee's job much easier in cases of complaint, and its decision fairer.

This complaints procedure also means, of course, that persistently sloppy judging or blatantly unfair actions on the part of judges will no longer be tolerated by exhibitors. Such a system is always open to abuse but it is in the interests of all concerned that the Judges' Committee is seen to be as fair and impartial an arbiter as possible. This has not always been the case (see Chapter 9 on Abuse of show horses) but it is to be hoped that the reforms in the selection procedure and the more comprehensive Judges' Committee policy will help to keep everyone on their toes. Certainly it was very noticeable that, during the season immediately following the introduction of the new policy, many judges were obviously being much more meticulous in their judging procedures. Let us hope this trend continues.

Also to be welcomed is the policy decision to encourage judges from other breeds and disciplines in the horse world to become Arab judges, provided they satisfy the Judges' Committee that they are competent to judge Arabians. There are many such people who, although they do not necessarily breed Arabians, have an immense amount of experience of them. Some may even have done more with Arabians, in a general way, than many members of the Arab Horse Society.

This expertise could be an invaluable way of counteracting some of the tendency to navel-gazing which has afflicted the Arab horse world for some time now. By this I mean a certain complacency, or assumption that all is well and for the best in the best of all possible worlds of Arab horse breeding and showing, even though there is ample evidence that this is not so. It might do certain sections of the Arabian horse world good to be shocked out of this complacency, as happened to Spanish breeders of the Andalusian in 1979 when Dr Lehrner of Piber (the Lipizzaner stud attached to the Spanish Riding School) judged Andalusian horses at the first Championship of the Pure-bred Spanish Horse (see Chapter 10, Breeding for Showing, for a description of what happened).

Those with less involvement in breeding and showing a particular breed, but with a comprehensive knowledge of that breed, can sometimes be far more accurate observers and judges than those who are so involved. This is not always the case, of course, but any fresh opinion, unaffected by personal interest, must be of value.

So far our discussion has been confined to in-hand judges, but what of ridden judges? There is a huge amount of variation in the riding ability of ridden judges. Some are very good indeed; others leave a great deal to be desired. Judges vary immensely in both style and level of ability; in addition they may be riding all kinds of horses whose abilities and level of schooling may be considerably less than their owners fondly imagine. Ridden judges face a daunting task: they may have a large class to ride, which, if it is a novice class, may include anything from quite well-schooled horses to those which have only recently been backed. The judge may obtain the sweetest ride imaginable or they may be in for a rough one. I have to say that they are braver by far than I. Even in an open class it is not like judging a dressage test, where: (a) the judge does not have to ride the horse: and (b) it may be assumed that the horse has reached a certain level of training for it to be able to execute the test at all. One cannot assume anything in a showing class, especially when the horse is ridden by a really clever rider who can enhance its good points while disguising its poor ones. Until, that is, the judge gets on board.

This is where things normally fall apart and it is seldom the horse's fault. I feel this exposes the true weakness of the system. A horse may be an extremely well-schooled, responsive ride. However, a sensitive horse, even if it is accustomed to being ridden by different people, may be upset by a ham-fisted or unbalanced judge's riding, to the extent where it does not perform anything like as well as it is capable of doing. In fact the better schooled a horse is, the more likely this is to happen. Any number of riders who consider themselves to be quite good have been astonished to find that, when given an opportunity to ride a horse schooled to a very advanced level, they could not even get it to turn a corner. Such horses are trained to respond to such subtle aids that anything else confuses them and they will offer what they think the rider wants. It might be rather disconcerting for a judge to be offered a *levade* when all they wanted was a halt, but the fact remains that with some very well-schooled, sensitive horses this is precisely what you would get if you used the kind of halt aids generally taught in Britain. In such a case the horse would in all probability be marked down for disobedience when all it was doing was what it thought was required. It must be very pleasing for a judge to have a good ride on a nice horse; however, they should sometimes ask whether it is not their own riding rather than any deficiencies in the horse that has led to a less than enjoyable ride.

Some diehards might argue that a well-schooled, well-mannered horse should be able to give anyone a good ride. I disagree completely with this argument. No horse is a machine, and particularly where hot-blooded, sensitive horses like Arabians are concerned, it is all too easy for their equilibrium to be upset by crude riding. I believe it behoves every ridden judge to ensure that their riding comes up to scratch. After all, it is not pleasant (and this has happened to me) to see one's much-loved horse, into whose schooling have gone many hours of patience, tact and effort, going flat with his nose poked and back hollowed because the judge was giving him a rough ride. I would not, however, go as far as one exhibitor whom I know who, when I asked her how her horse had fared in his ridden class, replied fiercely: 'That judge couldn't ride my f...ing bike!'

Conversely, to see one's horse ridden well gives a great deal of pleasure. Would that it happened more often!

No matter how strongly an exhibitor might feel that a judge has made a gross error in the placing (or failure to place) of their exhibit, and no matter to what extent this feeling is (or appears to be) justified, there can never be any excuse for attacking the judge (verbally or otherwise!) or arguing in the showring. There is no reason at all why a polite request for an explanation of the judge's decision may not be made but there is absolutely no place for verbal abuse or aggressive questioning. Nor is there any excuse for a disappointed exhibitor to storm angrily out of the ring. Whatever the provocation, such a lack of restraint betrays a certain lack of maturity, disgusts those spectators (and fellow competitors) for whom good manners are still a matter of importance, provides an unedifying spectacle for the vulgar, and adds a tone of unpleasantness to what should be an enjoyable occasion for all. The traditional British approval of the good loser has certainly been overdone in the past, to the extent that good losers have sometimes been seen as more important than good winners, but the opposite extreme view, that winning is the only thing that matters, is a corrupting influence which has all but destroyed the beneficial aspects of competition. Only the person who can handle defeat generously is equipped to handle success; so the bad loser is ultimately destructive of the whole process which makes showing a pleasure.

In the end, whatever doubts we may have about the knowledge, judgement and integrity of the judges at our shows, we must remember that they are no more or less subject to human failings than the rest of us and that, given the almost infinite number of ways in which a judge can commit a *faux pas*, it is so easy to blame them when they have simply made an unwelcome decision. If they are then honest (and courageous!) enough to explain *why* they have made that particular decision, they lay themselves open to being misunderstood and misrepresented. One breeder of Arabian horses, who often judges at local shows, was so abused and misquoted after giving a candid reply to an exhibitor's query, that she has vowed never to make that mistake again.

However, a judge at a large, affiliated show – particularly if it is a C-class show, at which qualification for international European shows may be at

Decisions, decisions . . .

stake – may well have to be prepared to justify their decision and I think this is the way forward if judges are to regain the respect and confidence of exhibitors and Arab horse enthusiasts in general. It may be irksome and time consuming, but if the suggestion put forward regarding written notes were to be adopted, I think it would be an invaluable tool for all concerned – for all those, that is, who genuinely wish to see fair, impartial, *knowledgeable* judging. How individual judges would regard such a proposal, and how they handled it, would be, I believe, a measure of their stature as judges.

Notes

1 Spooner, Glenda, *The Handbook of Showing*, p.150
2 Spooner, *Handbook*, p.150
3 Spooner, *Handbook*, p.150
4 *Arab Horse Society News*, No. 76, p.52
5 Burt, D., *Winning with Arabian Horses*, p.4
6 *Arab Horse Society News*, No. 77, p.48
7 Ratcliff, J. 'The Influence of Judging on Arabian Horses', *Arab Horse Society News*, No. 79, p.41
8 Zaher, Dr Ameen, quoted in *Arab Horse Society News*, No. 76, p.67
9 Edwards, Gladys Brown, *The Arabian: War Horse to Show Horse*, p.152
10 Finke, Betty, in *Arab Horse Society News*, No.76, p.30
11 Finke, *Arab Horse Society News*, p.30
12 Burt, D., *Winning*, p.69.
13 Burt, D., *Winning*, p.69.
14 Ratcliff, *'Influence'*, p.41
15 Ratcliff, *'Influence'*, p.41
16 *Horse & Hound*, 28 September 1995, Letters to the Editor, p.67
17 Arab Horse Society Judges' Committee Policy Document on the Training of Judges and Other Issues

Chapter 8

PROFESSIONALS *v.* AMATEURS

Professional: *'a person who engages for his livelihood in some activity also pursued by amateurs'*[1]
Amateur: *'a person who engages in an activity, esp. a sport, as a pastime rather than professionally or for gain'*[2]

IN OUR WESTERN culture, the word 'professional' carries a high value. Members of the emergency services are commended for the professionalism they display in carrying out their duties. Company executives pride themselves on their professional status, while employees in the public sector are constantly exhorted to improve their public image and to conduct their departmental affairs in a more businesslike and professional manner.

All of this implies a great respect for professional status. The word 'professional' is bandied about by people who are only vaguely aware of its true meaning. It is assumed that someone who, to employ one dictionary definition, 'engages in an activity for gain as a means of livelihood'[3] must be skilled or competent in order to be able to derive their livelihood from such activity. This brings us to another dictionary definition: 'extremely competent in a job, etc.'.[4]

It follows from this, then, that the *amateur* is accorded no such status. Indeed, one of the dictionary definitions of 'amateur' is 'a person unskilled in or having only a superficial knowledge of a subject or activity'.[5] 'Amateurish' is defined as 'lacking professional skill or expertise'. Any job which has been botched or skimped or lacks polish is dubbed 'amateurish'.

Yet it was not always so. The word 'amateur' is an eighteenth-century derivation from the Latin *amator*, a lover. An amateur was therefore someone who engaged in an activity or pursuit not for gain, but purely for the love of it. Such a person might or might not be of the aristocracy but they were almost invariably wealthy. They therefore had both the means and the leisure to pursue their chosen activity to whatever extent they wished. As they were motivated by passion and not by the prospect of gain, they could frequently take risks with ideas, theories and discoveries, which the professional, with an eye to their reputation, might well shy away from.

The eighteenth and nineteenth centuries saw the heyday of the gifted amateur. They were frequently polymaths, the range of their learning covering many disciplines, and a number of them had a command of languages that, in these days of ever-increasing specialisation, makes the head spin. Heinrich Schliemann, the passionate amateur archaeologist who discovered the ruins of ancient Troy, was the master of no fewer than fifteen languages by the age of 33. Going further back in time, the Russian Emperor Peter I (Peter the Great) became highly skilled in fourteen specialities. He learned masonry, carpentry, navigation and boatbuilding; among other things he could cobble boots, pull a tooth, shoe a horse or cast a cannon – all with as much skill as any professional. Moving closer to our own subject, Lady Anne Blunt was a mathematician, an artist (her drawing master was Ruskin), a musician, a linguist and a fine horsewoman. These people, and countless others like them, were motivated by an intense curiosity and interest in their chosen subjects (in Peter the Great's case he also wanted to master the skills needed to drag his nation into the eighteenth century). They were not professionals in any sense of the term, yet their skills were the equal of those of any 'pro'.

Nowadays we live in an age of specialisation. Few people have the means to pursue the variety of skills and learning that the great amateurs of the past took such delight in; those that have seldom seem inclined to do so. Learning, or physical skills, are rarely valued for their own sake; they must always be seen to serve some specific purpose in order to be considered useful. So we have an increasingly wide gap between the professional and the amateur. Because the latter does not earn a livelihood from their chosen activity, amateur status is perceived as being of lesser account than that of the professional who is considered skilled solely by virtue of that professional status.

This is especially apparent in the equestrian world. Here, professionals come in many guises. Quite apart from the myriad people whose skills are needed on an everyday basis – such as the farrier, vet and qualified riding instructor – there are many whose role is principally to take on those aspects of equine training and production that the average owner may feel they lack the necessary skill and/or experience to undertake. Enter the professional trainer or show producer who is, to a large extent, the successor to the professional 'nagsmen' whose job, in the days when the horse was primarily a form of transport, was to educate horses to a level where they were considered fit for a lady or gentleman to ride.

Nowadays the purpose of such training is most likely to be preparation for some kind of competition; nevertheless, the principle remains the same. Relatively few people feel they have either the time or the knowledge to bring on a green horse themselves, so (unless they decide to buy a green horse anyway and hope it will somehow turn out all right), they either buy a ready-made horse (which will prove expensive), or they buy a green horse and send it to a professional for training. This professional may be a qualified riding instructor who specialises in training horses, or they may simply be someone who has a great deal of experience of training horses and who has usually had a string of successes in their chosen aspect of equestrian sport.

In the showing world this usually means that they have a number of prominent show winners to their credit, perhaps a few major championships. In the case of the top professionals, they will almost always be among the first few places at all the major shows. These successes give them an aura of competence; to be so successful they must have talent, skill, dedication and an eye for detail. Many showing enthusiasts feel – with some justification – that if they want their horses to do well they need the services of a professional.

But how accurate is this perception? Are the professionals really so much more competent than amateurs, or is this an illusion created either by the bias of judges towards the big names, or by the triumph of 'showmanship' over genuine ability? As with so many such questions, the answer is both yes and no. Let us consider first the advantages the professional has over the amateur.

Firstly, the average amateur has to maintain a job as well as look after their horse(s); few will have the means to employ others to do this, although some may be able to coax or coerce members of the family into helping out. Many dedicated amateur horse owners also have limited facilities for schooling (although they may be fortunate enough to keep their horse(s) at livery in, say, a riding school with the use of an all-weather schooling arena or an indoor school). Many have no all-weather facilities at all, so that unless they are lucky enough to live in an area where hacking out on the road is not suicidally dangerous, they may have nothing more than a corner of a bumpy field to school in. In winter they may only be able to ride at weekends, if at all.

The professional, on the other hand, will most likely have access to considerably better facilities. Even where they have not, they will usually know how to make the best use of what they do have. If they can hack out in safety, some will be able to do almost all their schooling while riding out – this is by no means as difficult as it sounds. Others will have the knowledge and experience to make the best of natural terrain; much good work can be done on hilly ground, for example, in teaching a green horse how to balance itself. Indeed it may be said that the really good professional's greatest asset is this ability to make the best of a very little; this is why so many of them seem able to turn the proverbial sow's ear into a silk purse.

In addition, the professional has the advantage of *time*. Time, that is, to work on horses, instead of having to cram it all in at the end of a busy and possibly frustrating day at work in a mundane job. If a horse proves awkward in some respect, the professional will be able to schedule schooling so as to take account of this problem. It may be that the horse needs several short schooling sessions a day, rather than one (or two) longer ones. Again, the professional can accommodate this. If successful, they will almost certainly have at least one groom or stablehand to take over some of the day-to-day running of the yard, freeing the professional to concentrate on the actual production of the horses. If the yard is very successful, there may be an assistant to help with the training.

Nigel Hollings, himself a highly successful professional for many years, defines the situation thus: 'The role of the professional and the breeder in the showing world is to maintain standards, and the show ring is their shop window; this will create other business opportunities which will, in turn, hopefully pay the bills. For the amateur, who is the backbone of the sport, it is an opportunity to compete against and often beat the experts at their own game.'[6] He elaborates further: 'An amusing situation exists between amateurs and professionals: the amateurs envy the professionals, thinking that they are difficult to beat, and that they would love to be in their position; whereas the professionals envy the amateurs and dream of the day when they can afford to concentrate on just one or two exhibits like the amateur.'[7]

In the end, it comes down to sheer dedication, hard work and experience more than anything else. Caroline Akrill, herself a former producer of show ponies, sums up the good professional's work very neatly in her humorous and often hysterically funny book, *Not Quite a Horsewoman*:

> 'The truth is that it is not often that a horse or pony is so naturally per-

fect that it needs no artificial help whatsoever, but the same could be said of humans after all. A top showing yard is rather like a model school for equines; it's amazing what a bit of professional grooming and a few sharp lessons in deportment and good manners can achieve. In the equine model schools, where miracles are wrought daily, pig's ears are sent out to win looking remarkably like princesses. The end result is obtained by means of much grinding hard work and minute attention to detail. Only a handful of amateur producers have the know-how and the dedication to do the same'.[8]

This is not to say, of course, that the talented and determined amateur cannot achieve similar results. They can and do, but in the ridden classes it is evident that they are very much at a disadvantage unless they are so experienced that they have developed the same degree of polish in preparation, presentation and ringcraft as the professionals. The amateur may have a horse that is actually better than that ridden by the professional; they may be a far better rider, in the classical sense of the term, but, as we have seen, the nature of showing is such that it is the outward appearance that counts, and this is where the skilled professional scores time and again.

Is this really the reason why the professionals always (or almost always) seem to win? In many cases I would say that it is; but not all professionals are of the same calibre and there is a disturbing tendency for judges to put professionals up the line simply by virtue of who they are.

So, just who *are* the professionals? And why are they so often regarded (by the rest of the equestrian world) with a mixture of awe and suspicion?

Professionals come in all shapes and sizes, male and female, and from an assortment of backgrounds, not all of them necessarily 'horsy'. They may (as with the Hollings brothers, Nigel and Stuart) have ridden show ponies from earliest childhood and found it simply the most natural thing to carry this childhood pastime over into adult life and to make it their living. They may be dealers (again from a variety of backgrounds) who have, over the years, amassed a huge amount of experience with many different types of horse and pony. For them shows are both their shop window and their means of getting to know their clientele. They may simply be people who love the whole process of turning out horses and ponies to the highest standards and wish to make it their way of life.

Some professionals have no early equestrian background but, having been bitten by the 'horse bug', they have dedicated themselves to learning all they can about horses and horsemanship and have acquired the expertise to pass on to others. In fact, these people can sometimes be the most truly knowledgeable of all, and often the best horsemen and women, simply because they have *not* acquired a lifetime's accumulation of perceptions and assumptions which may not be accurate, and have had to develop most of their knowledge through a conscious learning process. It is too often assumed in the horse world that many years of experience equal true knowledge but this is by no means always the case. Experience is essential, of course, but it is the *quality* of that experience, not its quantity, that counts. Some professionals are not necessarily exceptional horsemen or women, simply very skilled in presenting the right appearances and in making a horse seem very much better than it naturally is.

Heaven forbid that I should seem to be presenting professionals in an unfavourable light; that would be grossly unfair as I am the first to acknowledge that many of them do a difficult job remarkably well. However, it cannot be denied (as it is well known and well testified in the showing world) that *some* professionals (and some amateurs) use some very dubious methods indeed. We shall take a look at this shortly but there is another disturbing aspect which is not generally commented on but which I think has profound implications for the way in which professional trainers and riders treat the horses in their care.

Presentation matters

This aspect appears common to all forms of training to do with horses – all those, that is, where a great deal of money is at stake. It applies particularly to trainers and riders of showjumpers, dressage horses, show horses and racehorses. I am talking about the curious phenomenon of the professional trainer and/or rider who doesn't actually appear to *like* horses.

There are those (and I used to be one of them) who are innocent enough to think, surely one must like horses to be able to work with them? Research has shown that this is far from being the case. If you observe, quietly and unnoticed, the goings-on in almost any large racing stable, for instance, you will see lads who appear to be actually afraid of their charges, to the extent that their fear makes them treat the horses with unnecessary roughness. If asked, some of them will openly acknowledge their fear and admit that they only work with horses because it was the only job they could get – usually in rural areas where job opportunities are very few.

Among racehorse trainers, some appear to have ambiguous feelings towards the horses they train. In an ITV documentary shown on 17 October 1995, entitled *They Shoot Horses, Don't They?* (which, admittedly, was unfair in many respects, although it made some very valid points), about the fate of ex-racehorses, one trainer was asked if he liked horses. He seemed very doubtful on this point, saying that he wouldn't exactly say he *liked* them, though he would like to think he respected them. One does begin to wonder why, if they do not have at least some liking for horses, so many people choose to work with them.

Some trainers and riders appear to regard horses as their natural adversaries, to be overcome and subdued at all costs. Some think of the horse as a living machine; in some cases, a rather stupid machine at that. I have heard any number of showjumpers express the opinion that a horse must be stupid: (a) to jump huge fences it would never need to jump in a natural existence; and (b) even more stupid to allow a rider on its back in the first place. We have seen in Chapter 4 how limiting these attitudes are but it is disturbing to think that 'professionals' can hold such potentially damaging opinions, so devoid of understanding of, and respect for, the horses in their care.

The best professionals, of course, do not think like this (or at any rate very few of them do so) but there are all too many lower down on the scale who do. This is a great pity, not only for the horses who fall into their hands but for the reputation of professionals as a whole.

The word 'professional' derives, of course, from 'profession' – originally an occupation requiring special training in the liberal arts or sciences, especially one of the learned professions – law, theology or medicine. In its turn, 'profession' comes from the Latin *profiteri*, to confess openly. It was associated with the taking of religious vows and the public affirmation or acknowledgement – in other words, open 'confession' – of one's faith. Thus 'profession' carried with it a quasi-religious significance which was brought forward into the later use of the term to denote an occupation in one of the areas of learning mentioned above. A 'professional', therefore, was, by implication, someone who took his occupation very seriously and applied to it considerable skill and integrity. Unfortunately, the demands of commercial reality mean that, very often, that integrity comes under intolerable strain.

Chapter 9 examines some of the abuses that are all too prevalent when showing becomes high powered, and it is inevitable that the professional's role in this must come under scrutiny. In cases where abusive methods of training and/or handling are used, it is easy to blame the professionals concerned (and just as easy to forget that amateurs, too, can be guilty of such practices). Certainly, those so involved must bear a considerable part of such blame. However the professional is, in these cases, in an unenviable position. He or she has a living to make; if an ambitious owner wants to win at all costs, and demands that the professional uses whatever means are necessary to achieve this end, what does the professional handler or trainer do? Personal and professional integrity demands that they should refuse absolutely to use underhand or abusive methods. However, in a harshly competitive world integrity does not pay the bills; and it may well be that in a toss up between integrity and complying with an owner's wishes, the former loses the toss. The professional with a cast iron reputation and an impressive record of show wins can afford to repudiate the use of dubious methods (though not all do so); the up and coming professional, struggling to make (and keep) a reputation, may not be in a position to be so choosy. I am in no way condoning the use of such methods, simply pointing out how difficult it can be to put integrity before mundane business considerations. The fault lies not so much with individuals but with an ethos that values results above all else.

This is the kind of dilemma which faces racehorse trainers. They know the damage that can be caused by racing immature two year olds. Most of them would infinitely prefer not to continue such a harmful practice but as long as owners pay vastly inflated prices for their bloodstock and insist on an early return on their 'investment', and so long as the Jockey Club not only condones but encourages this practice, it will continue. It is unrealistic to expect trainers to cut off their own means of livelihood; the impetus for change must come from the top. So it is with showing. While deploring the excesses of some professionals and trainers, I feel it is unfair to blame them solely. At least as much to blame are all those others – owners, judges, disciplinary committees, etc. – who knowingly or otherwise connive at undesirable practices.

However, that is to look solely at the negative side. As always, a balanced perspective must be retained and it would be absurd and unfair to suggest that all professionals (or even most of them) act under the same kind of pressures. While many professionals regard showing as simply part of their job, and damned hard work at that, many also still regard it as fun. After all this is what motivates people, whatever their status, to take on willingly all the fuss and infinite attention to detail that showing demands.

On the day of a show, many competitors will have been active even before daylight, especially if they have to travel any distance. In order to accommodate all the necessary classes, most shows commence classes at

Preparation for shows can be hard work

around 8 a.m. At mixed shows the classes for Arabians are often among the earliest starters, presumably because they are not regarded as one of the main attractions (a source of great irritation to Arab enthusiasts). Even at the all-Arabian shows, such as the Regional Group Shows and the two Arab Horse Society summer shows, classes must, of necessity, begin early, usually with broodmares and youngstock. As not all competitors are able to stay away from home overnight, this necessitates an early start for many. If – as in my own case – they also have other horses to attend to, this may entail feeding, turning out, and sometimes even mucking out before loading up the horses destined for the show and setting off on what may be a long drive.

Once there, they face the hassle of unloading, settling the horses, putting the finishing touches to the latters' *toilette* (and, if they are entered in a ridden class, to their own or to that of whoever is riding). For ridden classes the horse(s) must also be ridden in, which for some horses may take as little as half an hour, while for others it may take several hours before the horse is settled enough to be taken into civilised company!

All manner of disasters can befall exhibitors, and not only amateurs either. Many a professional has uttered a curse or two on discovering that, amidst all the scurrying preparations, someone has left out something vital, or that their favourite judge has gone down with the galloping lurgy and been replaced at the last minute with the one judge they have sworn never, ever to exhibit under again after that last débâcle. It is fair to say, however, that the more successful the professional, the less likely such disasters are to occur, as the well-seasoned professional (and amateur!) will have provided for such contingencies. However, almost all exhibitors will have some experience that they can recall with horror: such as setting off in the middle of the night in a sleepy haze, only to arrive at the showground and find that they have: (a) left the saddle behind; (b) left the jockey behind; (c) left the jockey's clothes behind; or (d) left the horse behind. They may even have ended up at the wrong showground on the wrong day. Such is showing.

Having got there and settled in, there is then the endless waiting around. Having made all one's preparations, if one is at all efficient, there will be time to spare before the start of the class. This may help to settle the horse or it may send it to sleep (which is not good for those exhibitors who like their horses to scuttle around like demented bananas). This is the point at which many exhibitors ask themselves: (a) what they are doing there; and (b) is it all worth it?

Why do exhibitors risk health, wealth or sanity (not to mention life and limb) for the sake of a rosette which, when one adds up the cost of entry fees, transport, stabling, etc., may well leave the exhibitor on the road to financial ruin?

The answer is that for many people it is not the rosette itself, or even the prospect of one (though that is naturally one of the reasons): it is the being there, the taking part. As we saw in Chapter 2, most human beings like to show off: it is a perfectly natural trait, so often wrongly despised (unless taken to excess: balance, as ever, is the key) by killjoy puritans. If we have beautiful horses, it is only natural that we like to show them off, too. Never mind that they may not always be the best; they are *our* best, and we want the world to see them.

Then there is the cameraderie. The format of the big shows means that a stay of a couple of days or more is often necessary and this, in turn, means that exhibitors are brought together more than they might be at all but the smallest shows. Groups gather together among the stable lines, renewing old acquaintances and making new ones; horses will be admired, discussed (and often disparaged but that is all part of the scene). Impromptu parties may be got up, and rivalries are frequently forgotten in the happy atmosphere that prevails where a group of enthusiasts get together to talk about the passion that unites (and sometimes divides)

Just happy to be there: B. Skipper with Guisburn Nivalis

them all. There will be disagreements, of course, but it is difficult to maintain sourness of mind when others are so clearly enjoying themselves.

For many people, going to shows is their main escape from a relatively drab weekday existence. Even the professional, for whom shows are, so to speak, part and parcel of their work, may still, after many years, find that shows have an irresistible glamour which makes all the grinding hard work worthwhile.

Sadly, many people are also finding that showing is becoming less fun than it used to be. Arab Horse Society judge and governor Barbara Campbell, in her article for the *Arab Horse Society Newsletter* (Summer 1995, referred to in Chapter 6), mentioned this fact, commenting that: 'this is not surprising when one realises that there is a great deal at stake for exhibitors who need to sell their stock'.[9] This feeling that it is all becoming too serious is reflected in an increasing resentment on the part of amateurs of the very apparent bias of some judges in favour of professionals.

The fact is that in the Arabian horse world the distinction between professionals and amateurs is sometimes blurred in the minds of outside observers. When one is considering the extreme ends of the spectrum, it is relatively easy to decide in which category an exhibitor belongs. The one- or two-horse owner, for example, who shows purely for fun, is clearly an amateur, however enthusiastic. On the other hand, the producer who accepts other people's horses for training and exhibiting is usually a

All worthwhile

professional, as in most cases they will receive a fee for these services. But what of those who do not fit neatly into either category? Is the large-scale stud owner who exhibits their own horses widely a professional or an amateur?

In the context of the modern show scene – and certainly where the showing of Arabians in-hand is concerned – the distinction may be less important than one might think. Perhaps the true distinction to be made is between those who are sufficiently successful and well known to be considered a 'name', and those who – whatever the merits of their horses – are not. As we have seen in Chapter 7, judges are far from immune to the influence of a 'name'. This has led many showing enthusiasts to reduce, or give up completely, their showing activities because they feel they can no longer compete on equal terms with others whose horses may have no greater merit than theirs but whose showmanship techniques and prestige appear to guarantee them success. The fact that this state of affairs has for so long been accepted is, to my mind, no reason why it should be allowed to continue. As I argued in Chapter 7, all exhibitors pay the same entry fees (except where these are reduced for members of specified societies) and are therefore entitled to be judged fairly. It is, after all, because of the widespread support of such people that the majority of shows can be held at all. Yet many now feel that major shows are dominated by a handful of 'names' to the extent that it is scarcely worth the small-scale exhibitor's while to attend. The same comment may be heard, with variations, all over the country. Take one look at the catalogue at the major shows and often you can see immediately who the winners will be, regardless of what horses they exhibit. One breeder recently commented to me that he believed a certain well-known exhibitor could enter a three-legged donkey and still win.

As with the lady whose comments regarding Welsh ponies were quoted in Chapter 7, it would be easy to dismiss this as sour grapes on the part of bad losers, were it not for the fact that most of these remarks come from people whose stock is very good indeed and who feel that they are simply not getting the recognition they deserve. Of course, one could argue that things are not so different from the days when it was the Crabbet, Hanstead and Courthouse studs which dominated the Arab showing world. However, those were the days when relatively few people bred or owned Arabians, and so it was perhaps inevitable that the big studs tended to walk off with the prizes. These days the Arabian horse population is enormous in comparison with what it was in the early days of the all-Arabian shows, and some of the finest horses belong to the small studs or

All exhibitors have the same right to be judged

to the one- or two-horse owners. Yet still the shows are dominated by the few. Certainly, a good professional handler may be able to show a horse to greater advantage than an amateur with little experience or know-how, but in the in-hand classes it is by no means always the case that professionals actually *do* handle the horses better (though they may display a great deal of showmanship!). If the gap between professionals and amateurs – perhaps we should say between 'names' and 'non-names' – is not closed by fairer judging methods, then shows – and Arab shows in particular – may well find that with a few exceptions the exhibitors are all 'names', and we will end up with the kind of sameness that afflicts some international shows – a kind of private club for a small core of exhibitors, with the rest looking on.

Such a narrow concentration cannot be good for the breed, for it is simply no longer the case that most, if not all, of the best horses are to be found in a few major studs. Besides, as I have already observed, all the major shows depend for their continued existence on the support, not of a few major exhibitors, but of those myriad minor players who deserve, at least, the chance to compete on level terms. If they are continually denied that opportunity they will inevitably start to desert the show scene in larger numbers. Mrs Campbell pointed out in her article that even if a judge does not like a particular horse on the day: 'the intense interest of the audience means that your horse will be studied with care by many people who frequently disagree with the judge and find a lot to like about the horse . . . this ensures the commitment of many exhibitors'.[10] This is perfectly true and this is indeed what brings many exhibitors back year after year. However, for many this is no longer sufficient recompense for what they feel to be biased judging, particularly as so many spectators will inevitably accept that the judge must be right and that the horse is somehow defective. This is very demoralising for exhibitors with good horses but little experience, who need to feel they can rely on judges to confirm their horse's merits. Chapter 10 discusses the negative effect this can have on breeding trends; it can also have a negative effect on exhibitors' attendance at shows. As we have seen, those who feel there is no chance of being judged fairly because of their status (or lack of it) are starting to give up on principle. If that happens on a considerable scale, the effect could be catastrophic. A number of major shows have in recent years dropped classes for Arabians because of lack of support. Often this support has not been forthcoming for the very reason that the minor exhibitors feel there is no point in attending where they cannot hope to compete.

How sad it would be for the breed if we were to see a reversion to the days when there were very few classes for Arabians in shows other than those run by the Arab Horse Society; sadder still if the exhibits at national and regional group shows were to consist solely of the entries of a few major studs and show producers.

What is the answer? I am afraid there is no easy solution. The Arab Horse Society must continue its avowed policy of educating judges, especially in the art of discriminating between genuine merit and effective showmanship. It must make it clear to them that they are judging horses, not names or faces, and that if they allow themselves to be influenced by the latter they not only raise questions about their own integrity but risk bringing the Society they represent into disrepute.

In the USA, where many judges blatantly judge faces rather than horses, this problem is to some extent overcome by running amateur-only classes, and some of the major shows in Britain hold similar classes. However, for breed classes and all-breed shows, this would be feasible only at the national and international shows as such classes would prove an impossible administrative burden for most regional and local shows. The costs of running duplicate classes – not to mention the problems of administration and logistics – would be prohibitive; and in any case, many people feel it would simply sweep the problem under the carpet. It would merely make amateurs feel like second-class citizens, as it would inevitably be the case that the professional classes were accorded the highest status as is normally the case in the USA. This is not what the enthusiastic amateur wants. They wish, in most cases, only for the chance to be judged fairly and without reference to status or whether the handler's face or the actual exhibit is recognisable. In any case, at some shows where amateur-only classes are held, show organisers have been known to allow professional riders and handlers to participate in such classes – which makes nonsense of the whole idea.

As long as so much emphasis is placed on show results as a criterion of excellence in Arabian horses, it seems likely that any system will lead to injustice. It is simply not fair or accurate to accuse all disgruntled amateurs of poor sportsmanship. Good sportsmanship (and by implication the ability to lose gracefully) is one thing; acceptance of injustice is another. As I said in Chapter 7, the fact that injustice is the way of the world does not mean that we should automatically accept it. To do so is to abandon principles and once we have done that we also lose not only our own self-respect, but respect for the horses that bring us so much pleasure.

Notes

1 *Collins English Dictionary*, 'professional', sense (6)
2 *Collings*, 'amateur', sense (1)
3 *Collins*, 'professional', sense (2)
4 *Collins*, 'professional', sense (3)
5 *Collins*, 'amateur', sense (3)
6 Hollings, Nigel, *Practical Showing*, David and Charles 1990, p.10
7 Hollings, *Practical Showing*, p.10
8 Akrill, Caroline, *Not Quite a Horsewoman*, Arlington Books 1982, p.104 (now reissued by J. A. Allen)
9 Campbell, Barbara, 'Some Thoughts on Judging', *Arab Horse Society Newsletter*, Summer 1995, p.1
10 Campbell, 'Some Thoughts', p.1

Chapter 9

ABUSE

'Love horses and look after them, for they deserve your tenderness; treat them as you do your children, nourish them as you do friends of the family and blanket them with care. For the love of God do not be negligent for you will regret it in this life and the next.'

OMAR, COMPANION OF THE PROPHET MOHAMMED,
EARLY SEVENTH CENTURY AD

MODERN WESTERN civilisation, in its arrogance, likes to believe that it alone understands the wisdom of treating animals with kindness and humanity. That this is not so is amply demonstrated by a mass of evidence, of which the above quotation is but one example. The great horsemaster of classical times, Xenophon, gives us in his treatise, *The Art of Horsemanship*, a set of principles for the training of the horse by a combination of firmness, kindness and reward, which should be compulsory reading for today's aspiring horsemen and women. The Prophet Mohammed himself exhorted his followers to treat their horses well. 'Each grain of barley given to a horse is inscribed in the ledger of good works.' Devotees of the Arab horse are universally aware that mares and foals shared the domestic lives of the *bedu*; Lady Anne Blunt writes in her journal of waking up one morning to find a foal lying next to her in her tent. Such trust in humans would only be possible where the creature had invariably been treated with kindness and gentleness and therefore had never learned to fear human contact.

How is it then that in the late twentieth century we appear to be regressing in the treatment of our horses? How is it that so much abuse – whether inflicted deliberately or through ignorance – still takes place? It seems that almost every week a new case of appalling brutality to horses

is reported. These range from wilful neglect of an extreme kind (often on the part of well-to-do people who could not even plead poverty or ignorance as an excuse) through the deliberate breaking of horses' legs with iron bars as part of an insurance fraud, to horrific cases of sexual abuse of mares and knife attacks of the most sickening kind. Horses, by their very nature, are easy targets for human abuse. The very manner in which they are kept – even though in most cases this is for their own safety – renders them virtually our prisoners. Unlike cats and dogs, they cannot run away when life becomes intolerable for them; and although some may lash out in fear or pain, the majority of ill-treated horses suffer in silence. Such is their willingness to co-operate and their general desire to please, that they will often continue to try their hardest even when the manner in which they are treated leaves a lot to be desired. Commandant Saint-Fort Paillard, of the celebrated riding academy at Saumur, wrote in 1974: 'Let us try to imagine for a moment what the atmosphere in the riding hall or around a show ring would be if the horses yelped whenever they were hurt as dogs do. Wouldn't certain jumping competitions be punctuated by howls of pain? And wouldn't certain dressage classes be punctuated by plaintive whimpers? What a nightmare!'[1] To this one might add: 'And wouldn't certain showing classes be punctuated by cries of discomfort and frustration?'

As previous chapters have shown, there is, and has been for some years now, a deep sense of unease among a growing number of Arab horse enthusiasts about much that takes place both inside and outside our showrings and this includes increasing concern about abuse. Abuse of show horses is not, of course, restricted to any one breed; I should make it clear, too, that in Great Britain, at any rate, only a minority of people mistreat their horses in or out of the showring. However, this minority seems to be growing, as the popularity of showing increases and more and more enthusiasts jump on the bandwagon.

Causes for concern range from overt ill-treatment of horses to much more subtle forms of abuse, often not immediately obvious and, to the less knowledgeable eye, not necessarily even recognised as abuse. Virtually every issue of the *Arab Horse Society News* carries either some comment on such abuses in the show reports or one or more letters protesting about what members have seen at shows. How, one may ask, has this situation come about?

George White, stud manager of the famous Barton Lodge Stud for 34 years until its dispersal on the death of Lady May Abel-Smith, recounts one occasion on which he was handling the great stallion Darjeel in the

OPPOSITE PAGE *The noble horse: 'Love horses and look after them, for they deserve your tenderness', Rusleem, Stallion Champion, UK International Show 1993 (Sweet)*

showring. Darjeel, always easily bored, needed waking up, so George gave him a tap – no more – with the whip. He unfortunately forgot that he had two pieces of leather attached to the end of the whip as a clapper and the sudden report started the judges. George thought he was in trouble, but one of the judges merely remarked, 'Darjeel's getting a reminder!', and Darjeel, in fact, went on to win his class.[2] This very mild use of the whip would not even raise an eyebrow these days, let alone be considered a cause for comment, but things were very different in Darjeel's heyday; which again raises the question of how on earth did we arrive at a situation where a horse can actually be beaten in the showring – not just tapped – with a whip, as happened to my certain knowledge at one show quite recently, *without any disciplinary action being taken?*

The answer lies in the sudden growth in popularity of the Arabian horse during the 1960s and 1970s, and the consequent Arabian horse population explosion, first in the USA and then in Britain and Europe. Large

Darjeel, Junior Male Champion 1965 Supreme Male Champion 1968, 1969, 1970 (Courtesy of George White)

numbers of people with little or no experience of horses, let alone of Arabians, wanted to own one of these beautiful living status symbols; more and more Arabians were bred, often indiscriminately, to feed the growing market; show winners changed hands at vastly inflated prices which bore no relationship to their actual value. Enthusiastic amateur owners, particularly in the USA where there were considerable tax benefits to be had, sent their horses to professional trainers and the pressure to win became and has remained enormous. In-hand showing classes started to become more like circus acts than the simple breed classes they were originally meant to be. Showmanship was all – the art of making a horse look like a potential champion even if it was a conformational nightmare. With the indiscriminate breeding referred to above, and also because of the sheer numbers being bred, a higher proportion of the animals had faults of conformation and type. The result was that all kinds of practices crept in, designed to alter the appearance of the less than perfect horse.

Some of the commoner practices have been known for centuries, such as that of inserting ginger into the unfortunate horse's rectum in order to raise its tail carriage. This does not really fool anyone with enough experience to know what to look for but, unfortunately, it can all too easily trap the uninitiated into thinking the horse has a superb tail carriage. That it causes the horse a great deal of discomfort goes without saying. To those who aver that it does not, or that any discomfort is, at worst, minimal, I would say, why not try it on yourself?

Another practice which has received much publicity of recent years is that of weighting the tail to make it snap up the moment the weights are removed. Again, this cannot be anything other than vastly uncomfortable, not to say painful, for the horse. This is quite apart from the damage it may do to the musculo-skeletal structure. The truly stupid thing about both these practices is that they are ultimately self-defeating; they are designed to cheat the observer into believing the horse possesses qualities that it does not. When an eventual purchaser (whether of the horse concerned or of its offspring) discovers that the horse they have bought does not, in fact, possess these qualities, whose reputation is going to suffer? The perpetrator's of course, but that does not seem to deter these people, who often appear to have hides a rhinoceros might envy.

Then there is the question of show bridles and halters. It is now very fashionable to show Arabians – even stallions – in very fine, often flimsy halters. Some of these are very decorative, even beautiful, but scarcely strong enough to hold a powerful creature like a horse. Indeed, there have been numerous occasions on which horses have broken their show halters and gone careering about the showring. I have witnessed this myself several times: in one case a filly got loose and barged into a First Ridden Pony class in the next ring; in another a colt broke his halter and crashed into the wooden barriers separating two rings. That no one was hurt in either of these cases was almost miraculous; that the colt did not break a leg even more so. In the context of this chapter, however, the real problem with some of these halters is that because of their flimsiness they can so easily cause the horse pain or at least discomfort. A broad webbing headcollar can easily dig into a horse's sensitive nose; how much worse it must be for the horse to have that broad webbing replaced by a very thin piece of leather, often with a wire core or metal inserts. Wire-cored halters have been outlawed by the Arab Horse Society, yet when one judge had the courage of her convictions and complained about a noseband that was digging into a horse's nose, her complaint was ignored. In this instance her own lack of experience was to blame; she should have called upon the steward to witness the reason for her complaint and she should have called the show vet. Trusting her own judgement, she did neither but, having admitted that she could have handled the incident better, she expresses great disappointment that she was not offered more support by the Arab Horse Society's Show Committee.

It is perfectly possible for show bridles and halters to be strong and comfortable, as well as fine and decorative, yet still we are seeing far too many of the flimsy types with potentially painful nosebands.

Such practices as rugging a horse up to ensure a smooth, early summer coat may hardly seem like abuse to most people yet in many instances this is carried to such extremes as to be actually harmful. A lightweight rug to insulate against severe cold is one thing; several layers of heavy rugs are imposing an unnecessary, unnatural burden on the horse. Imagine how much discomfort you would feel if you were compelled, on even a relatively mild day, to wear several overcoats, and were not allowed to take them off when you wished to but only when someone else decided it was time for them to come off! It is scarcely surprising that some horses, in despair, take to rug-chewing or tearing.

Nor is it surprising that so many horses, confined indoors for lengthy periods of time – sometimes imprisoned in darkened boxes to make sure they have plenty of sparkle and bounce for the showring – develop vices such as weaving, crib-biting and box-walking; or, in the case of stallions and colts, become difficult to handle or even nasty or downright dangerous. Horses have a physiological and psychological need for movement and for social contact with their own kind. If they are not allowed sufficient freedom to satisfy this need, they will tend to become depressed and apathetic, or take to the kind of behaviour described above, which is now believed to cause the release of endorphins to which the horse then becomes addicted. In spite of the amount of research that has been done on equine behaviour, many horse-keepers – including some 'professionals' – either remain ignorant of the effects of lack of freedom and exercise or choose to ignore them. Either way the horse suffers appallingly. I know of one Arabian stallion who spent almost six years shut in a stable because his owners were afraid of him. He had been a very naughty yearling and, although successful in-hand, by the time he was two he was almost unmanageable. By the age of seven he was a vicious and totally unruly horse with a bleak future ahead of him. Fortunately, he was bought by people who recognised that his problems were due to mishandling rather than real ill-nature. Thanks to their endless patience and tact with him, he is now a totally reformed character and is not only affectionate and well behaved but delightful to ride. Had the people who originally owned him possessed even half the patience, knowledge and understanding shown by his present owners, he would have been spared years of misery and desperation.

Even foals are not exempt. The effects of both overshowing and of the 'stretched' pose have been mentioned in Chapter 3. Fred Rice, speaking of what he saw at shows in the USA, said, 'they stretch them so in every way. Their bodies are extended. Lady Wentworth said, never do that, it hurts their insides, so she wouldn't ever have them extended.'[3] One might think that foals would be spared such excesses and allowed at least a little time in which to be babies and simply enjoy their freedom and play; not so in the competitive world of showing. We see foals that, at the tender age of five, six and seven months, are already 'veterans' of the show circuit, and are being made to stand in the 'stretched' pose. There is nothing wrong with teaching foals manners, to walk and trot in hand and stand up quietly for inspection; this is most desirable. But to ask such babies to behave like mature show horses is totally unfair, and when added to the endless round of shows some of them are expected to endure, this is nothing more or less than abuse.

Some showing practices are considered by the uninitiated to be so arcane that they give rise to mirth rather than disapproval. A friend of mine was reduced to a fit of the giggles when I described to her the use of neck-sweats; when I explained that they were used to reduce the excess fat off a 'cresty' neck, she said, 'Why not just prevent the horse from getting too fat in the first place?' A good question. Thankfully there is a grow-

This foal is being allowed to stand naturally; some others are not so lucky

ing trend now towards leaner-looking show horses rather than the over-weight creatures of the past. It is beginning to dawn on exhibitors that not only can show horses look good without being covered in rolls of fat, they are immeasurably healthier if kept slimmer. Many show horses, however, are still grossly overfed, often with the excuse that they need feeding up to give them 'sparkle' in the showring. Contrary to popular belief, Arabians do not need stuffing with feed; they evolved over thousands of years to survive on the most meagre diet. My own pure-bred gelding is what is euphemistically described as a 'good doer'. He is what Elwyn Hartley-Edwards calls the 'butty' type, and most of his weight is muscle. However some of it is not and when his neck starts to look like a Welsh Cob's I know it is time to take action. As for feeding for extra sparkle, one sees the regrettable results of this in so many classes where some of the exhibits turn silliness into a fine art and do much to confirm the prejudices of Arab-haters.

It is a moot point whether neck-sweats in themselves constitute an abuse. They are certainly a form of cheating as their function is to effect a change – albeit a temporary one – in the horse's natural appearance. While they can scarcely be comfortable for the horse, they are probably not much more unpleasant than many other things we do to horses in the process of taking care of their personal needs. However, what to my mind does constitute abuse is the use of excessively tight neck sweats. In her report in *Arab Horse Society News* of the 1990 Nations Cup, Betty Finke described seeing a stallion wearing a neck sweat so tight that it was impossible to put a finger between the neck and the band; the stallion was unable to swallow his feed without sticking his head up high.[4] What a sad and pathetic sight and how much better it would have been if the horse had not been allowed to become overweight in the first place.

Unfortunately, such is the vogue for a super-smooth topline that in some countries steroids are used to 'enhance' the horse's outline. I have seen horses with gross pads of fat as a result of this and other practices designed to alter the appearance. Apart from the fact that this, again, is cheating, it cannot be having anything other than an adverse effect on the horse's health.

Whip abuse is frequently mentioned in show reports and letters to the *Arab Horse Society News* from irate spectators outraged by what they have seen, yet blatant cases of whip abuse actually inside the showring are, mercifully, relatively uncommon. What we do see plenty of is what I call 'passive whip abuse' – that is, where the handler constantly waves a whip at the horse, presumably to remind it of what it may expect if it does not do as the handler wishes. As this kind of whip-waving is frequently accompanied by jerking on the lead-rein, or by a constant pushing and pulling of the horse (even when it is standing perfectly still and, to normal people, behaving itself), one wonders how the horse can possibly be expected to know what is required of it (in all probability the only thing it knows for sure is that no matter what it does, a good hiding awaits it). Such antics are not only senseless, they are a sure way to ruin a good horse as there is nothing like confusion and bullying to make even the most tolerant and good-natured horse decide, sooner or later, to withdraw all co-operation.

American judge Don Burt tells of several horses taken in by a friend of his for schooling under saddle. All had the same problem. They were unable to maintain a steady head-carriage when ridden and had a tendency to throw their heads up and bounce them up and down. The cause of the unsteadiness lay in the fact that all of them had been trained for halter classes and shown by 'one of the top trainers' in that field.

This trainer's methods had effectively taught the horses a form of resistance. As Burt says, 'many halter handlers jerk the horses continually to elevate the head and stretch the neck. They never let the horse alone – stetch, creep back, jerk again. I see it done every week with every age of horse. These horses were actually taught a defense mechanism from the very beginning. Every time something was just a little askew, a foot out of place or a tiredness in the back, it happened. The horse would brace for the jerk by putting the head up quickly to soften the coming jerk, bounce it up there as long as possible, and then relax completely after the ordeal was over. When ridden, the horse was doing exactly what he had been taught to do on the line.'[5] When one considers the thin – sometimes excessively thin – mouthpieces of the show bits so often used in in-hand classes, one can only cringe at the thought of the pain these horses must be suffering in their tender mouths.

Indeed, the whole question of bitting is a cause for concern. Many colts and stallions are shown in-hand with bits having these very thin mouthpieces. The potential severity of these should not need explaining to anyone with any pretensions to horsemanship and when one considers the lead-rein jerking described above, it is obvious that these horses are suffering a great deal of pain in their tender mouths. One reason often given for the use of such bits is that a thin mouthpiece gives greater control, and/or that a small bit ring is required for showing. Of course it is; no one wants to obscure the horse's head. But a small bit-ring does not have to mean a thin mouthpiece! There are all manner of bits available with small rings which are infinitely more comfortable and would give the handler all the control they need from the bit. If this is insufficient, I would suggest that it is a problem better addressed by education of the horse and better husbandry (perhaps fewer oats?), and that no educated and intelligent horseman or woman would attempt to control a horse by causing it pain!

Jane van Lennep, describing what she saw at the Masters Open Championship in Ostend in 1989, confessed to a nagging doubt that 'all that spinning round, chain-jerking and levelled off top lines from over-high heads must have serious negative effects if one wishes to ride one of these horses. In fact the ones we saw under saddle were generally very unsteady in their heads, lacking engagement behind and crooked.'[6] Tormenting the horse in this fashion is not only abusive, it is defective and ignorant horsemanship. We are back to Xenophon: 'what the horse does under compulsion . . . is done without understanding; and there is no beauty in it either'.

It is outside the showring that most instances of active whip abuse occur; one of the most respected Governors of the Arab Horse Society recently told me of an incident she witnessed at a show where a woman was beating a horse about the head in the collecting ring prior to a class, presumably to give it more 'presence'. She said sharply, 'Stop that!' whereupon the woman, rather shamefacedly, said, 'I do like him, you know.' This almost beggars belief; how can anyone who truly likes a horse beat it about the head in this way? It is true that there are some 'horsemen' (and women) who maintain that horses – particularly unruly colts or stallions – need to be 'kept in their place', and their method consists of administering a good hiding now and then. That this is counter-productive should be obvious to anyone with any real knowledge or understanding of horses; in fact, I can think of nothing more likely to turn a high-couraged colt or stallion into a real rogue. Of course, colts and stallions must be treated with firmness but this must always be accompanied by patience and kindness. Otherwise the horse will learn only fear and not respect.

Sadly, there are many so-called 'horsemen' who do not hesitate to terrorise the horses they handle with whips in order to give them 'presence' in the showring. There are few sights less pleasing to the discerning spectator than that of a horse clearly frightened almost out of its wits, whether by the whip, the highly charged atmosphere of the showring, or, in some cases, by the mere presence of the handler. Unfortunately, this is such a common sight, particularly at some international shows, that commentators in their show reports regard it as an occasion for comment when fewer horses appear so affected, in one instance even remarking that the horses exhibited by one particular handler appeared 'less terrorised' than in previous years! It is surely unacceptable that *any* horses should appear to be in a state of terror, either in the showring or out of it; yet very little appears to be done to prevent it. It seems that, as long as the horses in question appear spectacular, little thought is given to their mental or physical wellbeing. One can only wonder at the mentality of people who regard the sight of a terrified horse as an exciting spectacle, or of those who appear to think that only a horse in a state of near panic can have presence and sparkle. To quote a well-known and much respected breeder and authority on Arab horses: 'A frightened horse brings disgrace to its handler and all connected with it.'[7]

Much of the abuse described is the result of ignorance or lack of thought. Many of the perpetrators simply follow what they see others do, sometimes in the naïve belief that what an experienced exhibitor does must be acceptable; or that 'if X, Y, and Z do it then it really can't be as bad as people say, can it?'

Quite often it is sheer complacency, sometimes allied to an unwillingness to accept that horses are as physically sensitive as they are. There is also, among many people, a reluctance to believe that horses (and animals in general) have complex emotional lives and that although they may not respond to given situations or circumstances as humans would, and their emotional needs are not necessarily always the same as ours, nevertheless they *do* experience a vast range of recognisable emotions. Anyone who spends any time watching horses and communicating with them cannot fail to recognise this if they have any real feeling for them, yet a surprising number of people who work with horses scoff at such an idea.

Some of this ignorance is the result of that 'intellectual laziness' mentioned in Chapter 4. Many people simply can't be bothered to expand their knowledge of horses beyond their everyday experience. However, as I said in Chapter 8, it is not the quantity but the quality of the experience which counts and experience may be based on faulty knowledge and understanding. The more a true horseman learns, the more he realises how much more he has to learn. As the great Hungarian trainer and FEI judge Charles de Kunffy has remarked, 'Brutality begins where knowledge ends. Ignorance and compulsion appear simultaneously.'[8]

Too often, however, abuse is a calculated act performed in the full knowledge of the physical and mental trauma the horse is suffering. In many cases it is done, of necessity, with the full connivance of a veterinary surgeon. Not all of these people are monsters, of course; when prestige and personal gain are at stake, it is all too easy to persuade oneself that certain actions are justifiable. But one wonders how they justify to themselves some of the practices met with in the kind of shady sub-culture that haunts the top-level international show scene? What of the drugging of horses (and I do not mean relatively harmless drugs, but highly dangerous, illegal substances) to make them continually 'hyped up'? What of cosmetic surgery carried out to 'improve' the appearance? Quite apart from the fact that this is cheating on a grand scale, it is the sheer immorality of it that takes the breath away. It is one thing to administer drugs to combat a condition which may be causing the horse pain or discomfort, or to use corrective surgery where it is necessary to preserve the horse's health and/or mobility. There are many instances where the benefits of the treatment outweigh the short-term stress it causes. The administration of behaviour-altering drugs and purely cosmetic surgery, however, are quite another.

Humans make a choice as to whether they take drugs (and often, in the process, wreck their health and mental wellbeing). They make a deliberate choice when they have cosmetic surgery and, believing the results will render it worthwhile, accept the possibility that this will involve a great deal of pain and discomfort. The horse made to take drugs or undergo such surgery has no such choice. Even at the best of times, when drugs or surgery are being administered for sound clinical reasons, the horse cannot understand what is happening to it. It cannot understand why it is being subjected to such stress and, at the very least, discomfort (not to say pain). In such circumstances the caring horse owner can only soothe and comfort the horse as best they can, knowing that even though they cannot explain it to the horse, what has been done is in its best interest; although I do believe that some horses, particularly those that have a trusting relationship with their owners/handlers, do understand that the latter are trying to help them. But what of the horse thus stressed for such essentially frivolous reasons as stealing a march on rivals in the showring?

Some people might argue, with a degree of twisted logic, that as the horse cannot understand whether drugs administered or surgery carried out are for its benefit or otherwise, the motives behind such actions are irrelevant. I do not agree. They may be irrelevant to the horse, but not to the humans involved. If such actions cannot be justified in terms of benefit to the horse, then the only purpose they serve is, ultimately, to massage the egos of the owners and, if the show results raise the value of the horse sufficiently, to make a tidy sum of money. If that makes ethical behaviour irrelevant, what does that tell us about the ethos of the showring?

Cosmetic surgery is, of course, a blatant form of cheating: an attempt to alter the appearance of a less than perfect animal so that it fits the current image of the perfect show horse (whatever that may happen to be). As Betty Finke put it so aptly: 'If a horse has no refinement without make-up, no decent neck without sweating, no tail-carriage without ginger, and no presence without whipping, it simply does not belong at a show.'[9] But, surely, some might ask, would it not be simpler just to breed better stock? That may seem obvious but it is naïve. Breeding superlative stock takes dedication and patience, a deep knowledge of genetics and bloodlines, together with an eye for which lines 'nick' well together. The cheat, like the average criminal, seeks the easy way out, the lazy way: it may cost him more in the short term, but he will have his results that much quicker and is this not a symptom of the culture of 'instant gratification', the 'get rich quick' world in which we live? Time, patience and dedication often seem to have no place in such a world, so the cheats abound and abuses proliferate.

It is the sheer frivolity of all this that sticks in the gullet. It brings with it echoes of the kind of barmy genetic engineering which, never satisfied with what nature produces, bends all its efforts to produce such monstrosities as pale trout, straight cucumbers and square trees – a vision of a world gone mad, where essential values are corrupted. Strong words? Perhaps, yet surely anyone who truly loves horses, and in particular the Arabian, with its special affinity for humans, must feel acute distress to see them so degraded. For this subjection of a noble animal to the often ludicrous showing fads of its human keepers is a kind of degradation. Not only this: it degrades and diminishes the *humans* concerned. As classical trainer and rider Paul Belasik points out: 'The horse is nature. You are nature. Horse and man are in the same world, with a commonality. Brutality to nature is brutality to yourself. Brutality toward the horse is doubly destructive; destructive to the horse, as well as destructive to the person'.[10]

Yet it is only a minority of people within the Arab horse world who are actually guilty of such nasty practices. The truly sad thing is that so much of this abuse could be prevented. One can never legislate against what goes on out of sight in private studs and stable yards, but abuse on showgrounds themselves could be eliminated and this would, of itself, serve to put an end to much that goes behind closed doors, as it were, as abuse at home very often precedes what occurs on the showground.

Part of the problem is that, in Britain at least, the rules are often ill-defined. ECAHO rules are fairly specific with regard to the disguising of exhibits, whether by cosmetic operations, artificial methods of dilating the eyes or by any other means. However, under 'cruelty' Rule 33 merely states that: 'Excessive whipping, use of electric shock devices or infliction of pain by any means is forbidden in all parts of the showground, or stable areas, at all times.' Current Arab Horse Society rules regarding alterations to the natural appearance cover only trimming and clipping, and no longer mention equipment such as tail weights and neck sweats (banned under ECAHO Rule 31b). Rule 16 regarding cruelty merely repeats ECAHO Rule 33, quoted above. At the time of writing, the Arab Horse Society rules have been expanded to cover the misuse of drugs, including ginger and similar irritants but while this is clearly an improvement, and while it would be impossible for the rules to cover every eventuality, this is still insufficient. The American Horse Shows Association, under whose rules Arab horse shows in the USA are run, includes in its rules about cruelty not only the use of any substance to induce temporary heat, including ginger ointment; use of an electric device in schooling or showing, including an electrical 'hot-shot' or cattle prod (Heaven preserve us!); and use of any explosive(!) including fire extinguishers: the rules forbid *any* inhumane treatment of a horse by anyone at the showgrounds, whether or not the specific practice is identified in the AHSA Rule Book.

Surely it would not be beyond the powers of both the Arab Horse Society and ECAHO to expand their rules to include under cruelty a wider definition of inhumane treatment. While recognising that there are grey areas in any definition of 'inhumane treatment', these could be resolved by setting up a working party to examine, with the aid of recognised and suitably qualified experts in equine behaviour, this definition of 'inhumane treatment'; specific rules could then be laid down for disciplinary committees, judges and stewards *who should then be obliged to abide by this definition.* 'Inhumane treatment' should include the terrorising of any horse and it should be within the powers of any DC, judge or steward to disqualify, ban or remove any exhibit which shows signs (usually quite obvious to the knowledgeable observer!) of having been terrorised.

ECAHO rules (as current from 1 January 1996) already provide for widespread random drug testing, and 'Burns, cuts or other marks on the body of any exhibit in such places or positions as to indicate prohibited methods have been used, will be regarded by DCs with veterinary advice as full and adequate grounds for exclusion of any exhibit from competition,' (ECAHO Rule 30); although one must doubt whether these rules are sufficiently invoked. The rules could be expanded to include random checking of exhibits for signs of cosmetic surgery by DCs supported by veterinary advice (at the moment the rules only provide for random chemical tests or action in cases where a breach of the rules is actually suspected and/or detected). I simply do not accept that it is beyond the means of the regulatory bodies concerned to create, implement and then enforce such rules, and to invoke existing rules more stringently. If other organisations can do it, why not the Arab Horse Society and ECAHO, working together?

As far as a growing number of Arab Horse Society members are concerned, both the Society and ECAHO are failing in their obligations to safeguard the welfare of Arab horses. There have been far too many cases where justified complaints about broken rules have been made, or where obvious abuses have taken place, and yet no disciplinary action has been taken. This is to the credit of neither organisation. It is no defence for them to plead that in some instances the rules broken were minor and had nothing to do with the abuse of horses; if exhibitors see that one rule can be broken with impunity, this is positive encouragement to break all the others. Why bother to have rules if they are not going to be enforced?

One accepts that some minor rules may be irksome and can appear unnecessary. However, they are there for a reason and ignoring them simply because they are inconvenient is the beginning of a descent into lawlessness and anarchy, which, as history has demonstrated countless times, is the worst tyranny of all. In her editorial comment for the *Arab Horse Society News* (Winter issue of 1995), Emma Bennett commented that: 'there are those of us who remember the golden days of Kempton, Syon and Ascot, and who will also recall that many of the present day rules were unwritten and such things as fair play existed. It was not necessary to impose so many rules to curb bad manners and cheating.'[11]

Very few people welcome the introduction of rules for their own sake but as long as some exhibitors continue to lack the self-discipline either to refrain from abusive methods or from turning the showring into a free-for-all where anything goes, then rules will continue to be laid down, and disciplinary committees, judges, and show committees must adhere to them without fear or favour. Otherwise we are back to the tyranny of anarchy and all that it implies for the welfare of horses and the reputation of our breed. As one despairing member wrote to me recently: 'Until *all* the rules are obeyed, the horses are at risk.' The same member also wrote, 'I firmly believe that the majority of the abuse to show horses in the UK could be removed completely if the AHS and the relevant committees had the determination to act without fear or favour.'

If the Arab Horse Society (and ECAHO) took the action already referred to and redefined the rules regarding cruelty; if disciplinary committees, judges and stewards were made fully aware of the definition of 'inhumane treatment' and *of their obligation to enforce those rules*; if the ECAHO rules were expanded to allow complaints by spectators at shows to be investigated; if DCs, judges and stewards were able to act with the courage of their convictions and in the certainty that their actions would meet with the full support of the relevant Arab Horse Society committees; if, in other words, *all those whose responsibility it is to uphold the rules* were fully aware of, and committed to meet, their obligations, then I am convinced that most show abuse in Britain could be stamped out within twelve months. As the problem is much greater in Europe, the task would be more difficult there but, given sufficient commitment and determination on the part of ECAHO, European shows could be 'cleaned up' over a period of time.

Until this happens, the credibility of both the Arab Horse Society and ECAHO will continue to be undermined and both organisations will continue to be perceived – whether justifiably or not – as being run by persons governed by self-interest and dedicated to preserving the *status quo*. There is an even greater danger which both organisations ignore at their peril: the continued abuse of show horses provides fuel for the more extreme animal rights organisations who would use such abuse as fuel for their arguments that it is wrong to keep any animals for gain or pleasure. I believe it is not enough to dismiss such arguments as the drivellings of extremists; silly some of them may be but there are some valid points being raised, and if the horse world in general does not do more to put its house in order, it may well wake up one day to find its activities being called into question and limited by those who do not necessarily have real knowledge or understanding of horses but who may find some very powerful voices.

To its credit, the Arab Horse Society Shows Committee revised and expanded the show rules in 1996 but, although welcome, these changes are not nearly far-reaching enough. Still, it is at least a step in the right direction; we must hope that the Committee can continue the progress already made.

The Arab Horse Society was originally founded by people who were united by their love of the Arab horse. The Memorandum of Association states that the Society is established, among other things, to 'prevent cruelty to horses and ponies'[12]. Clearly it cannot take action in matters outside the UK but, within its jurisdiction, it bears a heavy responsibility. How desperately sad for the Arab horse, which the organisation was founded to honour and to cherish, if the Arab Horse Society and its members should be seen to fail in that responsibility.

Notes

1 Quoted by Sylvia Loch in *Dressage: The Art of Classical Riding*, p.202
2 Dykes, Diana, 'The Barton Lodge Stud', *Arab Horse Society News* No. 74, p. 71
3 Finke, Betty, *Arab Horse Society News* No. 76, p.36
4 Rice, Fred, *Chestnuts, Greys and Rodeo Days*, p.40
5 Burt, Don, *Winning With Arabian Horses*, pp.75–6
6 van Lennep, Jane, 'They Do It Their Way', *Horse and Rider* April 1989
7 Archer, Rosemary, Letters, *Arab Horse Society News* No. 79, p.63
8 de Kunffy, Charles, *Ethics and Passions of Dressage*, Half Halt Press USA 1993, p.76
9 Finke, Betty, *Arab Horse Society News* No. 76, p.37
10 Belasik, Paul, *Exploring Dressage Technique*, J. A. Allen 1994, p.133
11 Emma Bennet, editorial comment, *Arab Horse Society News* No. 85, p.41
12 Arab Horse Society Memorandum of Association, 3(b), 1967

Chapter 10

BREEDING FOR SHOWING

'An impure breed could never have maintained its essential sameness and characteristics so uniformly for so many thousands of years as the Arab has done, nor would men of all nations have so uniformly and so universally praised an animal which was not of surpassing excellence. If he pass away by human folly, you will never see his like again.'

THE HON. SIR JAMES PENN BOUCAUT,
EARLY TWENTIETH CENTURY

IN CHAPTER 2 we looked at how modern show winners differ from those of the past: the sturdy, more powerfully built creature of previous times has given way to the ultra-refined, modern, in-hand winner. The latter has emerged as the dominant type, and this is felt by many to be compelling evidence that an increasing number of breeders are aiming to produce this specific type of show Arabian.

The dangers of breeding for the showring – always subject to passing fads and fashions – cannot be exaggerated. To appreciate this, we need only look at what has happened to many breeds of pedigree dog. That great English country sportsman, Willy Poole, has commented that to become fashionable is the worst disaster that can overtake any breed of dog. It certainly seems to be universally true that when fashion takes over, common sense and ethics fly out of the window.

A team of distinguished veterinary surgeons at the Ontario Veterinary College recently carried out a study of the current status of the pedigree dog. They concluded that: 'The next hundred years look rather bleak for the pure-bred dog industry unless dramatic changes are introduced. We have a problem which, if not addressed and speedily rectified, may destroy for all time many beautiful breeds of dog. All dog lovers share the blame for not acting'.[1] This conclusion is quoted by David Hancock in a strongly worded article entitled, 'Are We Producing Pedigree Chumps?' (*The Field*, January 1995). Pedigree dogs, says Colonel Hancock, 'can now have distorted limbs, deformed heads, ears which drag on the ground, absurdly short legs, freak tails, sunken or protruding eyes, excessively long coats, superfluous teeth and overwrinkled skin, and actually be desired because of these exaggerations.'[2] Even worse, they can be 'mentally unstable, brainless, savage and psychopathic, have a brief life span, be carriers of some of the 300-plus inheritable diseases afflicting dogs and yet still be admired for just two assests: their cosmetic appeal and their pedigree.'[3] 'Such a fondness for disabled, useless animals', comments Colonel Hancock tartly, 'would have astounded our sporting ancestors, who dedicated their lives, in many cases, to obtaining functional excellence in breeds of dog which subsequently became revered all over the world.'[4]

Harsh words? Certainly; but more than justified. The evidence is there in front of us at any dog show. Willy Poole, never one to mince words, says, 'I am against dogs being bred just for showing. The Dog Show world is terribly susceptible to fashion. Breeders then alter the dog to fit the fashion. This seems to lead inevitably to the physical deterioration of the breed concerned . . . See what exaggeration has done to the Bulldog, for instance. There is no more bull baiting, but the Bulldog should at least look as though it would be up to the job; it does not seem to be able to do much except wheeze these days. It would also be hard to imagine the modern show Bloodhound tracking much more than its dinner.'[5]

'Many breeds of dog', Poole goes on, 'have become grotesques because of showing fashions and human vanity.'[6] David Hancock goes further. 'What', he asks, 'is the value of pure breeding when it is not working? The pedigree show basset suffers from eye and eyelid diseases, arthritis from bent legs and distorted feet, ear problems due to over-long and over-floppy leathers, and is susceptible to back injuries and slipped discs from a hyper-elongated spine. But they still become Kennel Club-recognised show champions.'[7] Colonel Hancock also regrets the deterioration of temperament in two breeds once noted for their good nature: the labrador and the golden retriever. Both now feature among the top three breeds in the UK displaying unwanted aggression.

The list of inheritable diseases and other genetic faults now rife is endless. 'It is morally reprehensible', says David Hancock, 'to allow dogs with faulty genes to be bred from; harmful exaggerations must now be bred out. We have got to the stage where ruthless culling is essential if the pedigree dog is to survive . . . if we do not act, many admirable breeds of dog will be destroyed for all time.'[8] Many of the working breeds have deteriorated to such a level that they would now be incapable of carrying out their original function. It is surely degrading for dogs whose ancestors formerly delighted in their working role (and anyone who doubts that working dogs *do* enjoy their work has never seen a really good working dog at his job) to be deprived, not only of the opportunity of fulfilling that role, but in some cases of even the ability to do so. A new association has been formed to save one such breed, the true working Bearded Collie, before its true characteristics are irretrievably lost. For many other once fine breeds it may already be too late.

So much for the damage inflicted by showing fads on pedigree dog breeds. But could the same happen to horses? More specifically, could it happen to the Arabian?

Of course it could. It *is* happening and there are signs that it is getting worse. The current disproportionate level of importance being attached to in-hand show results as determinators of excellence means that huge numbers of breeders are aiming to reproduce what they see winning at the highest levels. For many this means selecting for even greater refinement of type.

This is all very well; refinement is certainly one of the desirable characteristics of a horse of true Arabian 'type'. But how far does one go? One word constantly bandied about by breeders and show *aficionados* is 'typey' – a ghastly word used to indicate that a horse has the characteristics generally held to be desirable in the Arabian horse. We established these in Chapter 5 and it should, I hope, be clear from that chapter that 'type' is very much more than a matter of one or two such characteristics and refers, in fact, to the whole horse. Gladys Brown Edwards, in *The Arabian: War Horse to Show Horse*, writes of: 'the usual conflicts between type and conformation even though the latter should actually be incorporated into the former'.[9] Judith Forbis, in *The Classic Arabian Horse*, says, '*Type should come first* in the judge's or breeder's final selection, for without it the breed loses its identity.'[10] This is very true, but by implication this separates type from conformation and many breeders and judges have hearkened to Mrs Forbis's words *without* understanding that she is talking about a *final* selection. That is, the breeder or judge must first of all weed out all unsound stock – for, as Mrs Forbis points out in the same paragraph, no Arabian can be a good Arabian without being a good horse. *Then* the breeder or judge makes the final selection based on excellence of type. If, as I cannot emphasise enough, type and conformation are inseparable, then an Arabian of true type cannot fail to have good conformation. It is when type, conformation and function become separated that we encounter all the problems currently to be found in so many of those horses being bred – according to all the external evidence – specifically for the showring.

Successful show horses are very often referred to as 'typey', and this currently means that they have the 'ultra-refined' appearance referred to above, often seeming almost too ethereal to have real corporeal substance. Some appear so exaggerated as to be almost caricatures: extremely dished heads, tapering to very tiny muzzles; backs and croups so level that one could almost lay a table setting on them (what one senior and very experienced judge has called the 'Jersey cow' look[11]); and slender legs, so delicate in some cases that one fears for their integrity. Hazel Moss, commenting on the Northern Arab Show at Haydock in 1994, says that judges noted that we now see many more 'typey' Arabs with good heads in this country. They tempered this, however, by remarking on the increasing number of serious front leg faults. Here, again, we run up against the same problem. One of the Arabian's most outstanding characteristics has traditionally been good legs – 'legs fine and hard that seemed as if made of hammered iron'.[12] So how can an Arabian with poor legs *possibly* be classed as 'typey'? The answer is only if we isolate 'type' as referring to one or two characteristics – and that, as we shall see, is the slippery slope to hell.

Some of the faults seen in the showring are so serious that, should such horses ever be properly tested in performance, one wonders how long they would last before breaking down. Faults most commonly seen are: long cannons; small weak knees; back at the knee; narrow pasterns; lack of bone (though the density of Arabian bone renders this of slightly less importance, still it should not be discounted); lack of muscle in forearms and gaskins; small, weak, camped-out or, alternatively, over-straight hocks; and club feet. That any of these defects should appear in potential breeding stock to a significant degree should be unthinkable. That they appear as frequently as they do in show stock (which theoretically represents the best of the breed) makes one despair for the future of a breed hitherto noted for its soundness.

The long cannons often observed nowadays are in some instances the result of trying to breed specifically for height. This is similar to what has happened with the Thoroughbred, where increased height has been obtained at the expense of the short, strong cannon bones so necessary for soundness in the Arabian. However, as these long cannons are also often found in breeds noted for high action, it may be that in some cases they are the result of breeding for that kind of action – which may be very popular in some countries, but is quite wrong for the Arabian. Whatever the reason, these long cannons should never be present in Arabian breeding stock. It is worth remembering the old horseman's saying that 'taking bone off the head also takes bone off the legs'.

Equally disturbing is the increasing appearance in showrings, at both national and international level, of narrow, elongated horses with very poor quarters. Narrow fronts, slab sides, short, poorly muscled quarters and slack loins are the antithesis of how the Arabian should be put together. Apologists for the 'narrow' look say that this is how horses bred in the desert would look, because they were naturally leaner than our modern well-fed stock. Well, they would certainly be leaner, but the evidence from early descriptions of desert horses shows that even half-starved desert horses were notable for the roundness of their barrel, their breadth of chest, their powerful loins and their 'immense haunches' (see Chapter 5). The elongated weeds referred to above are a travesty of the authentic Arabian horse, yet we see them winning at the highest international level all over the world.

Immense Haunches: Mesaoud (Rosemary Archer)

If my objection here seems overstated, it is not simply because this type of horse is not one which I admire; it is because it offends against everything that is the essence of the Arabian, by which I mean his supreme harmony and balance. No matter how impressive its head, neck and tail carriage, an Arabian that does not fulfil these criteria of harmony and balance *cannot* be a representative of true Arabian type.

One might think that, with so much emphasis currently being given to exquisite heads, this aspect of show horses at least would be beyond reproach. Unfortunately this is not so. There are any number of horses whose heads seen in profile appear to be perfect, but seen from the front they are far too long and narrow, with insufficient breadth of forehead and width between the jaw bones. While the former fault may be of purely aesthetic concern (and even of personal opinion), the latter is a more serious fault, as it indicates insufficient room for the windpipe. In addition, I would also ask those who favour an exaggeratedly tiny muzzle and dish to the profile to consider that there is considerable evidence to suggest that such an exaggeration affects the efficiency of the horse's breathing; we must not be guilty of creating in the horse such deficiencies as have caused untold misery to many breeds of dog and cat bred with exaggerated facial features.

Sadly, one of the characteristics traditionally associated with the Arabian horse (and which I deliberately omitted from the chapter on type and conformation as I felt it merited discussion here) is also under threat; by which I mean the superb temperament. This is one area in which it is difficult to assess the depth of the problem. This is because it is always debatable how much of a horse's temperament is inherited and how much is the result of the way in which it has been handled. Some horses have been noted for their superb temperaments and their ability to transmit these to their progeny; of these Bright Shadow (Radi x Pale Shadow) was one of the most famous. Lady Anne Blunt, writing to Spencer Borden to allay his fears about the temper of the colt Rodan (Harb x Rose of Sharon), commented, 'Surely it is too soon to despair about the Rose of Sharon colt. I have never met with a bad-tempered Arabian horse in all my thirty years' experience'.[13] Lady Anne went on to say that her stud manager, 'an Arab of the Muteyr, the most famous horsebreeding tribe in the S. Eastern Nejd . . . declared that no Arabian horse could be innately or permanently ill-tempered, although young colts may sometimes be violent to begin with, from being above themselves and to let off high spirits, "before their intelligence is developed", as he expressed it.'[14] Yet we see so many stallions (for it is mainly stallions that seem affected), that appear to have extremely dubious temperaments, winning at all levels in the showring. This raises some serious questions. Are breeders becoming so careless that they no longer take temperament into account? There is much evidence that this is the case, judging by my own and others' observations and conversations with breeders. Or are these horses that appear so fractious and often downright dangerous merely protesting against some injustice in their lives? Either way, this has serious implications for the breed.

Finally we come to action. Here, too, as we have seen in the chapter on movment, there is much cause for concern. There is currently an enormous amount of emphasis being given by show judges to the action in trot. Too little consideration appears to be given to straightness of movement, so that a horse may be dishing or paddling in front, or practically brushing or moving wide behind in what has inelegantly been called the 'wet-knicker' trot, without apparently incurring penalty.

The lack of engagement of the hocks, mentioned previously in Chapters 3 and 6, is most clearly seen on video, especially one with a clean still/slow motion facility. However, a trained eye (and none other should be judging Arabians) can readily spot such deficiencies. When one considers that the horse's 'engine', its whole 'centre of operations', as it were, resides in the quarters and in the hind legs, the action we see so often at even the highest levels of showing is a travesty of what it should be. If the horse – whether in-hand or under saddle – is not moving through from behind, then any impulsion is going nowhere, no matter how spectacular the action of the forelegs may appear to be. A truly elevated, floating trot – the kind that seems to dance and sparkle – is, as we saw in Chapter 6, created by the power and impulsion of the hind legs, the spring forward from the hocks. If this is absent, then what we have is 'all show and no go'.

We must infer from the above, then, that in the pursuit of 'type' and 'action' (often spurious) many essential qualities and characteristics of the Arabian horse are in the process of being lost. Indeed, if one considers that 'type' and 'conformation' cannot (or should not) exist independently of one another, then we must ask, are many of the Arabians currently being bred for the showring really true to the Arabian type as described by Palgrave, Captain Roger Upton, the Blunts, Lady Wentworth and Peter Upton, and many others – in other words, true to the type that had remained unchanged for several thousand years? If one considers this description of a mare: 'a lovely strong grey Abeyeh, Hadbeh, a real desert type from the Nejd, small, tough and *as strong as a Welsh Cob*' (my italics)[15], we must conclude that they are not.

It must not be thought from all this that I am advocating plainness or lack of type. No. Quite the reverse. But I must say yet again, regardless of other considerations, any Arabian must – if we are to respect its nature – above all, be a good horse; after all, that is what the Arabian is: a horse, not a parrot or a poodle. Then, if it is a good horse, regardless of whether or not it is 'typey', it can at least stand a fighting chance of finding a decent home, of being allowed to fulfil its destiny as a horse and not merely as a living ornament. Whereas, if it is simply an example of the current ideas of 'type' divorced from conformation or function (which, as we have seen, often means over-refined and weedy) it does not, if it is not a consistent show winner, stand much of a chance of fulfilling anything.

It would be totally untrue to suggest that the horses of past eras did not have their fair share of faults. Of course they did; although among the best of those winning in the showrings and setting the standards, these faults were generally relatively minor and outweighed by their general excellence. And, of course, as with some modern champions, there were inevitably occasions when winners did not deserve to win. Moreover, it would be monstrously unfair, as well as untrue, to suggest that all modern show Arabians are poor representatives of their breed. This is patently not so; as we saw in Chapter 2, there are many very fine horses being bred and shown with great success, both in Britain and abroad. It is encouraging, too, to see that some recent examples of successful in-hand horses can participate equally successfully in other activities. Some of the top show horses have gone on to prove their worth as sires or dams of excellent, sound stock of *true* Arabian type. But when one sees *some* of the kind of horses that are consistently winning at the highest levels on the international scene, one must have serious reservations about the future of the breed.

These reservations have been expressed numerous times by judges, reporters at shows and Arab horse enthusiasts generally. One reader, who had been going to Arab shows for 23 years, wrote in to the *Arab Horse Society News* in 1991: 'Whilst there is nothing wrong with importing Arabs and these horses winning, must we have long, shallow bodies, flat backs, narrow fronts and bad limbs with their exaggerated action – is it a coincidence that at the International none of these imports, except one, was in any of the ridden classes. If we have been trying to prove that our Arabs are capable of performing, surely these are not the horses to do it with. Their breeders must be putting the hard work of thoughtful breeders back years.'[16]

Sadly, even some respected international judges appear to accept this situation with equanimity. Don Burt, in *Winning with Arabian Horses*, says,

'"Type" is a word that is always changing meaning. I have seen many changes in desired type over the years in every breed. What was "in" three or four years ago is "out" today . . . I just can't help wondering what type of horse we'll be wanting ten years from now.'[17]

I find this infinitely depressing. It suggests that we are all the helpless victims of fashion in the showring, and that changing fads and whims can enhance or destroy a breed willy-nilly. As we have seen with dog breeds, and as we shall see with other breeds of horse, this is indeed so, but surely it is the height of irresponsibility to sit back and let it happen. For goodness sake, we are talking about a living creature, with needs and feelings of its own, not the latest designer outfit!

We need look no further than the Thoroughbred to see what happens when breeding is carried on with one or two isolated characteristics in mind. The Thoroughbred, bred for generations with speed as the sole criterion, is still, at its best, a magnificent horse, but there are far too many weedy, narrow specimens of dubious temperament, stamina and soundness. Coralie Gordon, writing on this very subject, cites also the Appaloosa, which 'bred for colour, can be a gruesome caricature without spots'.[18]

Sandra Munro, writing about the Arab Horse Society Northern Show at Haydock in 1990, commented on the huge number of colts forward compared to the number of geldings, and concluded that many breeders were being unrealistic. She went on to say, 'There is also evidence that a specific type of in-hand show Arabian is being produced and unfortunately for them those that fail to make the grade in the showring are not going to be able to rely on the ridden market for a future career as their long cannons, table top lines and unsuitable temperaments (whether inbred or induced) are unacceptable to the experienced rider. The approach of 1992 and all its horrifying implications for unwanted horses should surely be uppermost in the minds of all breeders as each mating is planned.'[19]

At the time of writing Britain has been able to hang on to its minimum values legislation but the warning is still valid. One of the saddest equine sights is that of the by-products of the racing industry: the young Thoroughbreds who do not make the grade on the race-track, or those that break down in training. Too many of these, bred solely with speed in mind, have faulty conformation and dubious temperaments. Because of this they, like the Arabians mentioned by Sandra Munro, will be unlikely to find a home with a professional or experienced rider (although there are some who regard a dubious temperament as a challenge). Because of their drawbacks they are usually offered for sale very cheaply and so are most likely to be snapped up by novice riders or those with insufficient experience to handle them. The novice soon finds the highly strung bundle of explosive temperament too much; and if it has broken down in training poor conformation often renders the horse susceptible to injury or lameness. So it is sold on, each time more cheaply, until at last it finds its way to that ultimate degradation – the auction and the waiting meat-van.

It would be comforting to think that this is an exaggeration, or that such cases are few, but it is not so. I have personally seen far too many of them to accept such an argument. So severe has this problem become that a few years ago Carrie Humble set up the Thoroughbred Rehabilitation Centre in Cumbria, which takes in Thoroughbreds that have been rejected by the racing industry and reschools them and acclimatises them to a normal stable environment before finding suitable homes for them. It is good to know that something is being done, but the dreadful, frustrating truth is that it need never have come to this if Thoroughbred breeding were not, to a large extent, motivated by tunnel vision. How tragic if through the same short-sightedness we condemn many of our beautiful Arabians to such an undignified end as an appointment with the meat man.

Some might argue that, given the fact that so many Arabians are not ridden anyway, does it really matter if they are unsuitable for riding? I should say that it matters very much. The Arabian is, first and foremost, a riding horse. For the *bedu* the horse was to be ridden and to be admired, but the riding was always most important. Few people, then as now, could afford to keep horses just for looking at and even where a mare was a symbol of wealth and status, she would still be ridden. Nowadays there are few people who can afford to keep horses simply as pets and such a life of idleness is, for many horses as intelligent as Arabians, simply not enough. Without the stimulation and challenge of work, many become grumpy and withdrawn, as, indeed, do some broodmares whose entire lives consist of breeding, eating, and sleeping.

Many lovers of the Arabian have emphasised the fact that he is, first and foremost, a riding horse. 'Every aspect of conformation and breed type related to his function as a riding horse,' (Rick Synowski).[20]

As one reader wrote in a letter to the editor of the *Arab Horse Society News*: 'It is to be hoped, in the long term interest of the breed, that we do not lose sight of the fact that our horses, however beautiful, are working animals. In not using them as such, we are guilty of depriving them of their dignity, and reducing them to being playthings.'[21]

Another writer, considering the dangers of breeding specifically for the one or two characteristics felt desirable in the showring, says, '. . . if it happens on a large scale that horses are not continually tested for function and if they are selected over several generations on nothing more than the ability to look stunning when standing still, we pay a price for that, and the price is very high. It's the integrity of our breed of horse.'[22]

We must also consider where the biggest market lies for Arabian horses. The greatest demand for Arabians is starting to come from the people who want a versatile horse which can participate in a number of different disciplines. Regional Groups which run sales lists report that they are constantly being asked for ridden pure-bred mares and geldings, and that the demand exceeds the supply. So if the knowledgeable riding public wants a ridden Arabian capable of functioning well, what on earth are so many breeders thinking about?

Judges must bear a heavy responsibility in ensuring that only those representatives of the breed that are genuinely the best are placed highly in showing classes, and must not allow themselves to be hoodwinked or intimidated into accepting inferior exhibits disguised by clever showmanship. Newcomers to the Arabian breeding and show scene will naturally tend to believe that if a judge places a horse at the top of the line it must be one of the best. They do not always have the knowledge or experience to distinguish the truly excellent from the merely pretty and fashionable. Believing in this often spurious excellence they will naturally tend to use those stallions (and it is usually stallions who represent the extremes of fashion) that are consistently well placed in in-hand classes, regardless of whether these stallions have really desirable qualities (besides superficial looks) to pass on; even whether they are, in fact, likely to pass on these qualities. Indeed there is a startling and disturbing lack of understanding among many breeders of even the most basic laws of genetics and inheritance – knowledge which is essential for any breeder to produce consistently good stock.

Great breeders have always known, from a combination of knowledge, instinct and experience, that the only way to breed for true excellence is to study bloodlines, to find out what characteristics have emerged consistently; to discover which sires and dams have proved prepotent (i.e. having the ability to stamp their qualities on their descendants, sometimes through several generations); to know which lines 'nick' well together and which do not; how to breed like to like, and when to try a daring experiment; when to line breed, and when to try an outcross; how far one may safely go with inbreeding, and when such inbreeding would be dangerous

Mikeno, a very prepotent sire (Rosemary Archer)

– all this and much more. Only in this way can desirable characteristics be 'fixed' and passed on. The best of them have always recognised that their task is not to 'improve' the breed itself, for it needed no such 'improvement'; rather to seek improvements in the quality of one's own stock and to preserve what is best by breeding only from the best. As George White says, 'There are two ways to make a stud: the way of the unlimited purse that buys and buys, or the unlimited time way of retaining improvements you've bred. Look after the bloodlines!'[23]

However, as so many show exhibits prove, too many breeders seem to think that it is sufficient to put a show-winning dam to a show-winning sire to obtain show-winning stock. Not only is this a somewhat ignoble and short-sighted aim, it simply does not work – as many a frustrated Throughbred breeder trying to breed the next Derby winner will confirm.

This unsatisfactory state of affairs is exacerbated by the lack of any system to weed out poor quality breeding stock. This was highlighted during stallion performance testing (instigated by the Trakehner Breeders' Fraternity and now run by the National Stallion Association) over the last

An influential modern sire. Platoon HT, Senior Male Champion, Arab Horse Society Northern Show 1993 (Sweet)

few years. Performance tests of various breeds included a number of Arabians who all, very gratifyingly, did well, some extremely so. For the latter, two extra tests had to be devised, consisting of an assessment of conformation by three Arab Horse Society Panel Judges, using a points system, and an assessment of ride, tractability and gaits by an Arab Horse Society Ridden Panel Judge. The other breeds represented – Cleveland Bay, Irish Draught and Trakehner – had already all been selected as suitable breeding stock by their respective breed societies. Surely it is time a similar system of selection was operated by the Arab Horse Society? It would certainly be a fairer way of assessing conformation and type as judges would be freed from the pressures of the showring and enabled to concentrate on one horse at a time.

With such a system there is always the danger that good horses could be excluded because of a too narrow definition of suitable breeding stock but adequate safeguards could be devised to protect against this.

One argument against the introduction of such a selection procedure is that it deprives breeders of the freedom to select breeding stock entirely of their own choosing. This is not completely the case; it would not result

Imad, Grade 1 National Stallion Association Performance Testing (Diana Whittome)

in anything like the restrictions applied in, say, Germany. It would simply mean that potential breeding stock would have to satisfy certain basic criteria as regards type and conformation before being entered as breeding stock.

Freedom and rights bring with them responsibilities and while some breeders undoubtedly recognise their responsibilities to the breed and, accordingly, plan carefully, many others do not, as the amount of careless breeding of the type described in this chapter testifies. It is regrettably the case that, the more lawless and irresponsible a community or a nation, the greater the number of laws and restrictions needed to combat that lawlessness and irresponsibility. As with abuses, the remedy is in the hands of the breeders themselves.

No doubt objections would also be raised on the grounds of cost (although one suspects that some of the loudest protests would come from those with most to lose if their stock were to be subjected to a more rigorous selection process than that of the showring). However, the Arab

Horse Society is a very large organistion compared with the others and, surely, if they can find the resources, so can the AHS.

To their great credit, those responsible for administering the Arab Horse Society Premium scheme have continued, in spite of pressure to narrow its scope, to insist that participation in it is not decided solely by virtue of show results. However, excellent as it is, the scheme is not, by its nature, far reaching enough to ensure a nationwide excellence of breeding stock.

As we saw in Chapter 9, one of the greatest problems for the Arabian horse has been, paradoxically, its popularity. At shows in the USA the different performance classes are dizzying in their sheer variety and numbers, and there has been a temptation to cram as many of these into all-Arabian shows as possible. While it is certainly laudable that the Arabian should be given the opportunity to show his versatility, one must question the wisdom of trying to make the breed 'all things to all people'.

In his book, *Winning with Arabian Horses*, Don Burt discusses the 'ideal' Arabian as opposed to the 'optimum' horse for the job. He says, 'The ideal may be the mental image perceived in those classes that resemble the beauty pageants, but other criteria should be adopted in the riding sections . . . The horse having those traits or characteristics most conducive to the task involved – trail, cowhorse, hunter, etc. – would probably not equal the ideal at halter, but he'd be optimum using the traits necessary for that job.'[24]

After expanding on this theme, he then goes on to discuss angulation, which he calls 'the end result of each horse's individual capabilities' – the angle of the bones being what actually makes the horse work. Thus, shoulder angles affect the neck and back as to length and workability, the same way as angles in the hindquarters affect length of stride, propulsion, etc. 'What would be optimum for a race horse', says Burt, 'would not be the same standard for a Park horse. The angles would be quite different but could correlate to the ideal where breed standards are concerned . . . Breeders and judges are picking certain traits (optimums) that relate to jobs, while trying to maintain breed characteristics (ideals).'[25] Burt maintains that many evolutions are taking place in the breed, and he cites the Park horse optimum, the Western horse optimum, and hunter-style optimum as three separate distinctions that are emerging within the breed. He insists that it is possible to have optimum traits for a given job without losing the ideal qualities of Arabian type, and that this is the direction in which all breeds of horses are moving. 'Instead of just breeding horse to horse hoping for as close to the ideal standard as possible, the breeders of the future are directing their programs toward optimum efficiency for the job.'[26] He suggests that, when viewing a horse in relation to another, it is worth recalling the maxim,'Optimum relates to ideal for the job desired'. 'From the judge's viewpoint,' he says,'using that type of philosophy means that halter horses can look like halter horses and hunters can look like hunters while maintaining breed characteristics. This could rid us of much confusion.'[27]

This is an attractive view and one which provides much food for thought. However, in practice there are many difficulties with this idea. To begin with it, it is simply not true to say, as Burt does, that all breeds of horses are experiencing similar directional changes and his comments are probably very much related to American breeds. There are more than 200 breeds of horse in the world, and of these only a tiny handful are changing with particular aspects of performance in mind. Certainly the great warmblood breeding programmes of Europe have been geared towards specific aspects of performance; but it must be remembered that warmbloods are not pure breeds (although some of them, such as the Trakehner and the Hannoverian, do breed true to a certain extent). Other breeds whose stud books have long been closed are not, on the whole, evolving separate distinct types within the breed. Where this *has* happened within certain breeds, the result has been near-disastrous. Within the British mountain and moorland breeds, for example, selecting for various traits for a given job – in this instance showing in Riding Pony classes – is resulting in the loss of many of the characteristics which form the 'type' of these native breeds.

Just as breeding for one or two characteristics currently fashionable in the showring can change a breed, those who breed for specific aspects of competition are also faced with the temptation, very hard to resist, to concentrate on certain aspects which appear to be required. This has been particularly noticeable in the dressage world. Today's dressage judges and competitors have largely forgotten that the aim of dressage was never to compete, but to train a horse – any horse – to enhance its natural paces, and to render it supple, obedient and a safe, pleasant, balanced ride. The ultimate proof of this training was collection, with supreme collection being shown in the *piaffe*, *passage*, and canter pirouettes (and, in more classical times, the 'airs above the ground'). These principles applied to any horse, no matter what its breed (although, naturally, certain breeds found such training easier than others). With today's emphasis being almost exclusively on competition, and greater attention being paid to the spectacular extended gaits, horses are being selectively bred for dressage which display this bold, extravagent movement. In the process, as I mentioned in

Chapter 6, backs are getting longer and longer, to the extent that some horses' hind ends appear disconnected from their fronts, and they look as though they could accommodate another rider behind the saddle. This kind of back may be more flexible, but many of these horses find collection increasingly difficult, and at Grand Prix level it is a rare thing indeed to see even a passable *piaffe, passage* or canter pirouette.

Furthermore, I simply do not see how it is possible to maintain the ideal qualities of Arabian type while breeding for optimum performance in different categories of showing class, given the wide variation in the types of horse for which those classes were originally devised. I believe such a course is a potential recipe for disaster. It would be like trying to breed, say, Andalusians to race. They are a very different type of horse from the racing types, and to attempt to breed them for speed would inevitably result in a total loss of those characteristics which distinguish the breed (in fact this almost happened, for different reasons, as we shall see). Indeed, such a loss of type has *already* occurred to some extent among Arabians being bred on the continent for Arab racing; many of these, bred increasingly for speed, are coming more and more to resemble, not the Arabian, but the Thoroughbred. This seems like a pointless exercise; the Thoroughbred already exists – why re-invent it?

The Park horse classes mentioned in Chapter 4 are one of the most popular classes at all-Arabian shows in the USA. The Saddlebred, which is the type of horse for which the Park horse classes were devised, already exists; why seek to breed the Arabian specifically for such classes? This seems to me a classic case of trying to cram a left shoe on a right foot. Surely it would make far greater sense to accept the Arabian for what he is – a wonderful all-round riding horse – and to develop the talents of each individual according to what he is best formed to do (and, of course, what he enjoys), rather than to think of breeding Arabians specifically for certain aspects of performance.

Moreover, in spite of Mr Burt's comments regarding the meaning of 'type' (see Chapter 5), it seems to me that here he is falling into the trap of separating type from function. If (as I hope I have established) type, conformation and function are inseparable, then to change that function more than a very little will inevitably result in a change of type.

There are those who will argue that we live in a rapidly changing world, and that given that the horse's role in human society has altered drastically within the last hundred years, it is unreasonable to seek to maintain breeds unchanged. However, I see no virtue in change for its own sake and am a great believer in the maxim, 'If it ain't broke, don't fix it'. We must remember that the Arabian developed as he is *because* of his environment and the use to which he was put – i.e. as a war-horse and a hunting horse (the original sense in which the word 'courser' was used). If we truly love the Arabian, we must love him for what he is, not for what we would like him to be. He is surely destined for something more than simply trotting round or standing still at the end of a lead rope. He is not, after all, a leading-rein pony; he is a *riding* horse. If we want a horse that moves like a driving cob, then we buy a driving cob. If we want a hunter, then we either buy a hunter type or we take our Arabian hunting (which many of them take to like ducks to water). If we want to drive, or compete in dressage, or hunt, we have to accept that our Arabian is not going to be exactly like a driving cob, a hunter or a warmblood – or whatever. Nor, if we love him for what he is, do we want him to be. No. He is himself; let us leave him that way.

By the end of the nineteenth century, historical and political changes meant that high class Arabian horses were becoming scarce in the desert. It is largely thanks to the efforts of a handful of people – such as Abbas Pasha and Ali Pasha Sherif, Major Upton, the Blunts and Count Stroganov, among others – that in the nineteenth century so many superb specimens of the breed were saved for posterity. How tragic and ironic it is that the very popularity which arose from these efforts to save the Arabian from oblivion should now threaten the integrity of the breed.

Many breeders of Arabians are, of course, gearing their breeding programmes towards producing horses that are functional as well as beautiful and the preservation of those bloodlines which have consistently produced stock capable of high levels of performance. Others are concentrating on trying to produce the perfect Arabian and the best of these are conscious that this must automatically mean breeding for function as well as beauty. However, these breeders are widely scattered and while there are some prominent names among them, too many of them are unknown and unrecognised. Even where recognition has been won, there is no guarantee that their achievements will survive after them. Some of the great studs, such as the Courthouse Stud of Bill Musgrave-Clark, and the Barton Lodge Stud of Sir Henry and Lady May Abel-Smith, established bloodlines of great excellence; now they are gone, these bloodlines are in danger of being lost. Without a conscious effort to preserve what is good, the same fate may easily befall the life's work of some of the best modern breeders. If that happens, we may lose far more than a few bloodlines; we may end by losing our breed.

There are those who will argue that this is alarmist; that there are, and always will be, breeders who care sufficiently about the true type and character of the Arabian horse to continue breeding this traditional type and that given the huge numbers of Arabians being bred throughout the world there is no danger of our losing this true type.

This may be so; one sincerely hopes it is but we cannot afford to be complacent. There are even larger numbers of pedigree dogs of all breeds being bred throughout the world but this has not saved a number of these breeds from disaster – in fact, it may be said to have contributed to it. We must never underestimate the power of fashion to distort people's thinking. This is a situation in which other breeds of horse have almost foundered; mountain and moorland enthusiasts are becoming increasingly worried that the distinctions between British native breeds are becoming blurred and that as breeders strive to please judges in mixed mountain and moorland classes (judges, it may be said, who often do not appear to know the specific characteristics of, say, an Exmoor as opposed to a Dales or a Fell pony), the individual character of the breeds is being lost, together with the qualities that have fitted them so well for survival in their native habitat.

In her excellent study of Iberian horses, Sylvia Loch enumerates the qualities of the traditional Iberian (i.e. Andalusian and Lusitano) horse of function, the fighting and working horse. She calls these qualities 'the Iberian Factor'. They are very different in some respects from those of the Arabian, but they are superbly adapted to the type of work these horses have traditionally been expected to perform, whether on the battlefield, in the mounted *corrida*, or in the High School *manège*. However, some breeders, particularly in Spain, have aimed to produce an all-round pleasure horse. 'In this horse, the high-stepping action is encouraged but in order to eliminate features which have become unfashionable, such as the sub-convex profile or Roman nose, and the short-coupled back with its sloping croup, breeders favouring this more modern look have often sacrificed much of the agility which gives this horse his forward thrust, his handiness and his practicality.'[28] She goes on to say, 'So popular has this horse of parade become that at one time many people in Spain were in danger of convincing themselves that this type was the true type and horses bearing the Iberian Factor were shunned in certain circles. Fortunately, however, sense is once more prevailing.'[29]

However, the story might have had a different ending. In the 1920s and 1930s the military breeding establishments which were responsible for breeding the Arabian and Andalusian in Spain were not only changing the appearance of the Andalusian by breeding out the Iberian factor, but the strong hock action and impulsion and the superb temperament of the old war horse were also being diminished, though unintentionally. By the 1940s Spanish breeders of the old school, together with Portuguese breeders, were so concerned that in 1946 Dr Ruy d'Andrade warned that unless breeders returned to their original Spanish foundation horse – the Iberian prototype – and avoided the 'new' look, they were in danger of losing their breed altogether. It was not until the 1970s that the Spanish breeders of the Andalusian received a nasty shock, when the first Championship of the Pure Bred Spanish Horse was held in Seville in 1979. Herr Dr Heinrich Lehrner from the Piber Stud of the Spanish Riding School judged all the in-hand and ridden classes and shocked some of Spain's most illustrious modern breeders by marking their horses down for dishing and lack of impulsion. As a result of this, as Sylvia Loch comments 'Selectors are now rethinking their priorities and earnest efforts are at present being made to regain the straight forward action for which the Iberian horse was famed in history . . . Breeders continue to buy from Portugal which, because of the mounted *corrida*, has never diverged from its original prototype.'[30]

But what about the Arabian? As Peter Upton has pointed out, the breed's future is now in the hands of today's breeders: 'What is lost may never be regained: the burden is weighty but well worth the bearing.'[31] However, if we reach the stage where breeders, discouraged by lack of recognition, cease to breed the traditional, true type, then valuable bloodlines will be lost, and with them many of the characteristics that have throughout history made the Arabian so valued and sought after. What blood could we then draw upon, to return the breed to its true type? For thousands of years the Arabian blood was kept pure – to the extent that it is perhaps the purest breed on earth. This is, in part, the source of its immense prepotency, its ability to pass on its excellence and stamp itself on all other breeds with which its blood is mingled. If outside blood were introduced, the breed would no longer be pure; as Margaret Greely has said, if you take a glass of pure brandy and add to it one single drop of water, then it is no longer pure brandy.

The preface to the Arab Horse Society publication *Arabian Type and Standard* says, 'The Arab horse being an original breed, not subject to arbitrary alterations or passing fashion, has been unchanged in type for several thousand years.'[32] Yet, as we have seen, it is now subject to precisely those arbitrary alterations and passing fashions which are indeed changing the type. If we truly love the Arabian horse, we cannot, we must not, let this happen. If we allow the true character of the Arabian to disappear because

'If he pass away by human folly, you will never see his like again' Indian Magic (Rosemary Archer)

of the frivolous demands of fashion and the showring, not to mention the lure of gain on the racecourse, we will have betrayed the care and devotion of countless generations of horsemen who cherished their horses' excellence and the purity of their breeding. Once the Arabian's true characteristics are lost, they are lost forever.

Notes

1 Quoted by David Hancock in 'Are We Producing Pedigree Chumps?', *The Field*, January 1995, p.78
2 Hancock, 'Pedigree Chumps', p.78
3 Hancock, 'Pedigree Chumps', p.78
4 Hancock, 'Pedigree Chumps', p.78
5 Poole, R.W.F., *The Cheviot Ranter*, Michael Joseph 1993, pp.4–5
6 Poole, *Cheviot Ranter*, p.5
7 Hancock, 'Pedigree Chumps', p.79
8 Hancock, 'Pedigree Chumps', p.79
9 Edwards, Gladys Brown, *The Arabian: War Horse to Show Horse*, pp.291–3
10 Forbis, Judith, *The Classic Arabian Horse*, p.229

11 Quoted by Rosemary Archer, *The Arabian Horse*, p.137
12 Palgrave, William, *Narrative of a Year's Journey through Central and Eastern Arabia* vol. 2, p.93
13 Blunt, Lady Anne, letter to Spencer Borden, May 30th 1907. *Journals*, etc. ed. Rosemary Archer and James Fleming, p.437
14 Blunt, Lady Anne, *Journals*, p.437
15 Upton, Roger, 'Arab Horses in Saudi Arabia Part I', *Arab Horse Society News* no. 72, p.47
16 Letters, *Arab Horse Society News* no. 77, p.90
17 Burt, Don, *Winning with Arabian Horses*, p.67
18 Gordon, Coralie, 'Gilding the Lily', *Arab Horse Society News*, no. 82, p.60
19 Munro, Sandra, *Arab Horse Society News*, No. 75, p.64
20 Synowski, Rick, 'In Praise of the Riding Horse', *Arab Horse Scoiety News* no. 76, p. 48 (first published in the American magazine, *The CMK Record*, Fall 1990)
21 Letters, *Arab Horse Society News*, no. 76, p.67
22 Gordon, Coralie, 'Gilding the Lily', *Arab Horse Society News*, no. 82, p.61
23 Quoted by Diana Dykes, 'The Barton Lodge Stud', *Arab Horse Society News* no. 74, p.71
24 Burt, *Winning*, p.73
25 Burt, *Winning*, p.74
26 Burt, *Winning*, p.74
27 Burt, *Winning*, p.74
28 Loch, Sylvia, *The Royal Horse of Europe*, J.A.Allen 1986, p.154
29 Loch, *Royal Horse*, p.154
30 Loch, *Royal Horse*, p.160
31 Upton, Peter, 'The Pure Breed' *Arab Horse Society Newsletter*, Autumn 1995, p.1
32 *Arabian Type and Standard*, Arab Horse Society, p.3

CONCLUSION

'Observe, and reflect!'
CAPTAIN BEUDANT

'Complacency is the enemy of excellence.'
SYLVIA LOCH

NOW THAT we have reviewed the Arabian show scene, what conclusions may we draw?

I should say that depends very much on one's point of view. There will inevitably be many readers who will disagree with much of what I have written and this will undoubtedly include those who have a vested interest in maintaining the *status quo*. These people will argue that the Arab show world is bigger and brighter than it has ever been, the general quality of the horses higher, the showing classes well filled and exhibitors full of enthusiasm and, further, that I have painted a distorted picture of the problems identified. Others – and this will include people for whose views I have a very great deal of respect – may agree that there are some undesirable trends but that, in general, these are not of such a magnitude as to cause major problems and that, on the whole, the show scene does not present as black a picture as I have painted.

This might well be one's impression if only the surface is examined. However, under the surface, as I think should be clear from earlier chapters, there is a deep layer of unease and dissatisfaction, particularly at grass roots level, but extending through all strata of the Arab horse world. When I first started to gather material for this book, one breeder of Arabians, who has had considerable success both in the showring and in other forms of equestrian endeavour, wrote to me: 'The Arab show scene is bleaker than you realise.' At the time I hoped very much that I could prove her wrong; sadly, from my own observations, and the evidence presented to me by others, I found that she was only too right.

We have seen how the explosion of the breed's popularity has led not only to undesirable trends within the showring itself, but to careless breeding and the growth of outright, despicable abuse in training, handling and conditioning for shows. The fact that many of these trends and abuses are the work of a relatively small number of people does not make them any less insidious. The power of fashion to wreak havoc among otherwise perfectly ordinary people must never be underestimated. Peer pressure can be just as powerful among adults as it can among impressionable adolescents, particularly in the field of equestrian competition, where being seen to do 'the right thing' or to be 'in the know' is paramount in the minds of many. It is very easy for those who are inexperienced or unsure of their judgement to be persuaded that the actions of apparently successful show exhibitors must inevitably be correct. I have heard all manner of barbarous methods of dealing with 'difficult' horses accepted without a blink by people who should know better, simply because they have been recommended by someone who has x number of years' experience and a string of show or competition wins to their credit.

I think the options have been made plain: if the Arab Horse Society and other national and international Arabian horse societies do not take action to set their houses in order, their organisations will increasingly be split into distinct groups, each with its own agenda. Indeed, there are signs that this may already be happening, with reports of attempts by individuals to subvert rules and procedures to suit their own aims. This is to the credit of neither the organisation nor the individuals concerned. In any organisation which purports to be concerned with, among other things, the welfare of horses, this kind of fragmenting of purpose cannot be a good thing. It renders attempts at cohesive action in cases of cruelty, abuse and neglect difficult if not impossible; it hampers the formulation of any consistent policy designed to encourage the breeding of sound, well-conformed stock of correct type; and (in some countries at least) the lack of will to enforce rules at shows and to maintain standards can result in proceedings that, to all but those mesmerised by superficial gloss and glitter – or who have a financial interest at stake – appear increasingly distasteful and even repellent.

If this state of affairs continues, the Arabian horse world – and especially that section of it devoted to showing – will find itself increasingly marginalised. Already it is perceived, rightly or wrongly, by the rest of the equestrian community as a thing apart, peopled by eccentrics with scatty, ornamental but largely useless animals. This is infuriating and frustrating for the majority of Arab owners, who resent being typecast by the all too evident antics of what is, after all, a relative minority. If this general perception does not change, then as I pointed out in Chapters 3 and 10, the already finite market for pure-bred Arabians will dwindle; at the time of writing this market is already experiencing a kind of 'slump'. There are (as the enquiries for ridden Arabians mentioned in Chpater 10 show) people within the general equestrian community who appreciate the Arabian's special qualities but they are often discouraged by the perception (again, whether this is correct or not is not the issue) that good Arabians are becoming more and more difficult to find.

Remembering a former boss of mine who used to say, 'Don't come to me with problems if you can't suggest a solution', I have tried wherever a problem has been identified, to suggest a possible answer. Others may be able to think of better ones but the will to find solutions must exist, as must the will to implement them.

If this will does not manifest itself, I can foresee only disaster. Exaggeration, those who wish to maintain the *status quo* will say. Not so, is my reply. Look around at what is happening in the world at large. There have been dramatic changes in people's perceptions of animals and their relationship with humankind. An intense concern about animal welfare, while certainly commendable and desirable, has resulted in the increased blurring of distinctions between animal welfare and animal rights. Many people are not even aware that there *is* a distinction; general attitudes towards animals are, at the best of times, plagued by muddled thinking and often contradictory attitudes. Especially muddled and contradictory are attitudes towards horses and horsemanship. Horse ownership and riding are often perceived by the non-horsy person as somehow associated with class and status; an attitude that is encouraged by the news media and, of course, by the animal rights movements, many of whose motives are highly political.

This makes equestrian sports – even the most innocuous, like a children's gymkhana – particularly vulnerable to such movements, especially as such regrettable incidents as the death of a minority of horses in the pursuit of such sports is given so much (usually ill-informed) media attention – witness the fuss when three horses died at Badminton in 1992. Tragic as this was, three such accidents at one event was a freak, but this did not prevent the interested parties from clamouring for the banning of horse trials. Racing, particularly jump racing, is already suffering from the attentions of animal rights groups. Showjumping is another potential target, and one cannot doubt that other forms of equestrian sport will follow.

But surely, one might argue, dressage and showing, being two aspects of equestrian sport which are not likely to involve the injury or death of horses, will escape the wrath of animal rights activists? Not so. Dressage is regarded as a form of coercion, and by definition showing must also be so considered. Besides, in the view of many animal rights fanatics, showing is degrading to the horses concerned, as is any activity which requires them to subject themselves to the will of humans. Indeed, some extremists would go so far as to do away with all pet ownership, considering even the keeping of pet cats and dogs to be a form of slavery.

It is no matter that these arguments are fundamentally flawed, both logically and with reference to the natural world and our relative place in it. Indeed, such arguments frequently seem to stem less from any real love and understanding of animals than from a hatred of humans; and they often tell us a great deal more about their proponents than they do about animals. Nevertheless, the more moderate among them have some very valid points to make, while the extremists have gained a great deal of political ground. It might seem like political suicide for any party to consider the banning of equestrian sports or the 'phasing out' (as one animal rights spokesman puts it) of pet animals, but, once in power, political parties of any colour are notorious not only for treating the electorate with contempt, but for becoming spellbound by political dogma and ideology. In a century that has known Hitler and Stalin, Pol Pot and Nicolae Ceaucescu, we should not be surprised at anything politicians may concoct. Even Britain, once noted for its relative tolerance and inherent *reasonableness*, is now being stirred by the politics of greed, hatred and envy; while its people are becoming increasingly divided into narrow-minded, aggressive groups representing this or that 'ism' or 'ology'. In such a political climate, if current trends continue, I do not give much for equestrian sport's chances of survival.

We have only to look at what is happening to circuses. Many local councils have now banned them from performing on council-owned land. Yet an independent scientific study of circuses, commissioned a few years ago by the RSPCA, concluded that circuses have a valuable part to play in increasing our understanding of animals. This study, carried out by Dr Kiley-Worthington of the University of Edinburgh, involved more than 3,000 hours of observation of all aspects of animal care and training in a number of circuses. It found that, while some aspects of circus animal husbandry could certainly be improved, in general the standard of care and wellbeing of circus animals in British circuses is not inferior to that of the animal husbandry systems found in good zoos, private stables and kennels. Dr Kiley-Worthington further maintained that circuses, by virtue of the training they do with animals, are uniquely placed to do scientific research on how and what different species can learn, how and what they think, etc., and research on the human/animal relationship. 'On balance,' she wrote, 'I do not think that the animals' best interests are served by money and activities diverted to try and ban circuses either locally or nationally.'[1]

This objective, well-reasoned report did not cause councils to consider whether they were, in fact, serving animals' best interests by banning circuses; one can only speculate that they were either unaware of it (which suggests a somewhat careless and cavalier attitude to such a serious matter), or for reasons of what is generally known as 'political correctness' they chose to ignore it because it ran somewhat counter to received ideas about circuses. Either way this does not bode well for other activities involving animals which are 'perceived' to be contrary to certain political ideas or notions of animal rights.

There is no answer that will satisfy the strained, distorted logic of some of the animal rights fanatics; but much more could be done to ensure that the more extreme arguments do not take root. This involves all equestrian sports examining their activities thoroughly and with an impartial eye; perhaps a study comparable to Dr Kiley-Worthington's could be undertaken. Many unwelcome facts would undoubtedly come to light but this would enable them to be dealt with at the source, rather than by an outside (and unwelcome) agency.

For the showing world, and the Arabian horse world in particular, it would involve an even more rigorous self-examination, because for too long the various showing bodies have preferred to ignore much that was unpleasant, although, to their credit, some of these, the Arab Horse Society among them, *have* recognised that bad showing practices were harming their organisations. There must be, as I have said, the *will* to change what is bad and this involves accepting that change is essential before we are all revised out of existence by political ideology.

Unfortunately, by its very nature the contemporary equestrian scene tends to make life difficult in this respect. I am not against competition in general, any more than I am against showing. If I were, I would not take part in either. I do take part, however, and it is my personal observations made at such competitions and shows, as well as the observations of others, that lead me to believe, as I said in the introduction, that overconcentration on competition is one of the causes of a deterioration in general standards of riding and training and that this, in turn, is partly responsible for some of the disturbing trends in the showing of Arabian horses. In order to understand this and other causes, we need to step outside the Arabian show scene again and look at equestrianism and attitudes towards training in general.

In Chapter 9 I mentioned a widespread reluctance to accept that horses can experience emotion as we understand it. Recent scientific research, based on a wide range of case histories, has finally concluded that animals, in general, *do* have complex emotional lives. The only thing that astonishes me is that it has taken so long for scientists to discover what all the best animal trainers have always known – that animals, especially domestic ones such as dogs and horses – are capable of experiencing as wide a range of emotions as humans, although they will not necessarily always react to given situations in the way that humans would – much depends on their status in the animal kingdom, and whether they are predators or potential prey, etc. Indeed, it is the recognition of these emotions that has enabled the best horse trainers to obtain such outstanding results, which far exceed those obtained by people who regard the horse as merely a rather stupid animal with certain basic instincts such as greed and fear which can be exploited to a human's advantage. The latter type of trainer has always experienced difficulties, whereas those who truly know and respect the horse and treat him as a friend (thereby assuming that he can understand friendship) will invariably find their task much easier. The greatest philosophers and trainers have never been afraid to accept that animals can feel fear, pleasure, love, anger, jealousy and a host of other emotions, including pride. Here is Xenophon, Greek general, horsemaster, historian and philosopher, writing almost 2,400 years ago: 'if you teach your horse to go with a light hand on the bit, and yet to hold his head well up and to arch his neck, you will be making him do just what the animal himself *glories and delights in* [my italics].[2]

Granted, we have been partially brainwashed by generations of dreary behaviourists into believing that to attribute emotions (or even intelligence) to animals is dangerous anthropomorphism. Why this should be so I have no idea, unless it is that to deny animals a sense of personhood and the ability to experience emotions somehow serves to justify our use of them for our own purposes. Perhaps this explains why so many riders still treat their horses as if they were simply an animate piece of sports equipment.

We saw in Chapter 4 how classical principles were largely abandoned in Britain as a result of changes in social and cultural attitudes. Although the British Horse Society's Training Director maintains that its teachings adhere to classical principles, in reality these principles, resurrected but never fully entrenched, have become diluted to the point where they often seem to be non-existent. This is one of the reasons why Britain has always lagged behind other European countries in international dressage. Now that dressage is experiencing a popularity boom in Britain, the lack of good dressage trainers is becoming increasingly evident, with many top British riders seeking enlightenment from the most successful German and Dutch riders. In the field of showing, owners and riders of Arabian horses in particular, realising the benefits of a good basic dressage training, are looking to dressage trainers of all nationalities for advice and tuition.

Yet, paradoxically, it is precisely their success in competition that has led many continental trainers and riders to move further and further away from classical principles. I have recently (for purposes unconnected with the writing of this book) spent many hours watching and analysing video recordings, both commercially and privately produced, of top dressage competitors at work and in competition; and what I saw was profoundly disturbing with regard to the quality of both the riding and the training of the horses. With virtually all training aimed at competition work, there is a perhaps inevitable tendency for trainers to pass over what is correct for what is expedient. This is as obvious in Britain as it is abroad. The long, slow, painstaking work that the best trainers have always known to be necessary for the horse's full athletic development (and similarly the long apprenticeship the rider must undertake in order to become truly effective and well balanced, as opposed to merely being able to stay on a horse and get it to do more or less what the rider wants) take up far too much time for the hectic modern competitive world. As with so much in our current culture of instant gratification, trainers and riders want results *now*. This can lead to short cuts, and to the use of training (and riding) methods that are *ad hoc*, and ultimately forceful and crude, because superficially impressive results can be obtained by such methods. This can (and does) apply to the training of horses for in-hand show classes just as much as it does to ridden classes and, indeed, to all forms of equestrian sport.

Even at the highest levels, and in all disciplines, too many trainers pay lip-service to the idea of correct principles of training. When the chips are down, however, it is results that matter where competition is concerned. We are back to the idea that the end justifies the means, with all that this implies.

This overlooking, or ignorance, of true principles leads to a great deal of damage being inflicted on horses at all levels. Ignorant of these principles, riders blame the horse when things go wrong – 'He's so *tense*' – 'He won't bend round my leg' – 'I can't get him to go on the bit' – 'He rushes' – I can't stop him' – all these cries of anguish can be heard daily in riding schools and arenas up and down the country and, indeed, in other parts of the world where riding is a matter of pleasure and not a necessity. The advice given sometimes identifies the problem as emanating from the rider's attitude or way of sitting and applying the aids but, even where this is recognised, the rider's basic problems – which stem from an inadequate understanding of the biomechanics of the horse/rider interaction – are very often not corrected. What happens instead is that a variety of home-cooked ideas are tried out, which more often than not include the use of a greater or lesser degree of force. This may effect a temporary 'improvement', but it is the symptom that is being treated, not the problem. In addition, if the 'treatment' is not based on a thorough knowledge of the horse's biomechanics, considerable physical damage may result. This is how we see showjumping horses with unnaturally 'rubbery' necks and damaged back muscles, from having been forcibly flexed in a manner supposedly aimed at bringing the horse 'on the bit'. I have seen this, and the damage it can cause, more often than I like to think. We see show horses that carry their heads in a position that can only have been achieved by tying them down with draw reins, running reins or a similar gadget as their backs are hollow and their hind legs are trailing behind them. We see dressage horses whose natural beauty and fluidity of movement fool us into believing that they have been well trained, until it all falls apart when the horse is asked for true collection and can produce only a travesty of a canter pirouette, a *piaffe* or a *passage*. Many of them are tense and unhappy, being held in at the front by ferociously tugging hands while equally ferocious spurs jab them in the sides. The list is endless, and it is not pleasant to contemplate. All this may not be intentional; very often, certainly at the lower levels of competition, it is not. We are reminded of Charles de Kunffy's observation that: 'Brutality begins where knowledge ends. Ignorance and compulsion appear simultaneously.'

I maintain that all the evidence suggests that, at a time when more people than ever before are taking up riding as a form of recreation rather than as a necessity, we are no nearer to classical ideals than the Renaissance Italians who advocated tying live hedgehogs under horses' tails to make them go forward. Indeed, if we consider some of the methods used by certain show 'trainers' (such as fire-extinguishers or cattle prods), it seems as if the enlightened teachings of Xenophon, Pluvinel, la Guérinière, Podhajsky, Oliveira, etc. had never existed.

I wholeheartedly wish it were not so but much observation and analysis leads me to the inevitable conclusion that it *is* so. If I were alone in this opinion, doubters would have every right to dismiss me as a crank. However, similar misgivings have been expressed by some of the most eminent people in the realms of equestrianism; not just ultra-specialists who inhabit a world of impossible ideals, but people with a wide background of equestrianism in general, such as Charles de Kunffy and Brigadier-General Kurt Albrecht, former director of the Spanish Riding School. Both are FEI judges and so have more opportunity than most of us to observe just what is going on.

Many of the world's greatest and most talented trainers have long recognised this problem. Some of the great classical trainers of our time, such as Nuno Oliveira and Egon von Neindorff, have avoided competition altogether because they believe that it causes the horses too much stress and, furthermore, compromises true principles. Others, such as Alois Podhajsky, former Director of the Spanish Riding School, the Portuguese trainer, rider and FEI judge Francisco Cançela d'Abreu, and Arthur Kottas-Heldenberg, *Oberbereiter* at the Spanish Riding School, have successfully taken part in competition without compromising their classical ideals but examples such as these are relatively rare. Many other classical riders and trainers have found that competition, as it has developed in the late twentieth century, is simply incompatible with their ideals. Danny Pevsner, a classical trainer based in Britain who has worked with von Neindorff, Oliveira and at the Spanish Riding School, believes that the pressure of competition can spoil the pleasure of riding, and that training and riding methods are becoming more and more crude and unnatural because increasingly success in competition is the only criterion by which progress or excellence is measured. For each horse that is successful, he maintains, many will have been damaged. He says, 'Training methods which distort proper locomotion cannot be right and judging that is more affected by the superiority of horseflesh than by the correctness of schooling is also wrong.'[3]

This applies to all disciplines and aspects of equestrianism. Of course there are notable exceptions – there always are, at all levels – but the general picture is of horses trained not to unfold their potential and enhance their natural gaits through painstaking athletic development, but simply to present an impressive picture in the showring.

It doesn't have to be like this. While the number of true masters of equestrianism has dwindled and remains very small, there are compensations. Riders, trainers and all those who deal with horses in any way nowadays have access to a vast quantity of books and videos which can point them in the right direction. With regard to every aspect of equestrianism, there is absolutely *no excuse* for anyone to plead ignorance. Unfortunately, there are still those who obstinately maintain that one cannot learn about horses by reading books and that you shouldn't believe everything you read in books anyway. Both of these beliefs are partly true, but only partly. Of course, one cannot learn to ride, or to handle or train horses, simply by reading books; theory must be matched by practice and, above all, one must develop that elusive quality called 'feel' which, in any event, cannot be taught. However, Leonardo da Vinci (certainly no armchair theorist!) said, 'Those who devote themselves to practice without science are like sailors who put to sea without rudder or compass and who can never be certain where they are going.' Naturally, one cannot believe everything written by 'those madmen who write books' as the *bedu* used to put it. The reader must learn to be discerning, to judge whether the writer has based their statements on evidence or simply on personal opinion and, if the latter, whether that opinion can be respected. The same applies when one is evaluating the worth of any judgement or opinion, whether written or not. Those people who say, 'Oh, I never read those books' are effectively passing judgement on themselves. They are closing their minds to further knowledge and understanding; only they can know whether this is the result of arrogance (i.e. the belief that they already know all that can be known about equestrianism) or a wish to remain ignorant, lest wider knowledge should disturb their comfortable prejudices.

Then there are those who will maintain that I am exaggerating once again and that there is nothing wrong with current standards of equitation, whether in the showring or in the dressage arena; that where the showring is concerned a style which served past generations has proved perfectly adequate; and that much of what I am saying is based on personal opinion and theory. They are perfectly entitled to their opinions but I would ask them this: upon what criteria are these opinions based? If they are able to produce concrete evidence to counter my own observations and research, and arguments which refute the life's work and study of great masters of equitation past and present – in other words of people who, as Sylvia Loch says, 'spent not hours but every waking moment in the saddle and who dedicated their lives to understanding the psychology and physical ability of horses better than most of us will ever dream of'[4] – then I shall bow to them.

If not, it may simply be that they do not know what they are talking about and that their objections are based on nothing more than a (perhaps understandable) reluctance to abandon preconceived ideas or the prejudices of a lifetime.

So, as we approach the end of the twentieth century, what can we do to improve equestrianism in general and the Arabian show scene in particular? How can we stave off the attentions of people who would like to see all equestrian activities done away with?

There are a number of things that can be done. This involves large-scale education; not only the education of show committees, judges, trainers, exhibitors and riders, but of the general public. The latter must be taught that horsemanship and riding are not just about competition, but about the harmonious relationship between horse and handler and horse and rider. That we and horses are not simply two separate species but part of the same order of things; that, as Paul Belasik puts it, we and the horse are both part of nature. To try to separate horses and humans, animals and mankind in general, as some of the animal rights people would do, is to deny them and us our rightful position in nature. We both exist in the same world and whether we wish it or not, we share that world. I do wish it; I believe that horses and humans can enrich each other's experience immensely if only we learn to understand and respect one another rather more than we do at present.

There are encouraging signs that attitudes are already beginning to change in this direction and that equestrians in general want to see rather more than lip-service paid to the ideals of Xenophon and others like him. When Sylvia Loch set up the Classical Riding Club early in 1995, she originally envisaged a small group of like-minded people, bound together by a love of the horse and a wish to preserve the classical traditions which seemed in danger of becoming swept away. Within the space of a few months she was inundated with applications for membership from people from all kinds of equestrian backgrounds and from all over the world. These were not disaffected members of other organisations, but ordinary horsemen and women who felt that there had to be better ways to ride and train horses than those they generally saw in practice. These people realised that the effectiveness of classical riding and training applies to *any* breed, whether Arabian, Andalusian, Welsh Cob, Thoroughbred, warmblood or whatever. All of these will benefit if the trainer/rider applies classical principles; these are based on the correctness of the rider's posture in the saddle, of light, still hands, of aids clearly yet quietly given, and a system of training the horse based very much on reward rather than punishment, and which emphasises consideration for the horse at all times. They treat the horse as a reasonable creature, with considerable intelligence, a fine range of feelings and a strong sense of justice – surely the only valid approach for the truly thinking, feeling horseman or woman.

Then, too, there is the immense enthusiasm generated by the periodic visits of the Spanish Riding School. People who would not get out of bed to watch a dressage competition or go to a breed or general horse show, will cheerfully travel hundreds of miles to watch the magical displays given by the supreme exponents of the classical art. It is not merely the spectacle that draws them, attractive as that is; it is the feeling that they are witnessing a true union of humankind with another living species: total communication between horse and rider and horse and handler.

Many will feel that such an almost mystical union is beyond the average horse and trainer/rider and that it is therefore pointless to try to aim for such heights. Not so; I truly believe that if the will exists to work towards it, to try to understand the *why* and the *how* as well as *what* is required in working with horses, *every horseman or woman who truly loves his or her horse(s)* can strike a note on the same scale as the *bereiters* of the Spanish Riding School. It may be further down the scale but it is the same scale nevertheless. As the poet John Donne said, 'Aim for the stars, and you might yet touch the moon.'★

Shows, and in particular breed shows, could have a tremendously important part to play in demonstrating to those who believe that all equestrian activities are a form of coercion and beneath the dignity of horses, that this is not the case, but the leopard must be prepared to change its spots. Here, again, there are many signs that such changes would meet with wholehearted approval at grassroots level. As a committee member of one of the regional groups affiliated to the Arab Horse Society, and current editor of its magazine, I hear the views of many ordinary members – by which I mean those who are not necessarily prominent at our shows but who nevertheless form the backbone, both of the parent body and of the regional groups. These members are not only questioning much of what they see at our shows, they are actively turning away from what they see and disassociating themselves from what they consider brings themselves and their breed into disrepute. The will to change what is bad while preserving what is good certainly exists at these levels; what is needed is impetus from the top.

In the USA and Canada some breeders, disillusioned with the showing practices they see, have banded together to hold shows where horses are

★ With apologies to Sylvia Loch, who used this quotation in a similar context in *The Classical Seat*.

presented more naturally, with breeders and owners often showing their own horses instead of hiring expensive professionals. At one show in the USA not too long ago, the judges announced that no horse would be judged if it was shown 'stretched'. As a result, every horse was posed naturally. With many more owners and breeders in the USA, Canada and Australia expressing concern about show trends, let us hope that these groups will have a widespread influence, not only in their own countries but in Europe too.

As we saw in earlier chapters, in spite of misgivings about some of the judging we see at shows here in Britain, there is evidence that, in the wake of the Arab Horse Society's revised policy on the training and appointing of judges, a number of judges are being more meticulous in their approach and are finding the courage of their convictions. This is one trend that must be wholeheartedly welcomed; let us hope it continues and does not 'die a death' once the spotlight is off judging.

Also very much to the Arab Horse Society's credit is the introduction of a new championship show. The British Arabian Championship Show will have in-hand classes for geldings and ridden classes for geldings, mares

The Arab Horse Society wishes to promote high class geldings. Cakile, British National Champion Gelding 1991 (Sweet)

and stallions. The aim is to encourage breeders to have more good quality horses gelded and to reward ridden performance on the part of mares and stallions.

With regard to Arabian horse shows themselves, much could be done to transform classes so that they enhance, rather than detract from, the breed's reputation. Shorn of their excesses, in-hand classes could be restored to their proper place as a showcase for breeders. If the selection of breeding stock were subject to approval of type and conformation by an Arab Horse Society panel as suggested in Chapter 10, this would automatically mean that proper breed classes did, indeed, represent the best of the breed.

With more emphasis placed on performance, there could still be many opportunities for those who, for whatever reason, cannot or do not wish to ride their horses. In Chapter 2 I was rather severely critical of the so-called 'liberty' classes that are being held at some international shows. If we are going to hold liberty classes, then by all means let us do so: but for heaven's sake, let's get it right! To begin with, there should be a minimum age stipulated for entrants to such classes. I think the minimum should be at least four years old, as even older horses can easily become frightened in such circumstances, deprived of the support of the handler's close presence and physical control. Then rules must be laid down (yes, more rules! but, sadly, necessary to prevent abuse) about conduct in such classes so that they do not degenerate into a free-for-all. There must also be adequate safety precautions, to avoid the danger of loose horses injuring themselves and/or spectators. Above all, the horses *must* be adequately prepared. (It seems likely that some such provisions will be made in the future; at the time of writing the details are not yet known.) Properly done, liberty classes can be a joy to watch; anyone wishing to learn how to train horses for this kind of act can do no better than to watch such superb trainers as Yasmin Smart and Mary Chipperfield at work, and to read *Classical Circus Equitation* (published by J. A. Allen), by Henrik Jan Lijsen, translated by Antony Hippisley-Coxe and annotated by Sylvia Stanier. The latter, who worked with Nuno Oliveira and has stood in for Her Majesty the Queen at the rehearsals for the Trooping of the Colour, says in her introduction to the section on training horses for liberty work: 'To me the most important gain from Liberty work is the absolute rapport which is achieved between horse and handler.'[5] Further on in the same chapter Lijsen says, 'There is no better way of getting to know animals than by training them. It leads to mutual understanding, a fine appreciation of animal reaction – and, you will find, it greatly improves your patience.'[6]

Some purists have tended to be rather 'sniffy' about circus work, maintaining that it is merely teaching horses tricks, but the very best circus trainers have always been classically correct, and circus-trained horses of the highest quality generally display far greater suppleness, agility and collection than all but a tiny handful of Grand Prix dressage horses! Moreover, great masters such as Nuno Oliveira have never been afraid to acknowledge their debt to some of the masters of classical circus, while the late Colonel Hans Handler, former Director of the Spanish Riding School, has this to say: 'Circus training is primarily concerned with awakening, developing, and displaying various mental and physical qualities in the animal . . . Especially in the first phases of training, the classical school is no different'.[7] Those people who wish to train their Arabians properly and according to correct principles for in-hand work, could learn a great deal from good circus trainers – and have a lot of fun at the same time.

With the display aspect in mind, it would be nice to see more exhibitions such as the display of dressage to music given by Kandice Trusler and her pure-bred Arabian Dallal at the Arab Horse Society Summer Show at Malvern in 1995. This was received with great enthusiasm by the crowd, which showed that there is a definite audience for more of the same. Shows in the USA have, of course, been including such displays for decades, while the idea has also been taken up at some European shows. The execution has sometimes been somewhat variable, but the intention is good.

Ridden classes could be transformed from the safe but rather dull spectacles that, at the moment, are very much also-rans to the in-hand classes. In this context, it was pleasing to see Western-style classes included at Malvern in 1996. However, care would have to be taken not to fall into the trap of trying to cater for too many different styles of riding, as some shows have done both in Britain and in the USA. The ridden classes in the latter country are bewildering in their variety; the danger with such variety is that breeders then go to the extreme of trying to breed Arabian horses that fit the perception of the type of horses suitable for these classes, the folly of which we saw in Chapter 10. There is another objection that is usually overlooked: apart from the proper Western style (which, at its best, is truly classical, being derived from the Spanish *gineta* style of the *conquistadores*) and, of course, excluding racing (in any case, a world apart) there is *only one style of riding* on the flat which works in harmony with nature and with the horse: we may label this style 'classical' if we wish, but that is all it is – a label for riding that is correct and in balance. There are some people who say that such a style may be OK for

Dallal and Kandice Trusler: dressage to music display, Arab Horse Society Summer Show 1995. Dallal is here shown performing one-time flying changes (Pleasure Prints Area D)

international dressage but out of place in the showring. Surely good riding is never out of place anywhere. As João Oliveira, son of the great Nuno Oliveira, has observed, 'There is no "classical", no "dressage" – riding is either good or bad.'[8]

With this proviso, the ridden classes could, with some work on the part of all concerned, become real showcases for the breed. If greater emphasis were given to the *manner* in which the horses were ridden – rather than to whether the horse merely presents a pleasing picture to the judge and gives a safe, pleasant ride – then standards would automatically rise as it is the rider who largely determines the horse's peformance.

On a slightly higher note, more advanced equitation classes, such as some other breed societies run, could give riders an opportunity to show how well they have trained their horses. This could give rather more scope for riders to show off their horses' abilities than the normal ridden classes, where they are usually encouraged to 'play it safe' rather than attempt anything too ambitious. If the competitive aspect were played down and the correctness of the training and riding given greater consideration, this could be a tremendous opportunity to demonstrate just what well-trained Arabians can do. Some people might object that this would make it more of a dressage test than a showing class. Not at all. The idea would not be to ride set movements in a set order but a freestyle of the rider's own devising. If such classes were granted sufficient prestige, what a difference they could make to the way in which Arabians are regarded by the rest of the equestrian world!

In the end, it is only by aiming for excellence that we can attain excellence; it will not come on its own. As I said in Chapter 4, it would be unrealistic to expect the average Arabian to compete on equal terms in the higher reaches of most disciplines, for the reasons stated in that chapter. However, through the medium of our shows we have a unique opportunity to turn matters around completely and to demonstrate to the world at large all the Arabian's wonderful qualities: grace and beauty; fire and docility; lightness, sparkle and agility combined with power, strength and toughness; pride and independence coupled with affection and an endearing affinity with humans. If we choose to make the most of this opportunity, not only will we have enhanced the breed's standing and reputation, we will ourselves have gained immeasurably in knowledge and understanding of the horses we find so endlessly fascinating. This, however, will require the exercise of considerable effort and self-discipline on the part of the people who would effect this transformation of our show scene.

In spite of some of the weird and wonderful things that are happening in the breeding of Arabians, we still have in our breed some of the best riding horses in the world. There is an upsurge of enthusiasm for dressage and an increasing interest in the half-forgotten (in Britain at any rate) art of classical riding. How wonderful it would be if all these could be brought together in the showring and, instead of the somewhat uninspiring, apologetic performances we so often see, there could, instead, be seen displays of real horsemanship and pride in the noble, spirited creatures our Arabian horses can be, both under saddle and in-hand.

Pie in the sky? Perhaps, but at least it is something we could aim for. Surely we owe it to our horses to give them at least the opportunity to fulfil their potential and, in the process, to gain their lasting friendship.

As Sylvia Loch has observed: 'The noble horse, yes! But to be noble, to be himself, every horse requires a modicum of nobility from us.'[9]

Notes

1 The Kiley-Worthington report, further details of which may be obtained from the Secretary, The Association of Circus Proprietors of Great Britain, PO Box 131, BB1 9DT
2 Xenophon, *The Art of Horsemanship*, tr. M H Morgan, p.562
3 Danny Pevsner in an interview ('Pevsner's Principles') for *Dressage* magazine, August 1995, p.29
4 Loch, Sylvia, *Dressage: The Art of Classical Riding*, p.203
5 Lijsen, Henrik Jan and Sylvia Stanier, *Classical Circus Equitation*, p.11
6 Lijsen, *Classical Circus*, p.20
7 Handler, Col. Hans, *The Spanish Riding School in Vienna*, Thames and Hudson 1972, p.138
8 João Oliveira, quoted in 'A Profile of João Oliveira', *Horse and Rider* September 1990
9 Loch, *Dressage*, p.214

GLOSSARY

afnas – the dish in an Arabian horse's profile

airs above the ground (*aires relevés*) – movements in which the horse either leaps or raises its forefeet off the ground, e.g. *levade*, *capriole*

bedawin – term describing the nomad tribes of the Arabian Peninsula, their customs, traditions, etc.

bedu – collective term for the nomad tribes of the Arabian Peninsula

bereiter – rider at the Spanish Riding School

corrida – bullfight – in Portugal, refers to the mounted bullfight, which in Spain is called the *rejoneo*, to differentiate it from the bullfight on foot

courbette – a series of jumps on the hind legs

gineta – term used with reference to the horsemanship of the Iberian Peninsula (i.e. Spain and Portugal), which employs a shorter stirrup and a bent leg, in contrast to the straighter-legged style of the sixteenth, seventeenth and early eighteenth centuries

High School – the highest level of training of the horse, which includes the extremely collected gaits, *piaffe, passage*, and the airs above the ground

levade – an air above the ground in which the horse lifts his forehand off the ground with lowered hocks, at an angle of approximately 30 degrees. Up to the nineteenth century the movement was performed with the horse's body at an angle of 45 degrees from the ground; this older movement was known as the *pesade* and it would be this air that was performed by horses trained by M. de la Guérinière and his contemporaries

manège – arena, ring or other enclosed area where horses are schooled. The baroque or classical *manège* was considerably smaller than the modern arena as the emphasis was very much on the highly collected movements

mitbah – the curve of the horse's throat where the neck joins the head
oberbereiter – chief rider at the Spanish Riding School

passage – defined by la Guérinière as 'a measured and cadenced walk or trot'. Now used exclusively to mean a cadenced, elevated trot in which the moment of suspension is clearly defined

piaffe – 'a *passage* in place' (la Guérinière)

volte – a small circle

Appendix I

SADDLES AND THEIR FITTING

THE VEXED question of saddle fitting has, in the last few years, caused a great deal of controversy between various organisations and the saddlery trade. The equestrian press has highlighted – sometimes, perhaps understandably, with glee – the many shortcomings of saddlery design, some articles going so far as to suggest that most saddles incorporate serious design faults and may even be actually harmful to horses. Not surprisingly, the saddlery trade has leapt to its own defence, pointing out that these claims are exaggerated and that, yes, it accepts there is room for improvement, but design faults are by no means as widespread as has been suggested, nor can such a high proportion of saddles be responsible for poor performance or even injury to the horse.

I believe that both sides have a point and that the truth (as so often) lies somewhere between the two extremes. It would be silly to suggest, as some of the more enthusiastic proponents of the 'poor saddle design' theory have done, that almost all instances of lameness and back injury are caused by the saddle. There are so many potential causes of either that such an approach may easily lead one down the wrong path. It does make sense, however, to look first to saddle fitting as a *possible* cause of such problems; and in cases where the saddle *is* pinpointed as the cause, it is often not so much that the saddle is poorly designed (though some undoubtedly are), as that it has not been fitted properly and here the case is usually that the saddle is simply not wide enough, pinching at the withers and restricting the shoulder.

This is where problems with saddle fitting for Arabians come in. Most Arabians (of the kind that are ridden anyway) are fairly wide across the back and shoulder, and I have never known one yet that did not require a wide-fitting saddle – in some cases, the wider the better. There is an idea that if you get a saddle that is too wide it will bear down on the withers, but with the design of most saddles this could only apply if the withers were very high and of the 'knife-edge' variety which most Arabian withers are not. In any case, even with very wide saddles, I have not yet come across one that looked anything like bearing down on the withers. The reverse problem – a saddle that pinches at the withers and behind the shoulder blade – is a much more serious and widespread problem which can, indeed, cause all kinds of discomfort and physical damage to the horse, as can a saddle which is too narrow in the gullet. Fortunately, there are several excellent books on saddlery and tack and its fitting, notably by Susan McBane (herself an Arab-lover) and Elwyn Hartley-Edwards who also has a soft spot for the Arabian (see Bibliography). They give good practical advice on saddle fitting and also on choosing a suitable saddle for your purpose.

They also stress the need to ensure that the saddle fits the rider and that it puts them in the right position for the kind of riding contemplated. This is where I would really take issue with the saddlery trade. For jumping and cross country work, the average GP or eventing saddle is fine; for flatwork many of them are absolutely useless. This is because, as stated in Chapter 4, in most cases the stirrup bars are placed much too far forward, making it virtually impossible for the rider to sit correctly in a deep, balanced, upright seat, well forward in the saddle so that the rider's weight is placed over the strongest part of the horse's back. This compels the rider either to shorten the stirrup so that, in order to maintain balance, the upper body is then thrown too far forward, upsetting the horse's equilibrium and causing it to fall on its forehand; or, in an effort to retain the longer length of leg required for effective flat riding, to adopt a kind of 'chair' seat of the kind deplored in Chapter 4. In both cases the effectiveness of the rider's seat and lower leg is are drastically reduced, while the horse may, as well as flopping on to its forehand, suffer acute discomfort from the heaviness of seat and harsh aids which are the inevitable result of the chair seat.

The obvious answer would seem to be to buy a dressage saddle. However, most riders want to do some jumping at some stage and while it is quite possible to jump in a dressage saddle (my own instructor has done it, and a friend regularly hacks his point-to-point horse out in a dressage saddle with short stirrups because it is the only saddle he can find, other than a racing saddle, that actually fits the horse) they are not really suitable for anyone who wants do more than pop their horse over the occasional small jump. Besides, by no means all dressage saddles are free from the very fault that afflicts GP saddles; some of them, again, have the stirrup bars too far forward, with the same results.

What, then, is the answer? Many Arabian owners/riders like to do a bit of everything with their horses, including showing. They will not, in all probability, have sufficient resources to afford a saddle for each discipline:

few of us have! If they do not want (or cannot afford) to go to the expense of buying a good dressage saddle which will put them in the correct position, they might consider asking a saddler to fit a longer stirrup bar to an existing GP model. This should be possible and not outrageously expensive. Although it would be something of a compromise, it would at least help the rider to sit more correctly. If the saddler is really on the ball, they may even be able to fit a Wellep adjustable stirrup bar, which would enable the rider to adjust the bar setting to suit the riding position being adopted.

Quite a number of Arabian owners/riders like to take part in dressage as well as showing. For these riders it may well be advantageous to buy a good dressage saddle. I know that many professional showing people insist that these are not really suitable for showing but I suspect that this has more to do with tradition than anything else. Certainly a saddle which is high at the pommel and cantle will not flatter the horse's topline but any good judge should be able to see past that! Surely what is of paramount importance is that the saddle fits the horse and the rider and enables the rider to sit correctly and effectively. Anything else is of purely cosmetic interest. In any case, to judge by the number of dressage saddles one sees in the showring, most competitors are not impressed by this argument.

If you should, however, decide to go for a proper showing saddle rather than a dressage model, do ensure you get the right kind. Some of the older types had flat, 'soup-plate' seats that were hideously uncomfortable for all concerned and did nothing for the rider's position; again, the stirrup bars were usually placed much too far forward (although some manufacturers employed an extended stirrup bar). In addition, many showing saddles incorporate a cut-back head (as, indeed, do many dressage saddles). This tends to push the rider too far towards the cantle when what we want is the reverse, for the rider to sit as far forward as is anatomically possible (this then puts the actual seatbones in the centre of the saddle). As Elwyn Hartley-Edwards pointed out in an article for the *Classical Riding Club Newsletter* (September 1995, p.26), the German dressage saddles, which have provided a model for many of our saddle-makers, all use the cut-back head which is at least partly responsible for the 'back-seat' driving position so much in evidence in the dressage arena. 'The cut-back head', he says, 'was designed originally to allow for a high, knifey wither, which is not a noticeable feature of the German Warmblood – so why use it?' Nor, one might add, is it a feature of the Arabian, so it is difficult to see why the cut-back head has been included in some saddles designed specifically for horses of that breed.

There are now available some much better designs of showing saddle, particularly some of the working hunter types, but, whatever you fancy, if it doesn't enable you to sit as you would on a good dressage saddle, forget it and go for a decent dressage model instead.

The requirements, then, are quite straightforward: for the average Arabian, a saddle (whether modified GP, dressage or showing) needs to be pretty wide, in the gullet as well as the head; panels need to be as wide and flat as possible, to increase the surface area coming into contact with the horse's back and thus spreading the weight more evenly; the stirrup bars need to be in the correct position for the rider to sit properly; and the saddle needs to be *comfortable*. Nor should the head be too cut back, for the reasons just stated. If all these requirements prove difficult to fulfil, the Arabian Saddle Co., which makes saddles specifically designed for the Arabian horse, should be able to help. I have not had an opportunity to test one of their saddles but they have been recommended to me. They are not especially cheap but they do offer a saddle-fitting service which aims to fit the saddle specifically to your horse (which, ideally, is the way it should always be done but seldom is). Alternatively, you may be fortuante enough to find a second-hand saddle in excellent condition at a reasonable price, which fits all your requirements.

Or you might do as I did and have a saddle specially made for your horse. I experienced difficulty in finding a dressage saddle suitable for my Arabian gelding; they were all too narrow in the tree or the gullet, or had heads that were too cut back or stirrup bars set too far forward. In the end David Sayer of Yarm and Northallerton in North Yorkshire got his own saddler to make me a saddle to my specifications, including an extended stirrup bar (at no extra cost). The result is a lovely saddle which fits me and the horse and is beautifully comfortable. The price was very reasonable, too; much less, in fact, than I would have had to pay for a comparable design had I been able to find one which fitted the bill.

At the end of the day, listen to your horse. If he is not going as well as he should, or you think he could, what is the reason for that? Is he being naughty, or uncooperative, or simply lazy? Or – much more likely – could it be the saddle or the rider that is at fault? Does it pinch, or slide around on his back, bearing down on his spine? Is it helping you to sit in the correct position for effective riding, or is it hindering you? Is your riding, in fact, all it could be? Your horse cannot tell you in words. He can only tell you as best he can, by his reactions to being ridden. Very few horses are genuinely naughty or stubborn; so listen. You may be surprised by what you hear.

Appendix II

NOTES ON THE BIBLIOGRAPHY

NUMEROUS excellent books describing the Arabian horse have been published on both sides of the Atlantic during the last 150 years. The original classics were Captain Roger Upton's *Newmarket and Arabia*, a comparison of the respective qualities of the Arabian and the Thoroughbred, and *Bedouin Tribes of the Euphrates*, by Lady Anne and Wilfrid Blunt, in which, as well as Lady Anne's account of their travels among the tribes (edited, and considerably altered, by Blunt himself), Wilfrid Blunt gives a comprehensive description of the Arabian horse and his habitat. Much of the information in this book was later discovered by the Blunts to have been erroneous, particularly that given about strains and strain types. They were also, as their knowledge and understanding of the tribes and their horses increased, to alter their opinion of the kind of horse that represented the true Arabian type. Wilfrid Blunt's description of the ideal Arabian, given in 1900 in the *Encyclopedia of Sport*, differs considerably in certain details from his earlier description in *Bedouin Tribes of the Euphrates* but, because the latter became regarded as the authoritative work on the subject, many of the errors it contained have been perpetuated.

One example of this is Wilfrid Blunt's statement that the croup should be higher than the withers. It must be remembered that many of the horses the Blunts saw at this early stage were either immature horses (which, of course, tend to be croup high) or those that had suffered severe dietary deprivation in the desert. This, in the opinion of veterinary surgeons I have consulted on the matter, could quite easily have led to a kind of arrested development in which the croup and the withers did not level off, resulting in this croup-high conformation. Whatever the reason, it quickly became apparent that this was *not* correct for the Arabian, giving as it does an unpleasant, downhill ride. Unfortunately, this statement was taken up and repeated by several people who later became known as experts on the Arabian (one such was W. R. Brown), and numerous other authorities, including Lady Wentworth and Peter Upton, have found it necessary to point out that the croup should *not* be higher than the withers.

Lady Anne herself was always disturbed by the fact that the errors contained in *Bedouin Tribes of the Euphrates* and in *A Pilgrimage to Nejd* went uncorrected. She devoted many years to a thorough study of the *bedawin* tribes, their language, manners and traditions, in particular those relating to the Arabian horse. The fruits of this labour were never published in her lifetime but they were largely incorporated into *The Authentic Arabian Horse*, the monumental work of her daughter, Judith Lytton, Baroness Wentworth.

This is an immense labour of love, the result of a lifetime's experience of the Arabian horse, as well as of much scholarly research. Lady Wentworth has been much criticised, however, not least for some of her exaggerated claims on behalf of the Arabian horse. It is the greatest of pities that so much of her work is flawed by a tendency to make dogmatic statements apparently unsupported by evidence. For her admirers, the immense weight of her authority is sufficient to guarantee the accuracy of her facts. To her detractors, however, this lack of supporting evidence is a serious drawback. If she had only seen fit to give precise details of her sources, instead of somewhat bald statements, much of this adverse criticism could be rendered ineffective. As it is, one has to accept that her scholarship was by no means as scrupulous as her mother's and we must therefore treat some of her statements sceptically, particularly where some of her claims in respect of the Arabian horse's role in history are concerned (a prime example of this is her assertion that the Duke of Wellington's famous charger, Copenhagen, whom he rode at Waterloo, was an Arabian. In fact he was a Thoroughbred of very well-attested breeding. Lady Wentworth must surely have been aware of this but she chose to give her version of history). However, in spite of these caveats, her writings are endlessly fascinating, revealing an astonishing range of knowledge and understanding of a myriad subjects. *The Authentic Arabian*, whatever the faults of its brilliant but wayward author, must stand as one of the great classic horse books of all time.

Perfectly complementing the above as a handy and compact source of reference about the Arabian is Peter Upton's beautifully illustrated *The Classic Arab Horse*. This covers every aspect of type, conformation and movement and, perfectly illustrating each of these aspects, are the author's exquisite drawings. This book is indispensable for the true lover of the Arabian horse.

There are numerous other books giving a wealth of information on the Arabian horse but if I were asked to name half a dozen such books to take with me to a desert island, I should choose *The Authentic Arabian Horse*

(Wentworth), *The Classic Arab Horse* (Upton), Lady Anne Blunt's *Journals* and correspondence, *The Crabbet Arabian Stud* (Rosemary Archer, et al.), *The Arabian Horse* by Rosemary Archer and Margaret Greely's *Arabian Exodus*. Others may have their favourites among those listed in the Bibliography but these are the books that have been of most value to me.

In the field of equitation, if I were asked to name the books I have found most useful in learning about classical riding, I should say that, more than any other, Sylvia Loch's *The Classical Seat* has been the source of the greatest enlightenment. It describes the classical way of sitting on a horse, the aids, the use of the hands and the effect of all these on the horse in such a clear, precise manner, aided by simple, effective diagrams and illustrations, that the reader is left feeling as though a bright light has suddenly illuminated what for so long has seemed incomprehensible or impossibly complicated. One thinks, 'Of course! How simple!' Also of inestimable value in presenting classical riding simply, with clarity and precision, is Michael J. Stevens's *A Classical Riding Notebook*. I cannot recommend this, and its companion volume, *Practical Schooling*, too highly; the two should ideally be read in conjunction as they complement each other. For a further, and equally practical, look at classical principles, Erik F. Herbermann's *Dressage Formula* sets out those principles with equaly clarity. A former pupil of Egon von Neindorff, his love of, and respect for, the horse as a *partner* shines out from every page of this book. Another classic that should be in the library of every serious equestrian is *The Complete Training of Horse and Rider*, by Colonel Alois Podhajsky, for 25 years Director of the Spanish Riding School and one of the true heirs of Xenophon and la Guérinière.

For a more detailed look at the anatomy of horse and rider and how these interact with each other, Molly Sivewright's *Thinking Riding* is an absolute mine of information. If more riders and instructors read this book, there would be far less confused and confusing teaching in our riding schools. For those who are not natural riders and who find much of what they read and are taught difficult to apply in practice, Mary Wanless's *Ride With Your Mind* and *Ride With Your Mind Masterclass* explore the biomechanics of the horse/rider partnership with great thoroughness. If some of it appears superficially to contradict received equestrian wisdom, this is often, in practice, merely a different way of teaching the accumulated wisdom of the great masters of equitation.

Follow all this up by reading Sylvia Loch's inspiring history of the classical art, *Dressage: the Art of Classical Riding*; it is colourful, moving, and extremely thought-provoking. The author's depth of knowledge about her subject is evident at every turn and is attested by no less a person than Brigadier-General Kurt Albrecht, former Director of the Spanish Riding School, who wrote the foreword to this illuminating book. Then read *Riding Towards the Light* by Paul Belasik, who studied with Nuno Oliveira, *Dressage for the New Age* by Dominique Barbier, another pupil of Oliveira, and Mestre Oliveira's own *Reflections on Equestrian Art*. Finally, but perhaps most important of all, is the greatest classic of all: *The School of Horsemanship* by François Robichon de la Guérinière. The teachings of this master of masters, which form the nucleus of what is taught at the Spanish Riding School, are as fresh and relevant today as they were when he first wrote them in the 1730s. All aspiring horsemen and women – especially those who would advance beyond the basics – should read this marvellous exposition of the classical art of riding. If it were read – and understood – by all competitive riders and trainers before they ever set foot in the dressage arena or the showring, ineffective and coercive riding and training would surely become a thing of the past.

If you once become hooked by these books, I guarantee you will never be the same again.

For those with more of an interest in training from the ground (and also of inestimable value to those who do ride), there is *Training from the Ground* by the Marquis MacSwiney of Mashana-glass. This covers every aspect of controlling the horse from the ground with the minimum stress to both horse and handler: a real classic. I am sure if horses could be asked which books they would like their owners to read, this book would be high on the list. Also of great value to the trainer truly interested in making the most of the horse from the ground is *Classical Circus Equitation* by H.J. Lijsen and Sylvia Stanier. This covers liberty work as well as High School equitation and much else besides. It is a gem of a book.

For general information about conformation and movement, there is Susan E. Harris's excellent *Horse Gaits, Balance and Movement*, while Peter C. Goody's *Horse Anatomy* may help further with the understanding of how the horse's biomechanical system functions.

Finally, the serious show enthusiast can do no better than to consult the works of experts in the field: *Practical Showing* by Nigel Hollings, *Successful Showing* by Nigel's brother Stuart Hollings, *Showing* by Jane Holderness-Roddam and *The Handbook of Showing* by the late Glenda Spooner all give a wealth of practical inside advice.

Last, but far from least, are two books which illuminate the way the horse's mind works: Dr Marthe Kiley-Worthington's *The Behaviour of Horses* and Lucy Rees's much acclaimed classic, *The Horse's Mind*. Both of these explore life from the horse's point of view and show how inadequate understanding of the horse's needs can so easily lead to behavioural problems. If only more horse owners, riders, trainers and, indeed, all those involved in training and caring for horses (and *especially* those concerned with the management of colts and stallions) would read, digest and understand what is contained in these two books, there would be far fewer equine 'head-cases' and many more easily managed, contented horses. Both of these books are a must for the truly thinking horseman or woman.

These are only a few of the books that have helped me with the writing of this book and which, on the way, have given a great deal of pleasure. If readers have not already done so, I hope this may act as a spur to them to discover for themselves the riches that lie in wait for the enquiring mind.

BIBLIOGRAPHY

Arabia and the Arabian horse

Arab Horse Society, *Arab Horse Society News*

Archer, R., *The Arabian Horse*, J. A. Allen 1992

Archer, R. and Fleming, J. (eds), *Lady Anne Blunt: Journals and Correspondence 1878–1917*, Alexander Heriot 1986

Archer, R., Pearson, C., Covey, C. and Finke, B., *The Crabbet Arabian Stud: its History and Influence*, rev. ed., Alexander Heriot 1994

Blunt, Lady Anne, *A Pilgrimage to Nejd*, Murray 1881

Blunt, Lady Anne, and Wilfrid Scawen Blunt, *Bedouin Tribes of the Euphrates*, London 1879

Boiselle, G. *Grace and Beauty: A Study of the Horse*, 1992

Borden, Spencer, *The Arab Horse* (originally published 1906; reprinted 1961), Doubleday, Page & Co. 1961

Brown, W. R., *The Horse of the Desert*, Macmillan 1947

Burt, Don, *Winning with Arabian Horses*, Prentice Hall Press 1990

Byford, S. *The Arabian: A Guide for Owners*, Alpine Publications Inc., USA 1987

Doughty, C. M., *Travels in Arabia Deserta*, London 1926

Edwards, Gladys Brown, *The Arabian, War Horse to Show Horse*, The Arabian Horse Trust of America 1969

Forbis, J. *The Classic Arabian Horse*, New York 1976

Forbis, J. and Sherif, G., *The Abbas Pasha Manuscript*, Ansata Publications 1993

Gazder, Dr P. J., *The Arab Horse Families of Great Britain 1875–1973*, Alexander Heriot 1993

Greely, M. *Arabian Exodus*, J. A. Allen 1975

Guarmani, C. *Northern Najd: a Journey from Jerusalem to Anaiza*, London 1936

Hyde, Deirdre, *40 Years of British Arab Horse Champions 1953–1992*, Alexander Heriot 1993

Palgrave, W. G., *Narrative of a Year's Journey Through Central and Eastern Arabia*, London 1865

Rice, F. *Chestnuts, Greys and Rodeo Days: My Life at Crabbet Park*, Oran's Paddock 1993
Ridgeway, W., *Origin and Influence of the Thoroughbred Horse*, London 1905
Schiele, E., *The Arab Horse in Europe*, London 1970
Sherbatov, Prince A. G. and Stroganov, Count S. A., *The Arabian Horse: A Survey* (translated by G. I. Vassiltchikov; originally published in St Petersburg in 1900 as *Kniga ob Arabskoi Loshadi*), J. A. Allen 1989
Sherbatov, Prince A. G. and Stroganov, Count S. A., *Kniga ob Arabskoi Loshadi*, St Petersburg 1900
Smith, Lady May Abel and Forbis, Judith, *The Courthouse Arabian Stud*, Alexander Heriot 1992
Tweedie, Major-General W., *The Arabian Horse: His Country and People*, Blackwood 1894
Upton, P., *The Classic Arabian Horse*, The Arab Horse Society
Upton, P., *The Arab Horse*, Crowood Press 1989
Upton, R. D., *Newmarket and Arabia: An Examination of the Descent of Racers and Coursers*, Henry S. King 1873
Wentworth, Lady, *The Authentic Arabian Horse and His Descendants*, 2nd ed., Allen & Unwin 1962
Wentworth, Lady, *Thoroughbred Racing Stock*, 2nd ed., Allen and Unwin 1960
Wentworth, Lady, *The World's Best Horse*, Allen & Unwin 1958

Horsemanship and training

Albrecht, Brigadier Kurt, *Principles of Dressage*, J. A. Allen 1987
Albrecht, Brigadier Kurt, *A Dressage Judge's Handbook*, J. A. Allen 1988
Barbier, D. *Dressage for the New Age*, Prentice Hall Press, USA 1990
Belasik, P., *Riding Towards the Light*, J. A. Allen 1990
Belasik, P., *Exploring Dressage Technique*, J. A. Allen 1994
Crossley, A., *Dressage: The Seat, Aids and Exercises*, Pelham Books 1988
Crossley, A., *Dressage: An Introduction*, Swan Hill Press 1992
Guérinière, François Robichon de la, *The School of Horsemanship* (translated by Tracy Boucher; originally published in 1733 as *L'Ecole de la Cavalerie*), J. A. Allen 1994
Herbermann, Erik F., *Dressage Formula*, 2nd ed. J. A. Allen 1993
Kunffy, Charles de, *Ethics and Passions of Dressage*, Half Halt Press, USA 1993
Lijsen, H. J. and Stanier, S., *Classical Circus Equitation*, J. A. Allen 1993
Loch, S., *Dressage: The Art of Classical Riding*, Sportsman's Press 1990
Loch, S., *The Classical Seat*, Unwin Hyman 1988
MacSwiney of Mashanaglass, The Marquis, *Training from the Ground*, J. A. Allen 1987

Mairinger, F., *Horses are Made to be Horses*, Rigby, Sydney, Australia 1983
Oliveira, N., *Classical Principles of the Art of Training Horses*, Howley & Russell, Australia 1983
Oliveira, N., *From an Old Master Trainer to Young Trainers*, Howley & Russell, Australia 1986
Oliveira, N., *Reflections on Equestrian Art*, J. A. Allen 1976
Podhajsky, Colonel A., *The Complete Training of Horse and Rider*, Harrap 1967
Podhajsky, Colonel A., *The Art of Dressage*, Harrap 1976
Podhajsky, Colonel A., *The Riding Teacher*, Sportsman's Press 1973
Savoie, J., *That Winning Feeling!*, J. A. Allen 1992
Schaik, Henri van, *Misconceptions and Simple Truths in Dressage*, J. A. Allen 1979
Sivewright, Molly, *Thinking Riding*, Books 1 and 2, J. A. Allen 1984 and 1985
Stevens, Michael J., *A Classical Riding Notebook*, Kenilworth Press 1994
Stevens, Michael J., *Practical Schooling*, Kenilworth Press 1995
Wanless, M., *Ride With Your Mind*, Methuen 1987
Wanless, M., *Ride With Your Mind Masterclass*, Methuen 1991
Xenophon, *The Art of Horsemanship*, translated by M. H. Morgan, J. A. Allen 1962

General equestrian works

Akrill, Caroline, *Not Qute a Horsewomen*, Arlington Books 1982
Beamish, Huldine, *Cavaliers of Portugal*, Geoffrey Bles 1966
Bromiley, Mary, *Natural Methods for Equine Health*, Blackwell 1994
Goody, Peter C., *Horse Anatomy*, J. A. Allen 1983
Handler, Colonel Hans, *The Spanish Riding School in Vienna*, Thames and Hudson 1972
Harris, Susan E., *Horse Gaits, Balance and Movement*, Howell Book House (USA) 1993
Hartley-Edwards, Elwyn, *Encyclopedia of the Horse*, Dorling Kindersley 1994
Hartley-Edwards, Elwyn, *Horses: Their Role in the History of Man*, Collins Willow 1987
Hartley-Edwards, Elwyn, *Bitting in Theory and Practice*, J. A. Allen 1990
Hartley-Edwards, Elwyn, *The Saddle in Theory and Practice*, J. A. Allen 1990
Hartley-Edwards, Elwyn, *Training Aids in Theory and Practice*, J. A. Allen 1990
Hartley-Edwards, Elwyn, *The Ultimate Horse Book*, Dorling Kindersley 1991

Hartley-Edwards, Elwyn and Geddes, Candida, *The Complete Horse Book*, Ward Lock 1987

Hearne, Vicki, *Adam's Task: Calling Animals by Name*, Heinemann 1987

Hodges, Jo and Pilliner, Sarah, *The Equine Athlete*, BSP Professional books 1991

Holderness-Roddam, Jane, *Showing*, Threshold Books 1989

Hollings, Nigel, *Practical Showing*, David & Charles 1990

Hollings, Stuart, *Successful Showing*, Crowood 1991

Kiley-Worthington, Dr M., *The Behaviour of Horses*, J. A. Allen 1987

Langley, G., *Understanding Horses*, David & Charles 1989

Loch, S., *The Royal Horse of Europe*, J. A. Allen 1986

McBane, S., *Behaviour Problems in Horses*, David & Charles 1987

McBane, S., *The Illustrated Guide to Horse Tack*, David & Charles 1992

McBane, S. (ed.), *The Horse and the Bit*, Crowood 1988

Poole, R. W. F., *The Cheviot Ranter*, Michael Joseph 1993

Rees, Lucy, *The Horse's Mind*, Stanley Paul 1984

Smythe, Reginald H., *Horse Structure and Movement* (3rd ed., rev. Goody and Gray), J. A. Allen 1993

Spooner, Glenda, *The Handbook of Showing* (revised edition), J. A. Allen 1990

Summerhays, R. (ed.), *Summerhays' Encyclopedia for Horsemen* (revised edition), Warne 1975

INDEX

Page numbers in **bold** refer to illustrations